The Lady Was a Terrorist

THE LADY WAS
A TERRORIST

DURING ISRAEL'S
WAR OF LIBERATION

By

DORIS KATZ

Printed in the United States of America
by FUTURO PRESS, Inc.
476 Broadway, New York City

 200

To the memory of

Joe and Matie

and all those who sacrificed
their lives for our freedom.

TABLE OF CONTENTS

PREFACE

TO THE AMERICAN EDITION

THE realization of the Jewish State—a 2000-year-old dream—was not achieved only by the fierce ambition and bitter struggle of a handful of people, nor by the unaided efforts of one group or organization. It was achieved by a combination of grit on the part of a nation, and the political and material help of those who stood by her in her hour of need. Among these were the people of America, whose devotion and generosity played a noteworthy role in the successul culmination of a mighty and daring undertaking.

It was achieved by the suffering, courage and the self-sacrifice on the part of the youth; by the endurance and faith of their elders.

But before the State could be established, there was a difficult, and insurmountable, obstacle to be overcome. The manacles of a foreign power were clamped securely on the hands and feet of the people—preserving them from welcoming their suffering fellow-Jews to the sanctuary of a home, preventing them from going freely and securely about their daily tasks, and preventing them from taking the final stride toward statehood and liberty. The British ruled in Palestine; and before Palestine could become Israel, the British had to leave, or be forced to leave.

The task of fighting the British was undertaken by a small section of the youth—the members of the Underground. Their courageous foresight and indomitable spirit in the face of the enemy and of those of their people who did not, or would not understand, overcame this final formidable obstacle in the path of freedom. The British left Palestine and the State of Israel was born. Israel was born as America was born, in and out of a War of Independence.

But human memory is notoriously short-lived, whether by the blessed work of nature, the callousness of human feelings, or the misunderstandings common to all flesh. While the State of Israel has gratefully remembered those who came to her aid when she stood alone against the Arab hordes, her rulers have forgotten the men and women who fought her War of Liberation. They have forgotten the bereaved families of those who fell in a fierce contest with those of the British Mandatory Regime who prevented Israel from liberating herself sooner, who imposed arbitrary restrictions against the Jewish people in their own Homeland, who terrorized Palestine officials into swallowing the bitter pills of personal humiliations and suffering, who curtailed immigration into the one land of the earth that could yet save the surviving remnants of Europe's martyred Jewry.

Others may try to forget the glory and the goodness of these fighters of the heroic Underground. But the unforgettable cannot be forgotten. The twelve who died on the British gallows will long outlive those who would want them forgotten. The hundreds who were sacrificed and wounded will always bear witness to the eternal truth—so well epitomized in the American axiom—"that all men are created equal, that they are endowed by their Creator with certain unalienable rights, that among these are Life, Liberty and the pursuit of Happiness."

Let others try to forget, if they can. But as for us: For the sake of the living, we shall not forget the dead. For the sake of the dead, we dare not forget the living.

In this book I have tried to explain why the young men and women of the Irgun Zvai Leumi willingly, gallantly, proudly, and even flauntingly went to the gallows, died on the battlefields, languished for years in prisons and detention camps—for the sake of an ideal. If I have succeeded in giving to the public—and particularly the American reader—a better understanding of the background of a bitter struggle, then I have achieved my purpose.

But this American edition has another purpose too. It is dedicated to those who fought and fell in the fighting ranks of the Irgun, and to Shelach (Organization for the Rehabilitation of Fighters in Israel's War of Liberation), whose consecrated function it is to show, in a practical and material way, that these fighters and their dependents are remembered—and revered.

DORIS KATZ

CHAPTER I

A DREAM COMES TRUE

THE train journey from Port Said to Jerusalem had been long, uncomfortable and terribly disappointing. This last emotion was dissipated, however, as the train entered the defile between the rugged Judean hills. The wild grandeur of rock, softened by the profusion of flowers and shrubs growing luxuriously in the arm-pits of the mountain-side, was the real country, the real Eretz Israel, about which I had dreamed for so many years. The nightmare journey was forgotten; the dirt, the flies, the heat of the Middle East were part of the bad dream. In this majestic beauty, in these sun-tipped, rolling hills, stretching as far as the eye could see, lay the stories and legends of a proud, old race, and the dreams and aspirations of a new nation of pioneers.

The heat and noise of our crowded compartment dragged my unwilling thoughts back to the less inspiring aspects of the troubled and strife-torn Lilliput of the Middle East—Palestine in the year 1946. To any Zionist, brought up on the Utopian propaganda of the silver-tongued troubadours sent out by the Jewish Agency for Palestine, the first sight of his beloved homeland in those days must have come as a terrific shock— that is if he arrived via the Suez Canal and entered the holy territory by way of Kantara, the frontier control post between Egypt and Palestine. It is true that after Port Said with its screaming beggars and pedlars, its fly-infested children, its leprous outcasts and its thieving porters and officials, this was a veritable haven of peace. But where were the bluer-than-blue skies, the cows whose udders trailed on the earth, swollen and blessed with rich, creamy milk; and the golden oranges tenderly plucked by blonde, sun-tanned gods and goddesses? All were sadly lacking in the hot, dusty countryside at the Palestine border.

If the Zionist propagandists forgot to mention the questionable comforts of the Palestine trains, they may well be forgiven; for the railways were run by the Mandatory Government and were in no way the responsibility of the Jewish Agency. But they should have warned the unwary traveller to prepare for the six inches of dust in the carriages and for the

1

complete lack of water or sanitary conveniences on a journey which lasted twelve hours.

I cheerfully accepted the dirt and discomfort because Shmuel, my husband, assured me that my first sight of Jerusalem would compensate for this ephemeral sordidness. I waited patiently and good-humouredly at Lydda Junction for the branch train to Jerusalem, because I knew the real thrill was still to come.

Our fellow-passengers were a curious assortment of Arabs, goats and chickens, and an Egyptian doctor, who joined in the conversation when he heard Shmuel and me talking English to each other. He immediately started off on a long harangue against Britain and her claims on Egypt. "If only they would leave the Egyptians in peace," he mourned. "We don't want to interfere with anyone and we don't want to be interfered with." Shmuel asked pertinently why Egypt stuck her nose into Palestine then. The answer came with the patness of an oft-repeated argument: "Palestine is our business. The Jews are giving the fellaheen notions well-above themselves; and if the Palestinian fellaheen get such notions, so will the Egyptian fellaheen. And then what will happen to the effendis?"

I left Shmuel to discuss the age-old cry of the possessed against the unreasonable rebelliousness of the dispossessed, while I leaned out of the window just in time to watch the first of the Judean hills swim into my line of vision. Shmuel had not exaggerated. The hills were as beautiful as the words in which he had painted them, and the nagging sense of disappointment lifted as by magic, leaving me exhilarated and excited by the fulfilment of a centuries' old dream—the return to Zion.

* * * * *

Shmuel and I were not new converts to Zionism. We had always dreamed of the time when we would be able to come to Palestine not as refugees from oppression, but of our own free will, to contribute any few talents which we might have to the upbuilding of our own country. We could not realise this ambition until June, 1946, a year after the end of World War II.

The war years we had spent in London, arriving there from South Africa in February, 1940. I used to delight in telling puzzled enquirers that we had come to London from the security of South Africa to have a look at the war. But in actual fact we came because Shmuel had been

2

invited by Vladimir Jabotinsky to start a weekly newspaper advocating the formation of a Jewish Army to fight on the side of the Allies.

From London we saw European Jewry being destroyed under the sanctimoniously lowered eyes of the British Government. We knew of the situation in Palestine, despite having to rely almost exclusively on news presented with a British bias. But bias it as you will, the *Struma* still went down with everyone on board, after having been refused permission to land its cargo of human misery in Palestine; the British Parliament still contributed generously towards the saving of millions of Jewish lives by standing silent for three minutes. No amount of bias could hide this— and other acts of cold-calculated anti-Zionism on the part of the British.

Just as Britain's policy in Palestine had stirred the flames of revolt there, so did it intensify our burning desire to reach our own country and help the gallant fight of the resistance movements there, so as to ensure that Hitler's massacres should never again be repeated in the history of our people. This urge to immigrate to Palestine reached its zenith with the Labour Government's cynical and hypocritical betrayal of all their promises to the Jews, when they came to power in 1945.

At the time we arrived, Palestine could hardly be described as a haven of peace for war-weary travellers. The country was torn by internal strife and rebellion against the cold-blooded and oppressive methods of the British Mandatory Government. Of the three independent military organisations in the country the Haganah, under the official aegis of the Jewish Agency for Palestine, was sometimes considered legal by the British and sometimes illegal, depending on the whims and internal circumstances of the moment; while the "dissident" groups, who were not under the aegis of the Agency and did not consider themselves bound by any ties of discipline, were in all moods and all circumstances regarded as illegal military organisations by the British. They consisted of two groups: a larger group known as the Irgun Zvai Leumi (I.Z.L. for short) under the leadership of Menachem Begin, and a smaller group called Fighters for the Freedom of Israel (Lochameh Herut Israel, or L.H.I. for short) under the leadership of Nathan Friedman-Yellin. The three military organisations differed tactically in their struggle against the British. This difference could be summarised as follows: The I.Z.L. first warned and then acted; the L.H.I. acted without warning, and the Haganah warned without acting.

On my first day in Jerusalem I saw more barbed wire than I had seen in more than six years in war-torn London and invasion-threatened

3

England. I was in a constant dilemma as to whether to walk gingerly on the edge of pavements, which were a veritable forest of barbs and snares, and risk ruining my clothes on the malicious spikes, or whether to walk in the streets and be in constant danger of losing my life through the careless recklessness of the Palestinian drivers.

The police in Mandatory Palestine did not symbolise law and order as they do in any civilised community. Here they were hated and feared by the people as the chief instruments of the Administration's oppression. They, in turn, hated and feared the people, amongst whom, indistinguishable from the rest, were members of the I.Z.L. and L.H.I. who had sworn to rid the country of their presence—and were very effectively reducing thir numbers. That the lot of the British policeman in Palestine was not "a happy one" was evidenced by a recruiting poster calling on young Britons to "join the Palestine Police and see the world," and a realistic wit had added the word "next" to the word "world."

One of the most revolting sights to one unused to the manifestations of government by force was that of the spike-helmeted Arab Legionnaires from Trans-Jordan, brought in by the British on the somewhat feeble pretext that they themselves were not sufficiently strong to keep law and order in the country, and needed Abdullah's soldiers to help them.

* * * * *

Our first task in Jerusalem—by no means a simple one—was to find somewhere to live. The world was suffering from an acute housing shortage, and Jerusalem was no exception. After some days of searching, we finally rented a small, furnished house from a junior British official who was going on overseas leave for a few months. The house was in Katamon, then an aristocratic district, graced mainly by high British officials and rich Christian Arabs. This was one of the few parts of Jerusalem which remained unmarred by barbed wire and barricades, and here one could savour to the full the beauty and dignity of the pearl-grey stone houses set against the background of rolling hills. We discovered later that, before signing any agreement with us, the British official had asked the local C.I.D. whether Shmuel was persona grata. For some obscure reason, he was given a clean bill. I say "obscure," because Shmuel had been in Palestine for three years before the war, had known David Raziel (the first commander of the I.Z.L.) and his friends intimately and was already then suspected by the authorities of entertaining too much sympathy for the "terrorists." I thought that the C.I.D. considered Shmuel a

4

reformed character after his years in England, but he suspected, with more justification, that his dossier had been destroyed when the I.Z.L. blew up the C.I.D. headquarters in Jerusalem in 1944. At any rate, we started our careers in Palestine with a clean record from the C.I.D.

With the house, we inherited a young army captain who had lodged with our landlords and continued to lodge with us as part of the agreement. From Captain B we got an interesting insight into the lives of the young British officers in Palestine. They were terribly bored in a country where there was very little entertainment; and what there was, was very often debarred them by their own commanders or by the cold reception they got from the Jewish patrons. Their social life was limited to invitations from the British officials and their wives, from the few wealthy Arabs who entertained and from a handful of Jews who risked the opprobrium of most of the Jewish community to fraternise with the Army (as opposed to officials of the Administration—who had many friends amongst the Jews). For their female company they had the chance of a handful of young, European Gentile women who worked in the Administration or in the various consulates, or Arab girls. Jewish girls, for the most part, did not care to risk their reputations by associating with the British Army.

In their boredom the young officers drank copiously, and delirium tremens was, in their estimation, a much more formidable enemy than the "terrorists," for whom many of them had a sneaking admiration.

Captain B did not stay with us long. He, together with every other British officer in Palestine, was ordered into barracks—as protection against kidnapping—following the spectacular detention by the I.Z.L. of five British officers.

In an I.Z.L. attack on the Sarafand Army Camp, two of the young attackers, Simchon and Ashbel, had been wounded and subsequently captured. They were eventually brought to trial and sentenced to death. The I.Z.L., who had demanded that their men be given the status of prisoners-of-war, as the struggle they were waging against the British was in fact guerilla, underground war against an invader, determined to prevent the execution of the sentence. They kidnapped five British officers, threatening to hang them if Simchon and Ashbel were hanged.

Under this pressure, the Administration commuted the death sentence to life imprisonment. True to their word, the I.Z.L. released their hostages. The British had promised Mayor Rokach of Tel Aviv that they would allow the I.Z.L. a few hours grace to return the officers, unhampered by the British dragnet and revenge themselves subtly for this betrayal of trust, the I.Z.L. crammed the officers into a large, ventilated packing-case which they conveyed on a furniture-van to Rothschild Boulevard, in the heart of Tel Aviv. There they dumped the van in the middle of the street and drove off. The giddy and bewildered officers crawled out groggily to find themselves in the midst of a crowd of onlookers howling with laughter. This laughter echoed round the country and dealt one of the subtlest blows to British prestige which the I.Z.L. could have devised.

The G.O.C. Palestine, at that time General Barker, gave orders, in consequence, that all officers were to live in barracks and that all British military centers in the towns were to be barricaded and guarded. For the first time in their proud history, the British consigned themselves voluntarily to living in ghettoes.

Thus it came about that we lost our lodger. But we still retained other "heritages" from our landlord, in the form of some of his British friends who would drop in occasionally for a drink and chat. We were suspicious of these "chats." We knew that the Jerusalem C.I.D., although not very efficient, had numerous tentacles which it sent out in all directions. There was hardly a British official, businessman or newspaperman who was not consciously or unconsciously an agent or general source of information for the police. They used to visit Jewish homes and glean scraps of information here and there which they would, deliberately in most cases, or inadvertently in some few instances, pass on to their police friends.

The Jews, for their part did the same. The intelligence services of the Haganah, the I.Z.L. and L.H.I. were excellent, as the British often discovered to their cost.

Although we were well aware of the underlying significance of these chats we had with our British acquaintances, we were nevertheless outspoken in our criticism of British policy, and vigorously justified the attacks of the I.Z.L. We hoped we would be regarded as naively innocent, and therefore not dangerous; but, in any case, neither of us could have stomached kow-towing to our British acquaintances even for the sake of security.

One acquaintance in particular, a certain Major Y, who was also a neighbour, used to drop in at all odd hours of the night, whenever he saw a light burning. We suspected him of trying to check up on our late-night visitors, but I think we did him an injustice and that he was merely lonely. At any rate, he had a weakness, and I always had a bottle of brandy in the house, so that we got more out of him than he even got out of us. He expressed great sympathy for the Jewish cause and often criticised his superiors most energetically. Whether this was genuine or merely the Martell talking, we never discovered, but we did not trust him in any case.

This cat-and-mouse attitude of suspicion and distrust was prevalent in Jerusalem. The Jews distrusted the British and vice versa. And those who sympathised with, and belonged to the "dissidents" distrusted their fellow-Jews, as the treacherous betrayal of their people to the British by the Haganah in 1944 still rankled deeply. Every Jew in Palestine, whether a member of the underground or not, lived in daily danger of arrest on suspicion of subversive activities. It was, therefore, a great temptation to dispose of a rival in business, love or politics, by tipping the police off that he was a member of the I.Z.L. or L.H.I. As there was no such thing as the very simplest right of man, this false denunciation was sufficient to cause a man's arrest, internment and even eventual deportation to Eritrea. It must be said to the eternal credit of the Jews of Palestine, that there were very few cases of betrayal for personal needs. The vast majority of those who were sent into captivity by the treachery of their brother-Jews were victims of political viciousness and hatred.

* * * * *

As soon as we had settled in our new home, Shmuel contacted the I.Z.L. and offered them his services. As he had met Menachen Begin on a short visit to Poland in 1938, it did not take him long to establish his bona fides, and he was duly enrolled as a part-time terrorist, being still mainly occupied with his political work for the Revisionist Party. Besides being only part-time, he was also a passive terrorist, his work consisting mainly of writing proclamations and issuing news-bulletins in English. I was, at first, not accepted into the organisation as my ignorance of Hebrew disqualified me from doing any administrative or propaganda work, and I am not really the bomb-throwing type. If I had been, I could have been a valuable asset to the I.Z.L. in Jerusalem because of my deceptive personal appearance.

There is a general fallacy that all Jewesses have black hair, flashing black eyes, and hooked noses. I happen to have light brown hair, grey eyes and a retroussé nose. In addition, I speak English in what is known as a southern English accent. In consequence of my appearance and accent I was mistaken by the uninitiated in Jerusalem for an Englishwoman. If this purely coincidental resemblance to an Anglo-Saxon was not exploited to the full by the I.Z.L. it did at least serve to save me from some of the unpleasant incidents to which the Jews of Jerusalem were being continually subjected by the Administration.

On one occasion I was at a cafe with some friends, when the British threw a cordon around it and started checking identity cards. As very often happened to me, I was without identity card or passport, and not relishing the idea of being taken to C.I.D. headquarters for investigation, I brazenly walked through the cordon. A Cockney voice yelled loudly at me: "Hi, where d'ya think you're going?" I turned around, looked at him coldly as only an Englishwoman can look and said in my haughtiest Oxford accent: "To whom do you think you're talking?" He mumbled an apology, touched his cap and I stalked off with a dignified air of injured innocence, to the great delight and secret envy of my friends.

On another occasion I had to visit someone in the King David Hotel just after it had been partially wrecked by the I.Z.L. It was the most difficult place in the world to get into, especially for a Jew. I went along without my passport and told the officer in charge of the guard at the barbed-wire cordon, that I wanted to see Captain X. very urgently. Without any hesitation, he sent me through to the main building where I repeated by request. Here the guard tentatively asked to see my identity card or passport. As the British did not have to have identity cards, I said very coldly that I did not carry my passport around with me. That worked miracles. I was politely conducted through the whole building and could eventually give a good account of the extent of the damage which had been done.

To complicate matters still further, I had a blue British Passport. My own passport, a South African one, I had lost in a typical Palestinian accident. We travelled from Katamon to town in an Arab bus which was always crowded with people, children, baskets and chickens. There was one driver who always drove with his eyes closed, but never sufficiently closed to avoid seeing a pretty girl go by. Then he would open them wide, lean out of the window and, for the next few seconds, continue to gaze at the disappearing back of the fair damsel. On one such occasion he did what he had till then miraculously avoided doing—he collided with an oncoming vehicle. The jar of the collision caused my handbag to fly out of my hand and when, a few seconds later, the bus caught fire and the fear-stricken passengers started to stampede, I decided to forego the pleasure of being trampled to death by a horde of screaming Arabs and chickens while grovelling for my handbag, and took a neat, ladylike header out of the nearest window. We were all extremely lucky that the bus was new and that the iron cross-bars usually on Palestinian buses had not yet been affixed to the windows. My passport had been in the ill-fated bag and I had perforce to apply for a new one. As there was no South African consul in Jerusalem, the British Mandatory Government, out of the goodness of its heart, gave me a blue British passport instead of my brown South African one.

I lay special stress on the colour of the passport because of its significance to the Arab guards at all Government and public buildings. At this period in the history of Jerusalem, it was impossible to enter a post-office, police-station or any government or public office without first producing an identity card and submitting onself to a search by Arab guards. At least 90 per cent of these guards could not read, but they could distinguish colors. A brown passport meant you were Palestinian and therefore a potential terrorist, but a blue passport dubbed you immediately as British and therefore completely above suspicion. All I had to do was to produce my blue passport and I was never subjected to the indignity of having my bag and pockets searched by an Arab guard.

*   *   *   *   *

None of our friends, even the closest ones, knew of Shmuel's connection with the I.Z.L., a fact which I regarded as a direct tribute to my own acquired clamishness. At this stage, Shmuel still did not let me into all the secrets, or rather all those that he himself knew, as I had still to prove my ability to keep my mouth shut. But I did, of course, know of his own activities and also knew some of the younger members who acted as liaison officers and messengers. The latter were constantly visiting the house with messages for Shmuel which they delved out from the most unlikely places on their persons. My particular favourite was a 17-year girl, fictitiously known as Adina. She was shy, pretty and terribly punctual. If she were due at any specific hour she would arrive as the clock was striking. Never once did she arrive after the appointed time, curfews or police-searches notwithstanding. I was fascinated by this punctuality and secretly despaired of ever being accepted into the organisation if this were one of the criteria.

CHAPTER II

THE BRITISH AT WORK

L ESS than a month after we arrived in Jerusalem, the mounting tension between the Mandatory Government and the Jewish Agency culminated in the arrest of the latter and their internment in the detention camp at Latrun. Some of our more cynical friends were convinced that this was an understandable error on the part of the British. What had really happened, they maintained, was that each member of the Agency had submitted a list of suspected terrorists to the CID, signing his name at the end of the list, and so inadvertently including himself. It was a good story anyhow.

A little while after these arrests, the IZL carried out a long-standing plan to blow up that part of the King David Hotel in Jerusalem which housed the British Administration offices and military GHQ. I naturally knew nothing about this plan and drove by in a bus about five minutes before the explosion. There seemed to be a large number of people standing around in the street outside the hotel, and I wondered who had arrived or was about to arrive. A few minutes later I knew. A journalist friend, who was amongst the crowd outside the hotel, told us that hundreds of people appeared to have heard of the IZL's warning about the impending explosion and had turned out to watch it.

One Arab who escaped by jumping out of a window before the explosion occurred, told him the following story: "You see, in my village I am known as the village idiot. When I heard that the Irgun had said they were going to blow up the building, I wanted to run away. My boss ordered me not to leave as everything was being taken care of. But I am the village idiot, and I couldn't understand how they were going to take care of the Irgun; so I jumped out of the window."

I later heard that the young woman who had given the warning was Adina. Unfortunately, the warning was not heeded, and many innocent victims lost their lives—amongst them some staunch supporters of the IZL. That was a black day for Jerusalem's Jewry, and a still blacker one for the Mandatory Government, which never recovered from the complete chaos and disorganization which resulted from the loss of their records and the deaths of numerous high officials.

Captain B, still our lodger at this time, also worked in the King David Hotel. I never was more pleased to see anyone than I was to see him walk in alive and whole after the explosion. Similarly, there were many Jews in Jerusalem, many of them supporters of the IZL, who mourned the deaths of British officials whom they had known intimately and who had fallen victims to an ill-timed manifestation of British pig-headedness and pride—the "we won't be intimidated by those damned Jews" attitude.

After the King David Hotel episode, the British authorities were very quick to respond to every warning. It soon became a national sport to phone a warning through to some government building and then watch the officials scurrying out at full speed, sometimes with the aid of specially-prepared firemen's ladders. The officials' lives became quite impossibly harassed and the administration remained permanently semi-paralysed. the Post Office used to be evacuated three or four times a day, until people simply stopped using it. And the worst of it all was that they never knew when the warning was a hoax and when it might not be in dead earnest—and no one was taking any more chances.

*   *   *   *   *

Stories of British brutality had been so much hearsay until I saw signs of it at first-hand. After the blowing up of the King David Hotel, the Army carried out searches in various Kibbutzim, ostensibly for arms, but actually as a subtle warning to the Yishuv of what they could and would do to settlements if the Agency and Haganah did not cease their co-operation with the "terrorists" and renew their previous idyll with the Mandatory Government.

Two kibbutzim which received special attention from the Army were Ruhama and Dorot in the Negev—the southernmost part of Palestine. A party of journalists was taken out by the Jewish Agency to see these settlements a few days after the British had finished with them. One of our journalist friends invited me to come along and I grabbed at the chance.

We passed Latrun on the way. Besides the VIPs there, who received special attention, there were hundreds of young men, suspected terrorists, who had spent years behind that barbed wire. This happened to be a relatives' visiting-day. As we turned off the main road to Latrun we

11

passed a long string of people walking the mile from the road to the camp gates. It was a scorchingly hot day and the sun blazed on those tramping silently down the dusty highway each carrying a basket and numerous parcels—delicacies, clothes, books, games, anything to make their beloved ones see that they were remembered. As in most cases the ones behind the barbed wire had been breadwinners, those pitiful packages symbolised constant stinting, scraping and self-sacrifice.

At the gate there were already a crowd of people, standing quietly, patiently and waiting—always waiting—while the pitiless sun beat down on their defenceless heads. I could have wept with pity and humiliation.

We left Latrun with its sad, sun-scorched line of straggling visitors behind us, and continued south into the desert of the Negev. After miles and miles of hot sand, we were suddenly startled to see brilliant patches of bright green and silvery cascades of water leaping joyously from the sprinklers of the irrigation pipes. We had reached Dorot.

As we turned into the gates of the settlement, the first thing we noticed was a young plantation of saplings, which had been practically uprooted. The settlers who came to greet us explained that the Army had used the plantation as a parking-ground for their armoured cars and bren-gun carriers. Those saplings which had not been destroyed by the heavy vehicles had been deliberately uprooted in the search for hidden arms. There had been considerable damage done to Dorot, but we spent only a short time there as we were intent on getting to the real showpiece —Ruhama, our next place of call.

Here the sprinklers were not operating, as the soldiers had broken the water-pumps. The settlers were working hard against time to repair the pumps before the year's crop was lost in the blazing heat of the sun.

We were met by the secretary of the settlement, and taken for a tour of the "battle area." On the way, various members of the Kibbutz joined us and told us what had happened. The soldiers had been sent into the settlement without officers and instructed to behave as they would in conquered enemy territory. They imposed a 24-hour curfew while they conducted their search, and allowed no one out to get food or visit the lavatories which, as is customary in Kibbutzim, were in a separate building set some distance away from the living quarters. The soldiers did, however, milk the cows and brought some food to the children's house. A pregnant woman was dragged to her room by her hair when she did not hurry to carry out the curfew orders quickly enough; soldiers at-

12

tempted to break into the girls' rooms at night but were frightened off
by their screams; some of the young men were punished for breaking the
curfew by being made to stand bare-headed in the hot sun, holding heavy
stones above their heads. Anyone whose arms drooped had his elbows
severely punched with the butt of a rifle. Others, for some minor offence,
were made to run round in a circle for hours and when their pace lagged
they were reminded none too gently with the point of a bayonet to pick
it up.

Some of the settlers had been in Nazi concentration camps and they
said, with terrible bitterness, that the British were no better than the
Germans. But these were all stories; we wanted to see the facts, with our
own eyes. And we saw quite a good deal. Practically every house had
its floors torn up and large holes ripped in the ceilings and walls. Destroyed furniture lay scattered all over the rooms. In the dining room
there was a veritable mountain of soil where extensive digging had taken
place.

One of our guides told us that the British had brought mine-detecting
dogs with them and that every time the dogs sensed metal—usually pipes—
digging had been instituted. Another maintained that each time the
dogs felt tired and sat down, the soldiers dug up the floor at that spot.
But I suspect the latter of having a sense of humor.

The two or three British journalists in the party insisted that these
were all legitimate measures in the search for arms. Perhaps they were;
but the situation began to look ugly when we visited the workshops and
found the walls bare of tools, and everything that was not removable,
destroyed; when we visited the food-stores and found that paraffin had
been poured over edible goods, that food had been mixed with manure—
and other such refinements; when we found hay-ricks spitefully set on
fire, shower-baths completely ruined, the generator, water-pumps and
bread-ovens deliberately damaged, and visible evidence that living quarters and store-rooms had been used as latrines. Any further doubts which
any of us might have had about the intentions of the British were
completely banished when we visited the secretary's office and the clothes-
stores. In the secretary's office the pictures on the wall had been slashed,
papers had been taken out of files and torn to shreds. The typewriter
and duplicating machine were wrecked; gramophone records lay on the
floor smashed to smithereens. In the clothes-store there was a veritable
shambles. There were practically no men's clothes, or fragments thereof,
visible, as these were probably considered fair loot; but women's and

children's clothes were very much in evidence—swept off the shelves, ripped open, torn, ragged and trampled into the ground by heavy boots. The crowning evidence of British "kultur" was the writing on the walls. Wherever there was a nice, white expanse, there were swastikas and slogans such as "Hitler started the job, we'll finish it!" or "We'll turn this whole bloody country into a concentration camp" and so on.

There was, however, one saving grace. Some more kindly-disposed soldier had drawn a replica of the wistful-looking man peeping over a wall—then very popular in England—and underneath it had written: "Wot! No arms?"

By the end of our tour we were thoroughly sick at heart and even the lone British correspondents looked somewhat crestfallen and shame-faced.

We had a late lunch at Ruhama—a typical kibbutz lunch, with the soup, meat and vegetables all dished up together in a tin plate, and eaten with a spoon and fork (there seems to be a general boycott against knives in all communal establishments in our country) and were each given half a cup of precious water to moisten our extended tongues.

As we took leave of the settlers and commiserated with them, one of them remarked sadly: "This is what they did to us in spite of the fact that we told them we hated the terrorists as much as they did, and that we were Socialists, just as they were." As we looked back, we saw the red flag of the Shomer Hatzair waving proudly in solitary splendor on the roof of what once had been the dining-hall.

*   *   *   *   *

In September, 1946, Shmuel was asked by the Revisionist Party to go to Europe on their behalf. At the same time, he was asked by the IZL Command to become one of the few full-time members of the organization and to initiate his new status by undertaking a mission for them too, while he was in Europe.

While he agreed unquestionably to carrying out this commission, he was nevertheless worried about what would happen to me. Jerusalem was not a very savory place at that time for a solitary Jewess, for reasons which I will explain later; and, in addition, both the country and the language were still very strange to me. I confess to having shared Shmuel's misgivings.

14

We found a solution to our problem: I would visit South Africa, while Shmuel was in Europe. For nearly seven long years we had been separated from our families there. During that time my father and both Shmuel's parents had died. Due to the complete lack of transport for civilian passengers during the war-years, and immediately after the war, I had been unable to visit South Africa since the day we set sail for England early in February, 1940. Shmuel, in his capacity as a newspaper man, had made the dangerous sea-trip there and back during the height of the U-boat season, but I had remained in London. It seemed, therefore, a very opportune time for us to split forces, he to journey north-west and I south.

The night before Shmuel left for Europe I was awakened by the sound of sirens. I still needed to think hard for a few seconds before orienting myself to the Jerusalem sirens. In the distant peaceful days of our youth in South Africa the shriek of sirens had indicated nothing more drastic than the approach of an ambulance. In London, the dreary wail presaged a storm of death and destruction from the skies; but in Jerusalem, the sirens, the symbol of man's puny attempts at self-preservation, was used to warn the security forces and the public that the underground army had carried out an operation. The security forces were warned to be in a general state of alert; while the public was warned that motorists should pull up immediately and remain stationary till the all-clear signal was given.

Soon after the sirens sounded, at two o'clock in the morning, I heard a car pull up outside our house. English-speaking men jumped out of it. I rushed to the window looked out `and saw a police-car. My heart throbbed painfully in my throat and I thought: "They've come for him at last!" My thoughts dashed wildly around: thinking of a suitable hiding-place for Shmuel, formulating lies and excuses for not letting the police into the house. In the midst of my panic I prayed fervently that I would be able to control myself and behave with dignity before the police. By this time my heart-beats had quietened down sufficiently for me to hear what was going on outside. I discovered to my intense relief and chagrin that the British were as scared as I was. The police-car was a wireless car which had by chance pulled up outside our house, the better to receive and send messages. To say that its occupants were jittery is an understatement. I heard the officer-in-charge tell his men in very picturesque language to pull themselves together, and went very shakily back to bed, with difficulty restraining myself from venting my feelings on the peace-

fully-sleeping, unconscious object of my agitation. This experience strengthened an already well-established suspicion in my mind—that fear is a
most pitiable sensation and decidedly uncomfortable.

*   *   *   *   *

Shmuel flew to Europe and I set about preparing to visit South
Africa. I discovered with something of a shock that we had both been
somewhat naive in our presumption that all that was necessary was a
decision in principle that I should go to South Africa—and then I would
go. When I attempted to do that I found that it was practically impossible for any ordinary human being to get from Palestine to South Africa
without very liberally crossing with silver the palm of a certain British
official. The ultimate purpose of this excursion into the realms of bribery
and corruption was to obtain a "Priority 3" for an air-passage.

Any civilians travelling for personal reasons were given Priority 4,
which entailed a period of waiting of anything up to three months in Cario
before securing a seat on a plane to South Africa. Priority 3 was sufficient
to get a seat from Cairo within two or three days. A close friend of ours
had actually returned to Palestine after waiting six weeks in Cairo, and
had then managed to secure Priority 3 with the judicious use of £100.

While I had neither the time, nor the money, nor the inclination
(with visions of Port Said still fresh in my mind) to spend three months in
Cairo, nevertheless my whole being revolted at the thought of lining the
pockets of a British official. I sought means of transportation in the other
elements.

There was no shipping accommodation whatsoever as the very infrequent ships which went through the Suez Canal en route to India or Aus-
tralia were already badly overcrowded when they left England. An obliging young man at Cook's worked out a fascinating overland trip for me.
It entailed travelling down the Nile by sampan, crossing various deserts,
penetrating through lion-infested jungles, doing interesting and lively
stretches by ox-wagon, and eventually ending up in a prosaic train-journey
to Johannesburg. My spirit of adventure was enthralled by the idea, but
I had to turn it down very sadly, on practical grounds—it would have taken
three months and cost hundreds of pounds, as no one else had volunteered
to join the expedition and share the expenses.

I was becoming quite desperate when, by a stroke of good luck, someone offered to get me an appointment with the great panjandrum of the

priorities, himself. (Incidentally, not the recipient of the bribes, who was an official lower down on the ladder. Whether the "big boss" got a cut or not, I do not know. I rather hope he did, as he was not at all a bad fellow.) I was warned that my story had better be good if I hoped to succeed in persuading Mr. C.

When the momentous hour arrived, I put on as tragic an expression as I could muster and this, together with my extreme nervousness, must have made me a very picture of femininity-in-distress. At least I did appear to have plucked at Mr. C.'s heart-strings. When, in addition, I told the sad tale of a poor fatherless young woman thousands of miles away from her loving family, of a distracted mother longing for one more sight of her favorite daughter, he was so visibly touched that I expected him to wipe away a surreptitious tear at any moment. Instead, he patted my shoulder in what I hope was a fatherly way and clucked consolingly: "But, my dear, my dear, of course we *must* give you Priority 3." I brightened up so considerably at this that by the time I had the precious bit of paper safely in my hands I was exchanging pleasantries with him and promising to give his regards to acquaintances in Johannesburg.

I spent a whole month after Shmuel's departure on all these manoeu-verings and contrivings to get away. And all the while I stayed, alone, in the little house we had rented from the British official. Our Jerusalem friends were appalled at my living alone and at my habit of walking around, unaccompanied, at night. Their misgivings were not without foundation. Our little house had only one story and stood isolated from its neighbours. It was consequently an easy target for prospective burglars and intruders, especially Arabs, who would not have been averse to attacking a lone, unprotected Jewess.

The danger of my walking unaccompanied at night came both from Arabs and from the British soldiery. The latter had, during this period, committed a number of atrocities against young Jewish girls and women. Several girls had been waylaid, assaulted and raped. Among them was a young member of the IZL who had been caught by a military patrol whilst pasting up the underground newspaper on the walls.

I had become too accustomed to independence and freedom from fear to be influenced by the well-meant adjurations of my friends; and I laughed off their anxieties, with the pious hope that the proximity of our dwelling to that of the head of the CID, Mr. Giles, and to various other police officers would ensure its immunity against burglars. As for my being accosted at night, I relied on my English accent and light hair to frighten off both Arabs and British. The former knew very well that the Administration would not tolerate any interference with English women, while the latter would not take the risk of assaulting the Colonel's wife by mistake.

Whilst the proximity of my house to that of Mr. Giles' might have earned me immunity from burglars, its strategic disposition had some decided disadvantages. Mr. Giles and his friends were guarded day and night by Arab guards. In the daytime, when there was traffic and company in the streets, these guards were comparatively tame. But at night, when the streets were practically deserted and when every shadow could be concealing a "terrorist," these guards were extremely jittery and trigger-happy. On many an occasion as I walked passed Mr. Giles' walled garden on my way home, I would look up to see the ugly barrel of a Sten-gun pointed at me over the wall, and would see this ominous-looking object swivel round to keep me covered all the time I was within bomb-throwing range of the domain over which it presided. Any falsemove on my part would possibly have earned me a back-full of bullets. These precautions were rather laughable in the light of the fact that I occasionally visited Mr. Giles' British neighbours and could have leaned out of their bathroom window and planted a grenade safely and soundly in Mr. Giles' bathroom. Neither Mr. Giles nor his Arab guards knew this, so the latter persisted in keeping a nervous watch over me, or rather over my shadowy outline as soon as my footsteps resounded in the dark streets.

CHAPTER III

RETURN OF THE PRODIGAL

As soon as I had my plane passage booked, I got in touch with Adina to arrange an appointment for me with Avraham, Menachem Begin's Chief-of-Staff, whom I had met a few months earlier with Shmuel. When Avraham had heard that I was planning to visit South Africa he asked Shmuel whether I would be prepared to try and raise some money for the IZL while I was there. I had had some compunctions about leaving Palestine, at a time of trouble and stress, for the comforts and leisure of a pleasure-trip to the sunny south, and this commission served to ease my conscience. I readily agreed, in spite of my intense aversion to the thankless job of appealing to people for donations.

I met Avraham in Tel Aviv. In the street, outside our meeting place, a group of young boys and girls loitered innocently. These street-gatherings were a common sight in Tel Aviv, and this one had no particular meaning. But in my romantic ignorance I read something conspiratorial and significant into this particular group of young people. No one would have been more surprised than Avraham to learn that I was convinced that they were his bodyguards and were, with ostensible innocence, guarding the building while our interview was taking place. I even went so far as to describe this meeting, and the aura of protection afforded by the young guards to my friends in South Africa, a few weeks later. It was only when I really lived "underground" that I learnt how badly I had misinformed my enthralled audience in Johannesburg. Nobody ever had any bodyguards! The boys and girls outside our place of rendezvous were as completely impervious to and ignorant of Avraham's presence as he was of theirs.

So that I should be able to carry out my commission for the IZL with some sort of legal status, Avraham enrolled me as a member. My initiation was decidedly disappointing. I had expected the solemn swearing-in process which all other members went through, but in my case this was dispensed with. I suspect the reason for it was that I was then, and until the IZL disbanded, regarded as a queer, lady-like species of terrorist, to be treated gently and sheltered from the crude, stern side of life. But, however hum-

19

drum the initiations, I was at last a full-fledged member of the Irgun Zvai Leumi!

Avraham gave me detailed instructions of how to send any money which I might collect and taught me how to use the IZL code in order to enable me to send him regular reports. Before we parted he handed me a speech, in English, which he had had prepared for me. I humbly accepted the implication that he did not consider me capable of preparing one of my own. That speech was an absolute masterpiece. It consisted of fine-sounding, flowery, Biblical phrases, in no wise improved by having been literally translated from the Hebrew. Unfortunately, I thought it wiser to destroy it before returning to Palestine, otherwise I could have quoted it in full for the delectation and education of those unacquainted with the quaintness of Hebrew style rendered in an imitation of modern English. If I had ever used that speech I am certain I would have been a sensation. Never since the days of Deborah would such thundering phrases, such god-fearing panegyrics, such fire and brimstone have been hurled at the heads of a defenceless audience.

To my regret I had to confine myself to language a little more suited to a South African audience in the year 1946; but I felt a sentimental attachment to that speech and took it with me wherever I went. A glance at it would restore my spirits when they wavered and imbue me with the fire and courage of my prophetic namesake. If that was all that Avraham intended, he succeeded admirably.

* * * * *

Cairo was an improvement on Port Said, as long as one did not penetrate too deeply into the noisome little side streets. The hotel was luxurious and orientally lavish, and the service was excellent. But none of this compensated me for the shock I received at the offices of the air company.

I arrived in Cairo on Thursday, the 31st of October, with every intention of flying to Johannesburg on Saturday. But the BOAC had other intentions. They told me regretfully, but firmly that there were only another thirty people in Cairo waiting for the same plane which, in any case, would probably be full when it left England. They assured me I would not have to wait more than two weeks in Cairo. As I had left Jerusalem with £10 in my pocket this prospect was, to say the least, somewhat disheartening. I immediately started a wearisome trek from official to official, from one travel agency to the next, in an attempt to save the situation. I tried

being angry, distraught, haughty and pathetic. I out-Sarahed Sarah Bern-
hardt in my histrionic achievements. Then I became the ultra-feminine,
helpless, clinging-ivy type. I played this act to such a pitch that I almost
convinced myself of my complete debility. But of no avail. When by Friday
evening I had still not secured myself a seat on the plane, I gave up the
struggle and sought to drown my sorrows in the company of a Cairo
acquaintance, who undertook to show me some of those vaunted fleshpots
of Egypt. We returned to my hotel rather late to find a man from the
travel agency impatiently awaiting me with the good news that I was, after
all, leaving early the next morning. My guardian angel had certainly
worked over-time. One of the passengers on the plane from England had
been an outsize man with outsize luggage. The authorities in Cairo had
given him a choice: either he travelled or his luggage travelled—but not
both. He chose to remain with his luggage and I was sent in his place. This
experience convinced me finally that anyone in skirts, who is under fifty
and not positively repulsive, can manage very nicely in the Middle East.

*   *   *   *   *

I walked in unexpectedly on my family in Johannesburg, having, char-
acteristically, neglected to let them know I was coming. My welcome was
both enthusiastic and tumultuous, the tumult sometimes reaching deafening
proportions when too many of my approximately five hundred relatives
foregathered in one place at one time. My reception was both overwhelming and somewhat frightening. After seven years of being completely
family-less, this sudden transplantation into the bosom of a prolific clan
was dizzying.

When the nine days of wonder were over and I had rested awhile from
the super-abundant display of familial affection, I turned my attentions to
campaigning for the Irgun Zvai Leumi. I found that the activities of our
organisation had made an immense impression in South Africa, and not
only on the Jews.

The South African white population is divided roughly into three
categories: the English, the Afrikaans and the Jews. There are two large
political parties: the United Party, which consists of the English and a
minority of Afrikaans; and the Nationalist Party, consisting almost exclusively of Afrikaans. The vast majority of the Jews had always thrown in
their lot with the United Party, spoke English and sent their children to
English schools. Because of their pro-British, pro-United Party orientation,

21

they were generally disliked by the Afrikaans of the Nationalist Party, this dislike varying from the bitter hatred of the extremists to the indifference of the moderates, like Malan. At the same time, it would be very far from the truth to describe the attitude of the English to the Jews as that of brotherly love. It is among the English in South Africa that you find the real anti-semites—they dislike the Jews without reason, whereas the nationalistic Afrikaans at least think they have natural, legitimate reasons for disliking them.

The struggle of the IZL against the British in Palestine was a revelation to the Afrikaans. Firstly, it showed them that not all Jews were Anglophiles *causa Anglophiliae,* and, secondly, it revealed the astonishing fact that the "Jew-boys" knew how to fight and give better than they received. A great respect for this new generation of Maccabeans was born in the hearts of the Bible-loving Afrikaans. Their admiration for the exploits of the IZL was unbounded. If we had collected money amongst them we might have had even more of a success than we had amongst the Jews.

The feelings of the English in South Africa towards the revolt in Palestine were mixed. The handful who understood its motives and aims sympathised with it. But the English are notoriously insular—not less so in South Africa than in their Home Country—and the majority of them neither knew what the conflict was about nor cared to take the trouble to find out. They knew only that the British and British interests were being attacked in Palestine and that the Jews were to blame for all the bother. This served to make them just so much more anti-semitic.

The Zionists in South Africa, brought up in an atmosphere of comparative freedom, completely devoid of any of the ghetto-complexes which had crushed the spirit of independence of many European Jewish communities, unanimously approved of the struggle against the British in Palestine. There were differences of opinion amongst them on the question of what form this revolt should take—that of the Jewish Agency or that of the "dissidents." The majority of those who belonged to the so-called Old Zionist Organisation stood solidly behind the Jewish Agency and gave their financial support to the Haganah. A large minority, consisting of members of the New Zionist Organisation, gave their whole-hearted support and sympathy to the IZL and LHI—the "dissidents" or "terrorists."

Among the Jewish non-Zionists, or anti-Zionists (of whom there are not overmany in South Africa) there were many who supported the IZL because they believed in freedom from oppression and because they were

22

filled with admiration for the courage and idealism of men who could undertake so unequal a battle against the mighty British Empire. Others disapproved because it spoilt their relationship with their English friends, and a third category wavered while waiting on a lead from Moscow.

Everyone whom I met was eager and hungry for news of Palestine. I could not tell everyone, indiscriminately, about the IZL and its activities, but I did give them a general picture of the complete reversal of history in Jerusalem—where the proud British had been forced into ghettoes and lived in daily fear of their lives at the hands of the once-cowed and trembling Jews. They loved to hear this and I loved telling it. I took particular pleasure in describing how the notorious General Barker—one of the most anti-Jewish of all the British GOC's who succeeded one another in Palestine in a dismal parade—went to work in the mornings with an armed guard on either side of him, two soldiers with tommy-guns preceding him and two walking behind. He needed only a steel umbrella to complete the picture. My listeners, whatever their sympathies may have been, were delighted at the blow which the underground in Palestine were dealing to British prestige.

Whenever anyone asked me curiously whether it wasn't rather frightening to live in Palestine, I answered with a great show of bravado that only two things there really frightened me: crossing the streets, especially Allenby road in Tel Aviv, and the thought of having to share a kitchen with another woman. The latter fear was by no means academic, in a country where the acute shortage of accommodation had driven thousands of unfortunate women to suffer just that very purgatory.

* * * * *

My friends and I discussed ways and means of raising money. We did not want any large-scale, country-wide campaigns with the concomitant propaganda and expenses. From all points of view, the less the general public knew about our activities the better; and from the specific point of view of expenses, we were determined to keep these down to the barest minimum, so that every penny we collected could be used to buy guns and bullets in Palestine. We were all voluntary workers and any of the small expenses which we did incur were paid out of our own pockets or by one of the richer members of our small working committee.

We at first concentrated on approaching people personally and asking them for donations, but towards the end of my trip I dropped my caution to some extent and addressed meetings of about seventy-five people at a

23

time. Although not all the people who attended these meetings were sympathisers, nevertheless no one ever betrayed our trust by talking about my identity or spreading the news about my activities. For this I was very grateful, as I still had to return to Palestine.

In lieu of any ability as a public speaker, I had to call on the latent histrionic talent which I had discovered in myself. As I am not anything like the popular conception of a "terrorist": someone who stalks around in riding-boots carrying a sten-gun—a kind of cross between a Hollywood cowgirl and a Russian partisan—I emphasised the contrast by appearing before my audiences as a well-groomed, well-dressed young woman straight from a finishing-school in England. I immediately produced the right dramatic effect. From the audience came the inevitable stage-whisper: "Is *that* what the terrorists look like?" and "If all the terrorists are like that, then they can't be such terrible people!"

I started my speeches by introducing myself as a very, very humble member of the Irgun Zvai Leumi. This was literally true, but nobody believed me. Many were quite convinced that I had personally blown up the King David Hotel and daily wrecked trains and bridges. I really did try my best to deny it, but it did not help.

I told my audiences as simply and clearly as possible about the position in Palestine, about the struggle and aims of the IZL and why they, the South African Jews, should help in this struggle. I usually anticipated the objections of many people to the killing of "innocent Tommies" by proclaiming beforehand that in any war the ordinary soldiers were innocent victims of their Government's quarrels and no less so in the war in Palestine. In an appeal to my audiences to choose between innocent Tommy Atkins and innocent Isaac Cohen, I told them this story of one of many unfortunate so-called illegal immigrants—a true story and one typical of many of the tragic tales of the pitiful remnants of European Jewry.

A young Jewish girl had been in a German brothel where she contracted syphilis. According to Nazi practice the punishment for this crime was the gas-chamber. As she was already in the queue, patiently awaiting her turn for death, the Russians bombed the camp. In the ensuing panic and disorder she and many of her companions escaped to the surrounding forests. There they made contact with the partisans, one of whom was a young Jew, "Isaac Cohen." Isaac befriended the young girl and took her to the nearest hospital, where she received treatment and was cured. She returned to fight with the partisans and married Isaac. When the

24

war ended, the two of them decided to go to Palestine and start life anew, forgetting the horrors and atrocities of the past. They walked across the whole of Europe, from Poland to Italy. For many weary weeks they suffered hunger and cold and hardships, until they reached Italy, the last stage in their journey. From there they sailed in one of the small, overcrowded "illegal" ships to Palestine—the land of promise. Off the shores of Haifa their tiny ship was intercepted by a British destroyer and the passengers were forcibly transferred. They resisted, armed only with bottles and sticks against machine-guns. In the ensuing fight, Isaac Cohen was killed. His young wife was left alone—without the friend who had encouraged her in her fight to regain her health, without the husband who had been her prop and mainstay on the long Odyssey across Europe, without the sole remaining person on earth who was close to her and loved her.

I appealed to my audience to decide whether they had enough room in their hearts for both Isaac Cohen and Tommy Atkins. My speeches usually ended with a grand Churchillian epigram: "Give us the gold and we will turn it into iron!"

Question-time after the speeches was the most trying time of all. Sometimes, I had to confess to my complete ignorance of the answers to questions such as: "What are the exact numbers of members in the IZL and LHI?" or "What does Menachem Begin look like?" At other times I had to hide my irritation under a calm and patient exterior while answering questions such as "What is the national food of Palestine?" or "How does one cook the Palestinian egg-plant?" But generally the questions were a good deal more pertinent. One question which invariably cropped up concerned the Irgun's debut into the bank-robbing industry. This thorny problem had been discussed and rediscussed by the High Command before it was decided that the urgent need for money necessitated its being taken by force—from British banks only. It had been a very difficult decision for the High Command to take, and the boys who carried out these operations really could not stomach them. This was obvious from the numerous bank-robberies which failed, in contrast to the brilliant success of nearly every military operation carried out against the British. The IZL were very bad bank-robbers—a field in which they were admittedly outdone by the LHI.

The question, with implied denunciation, usually came from one of the nastier members of the audience, and was framed as follows: "How can the speaker reconcile the so-called high ideals of the IZL with the

25

common robbing of banks and the extorting of money from the public?" The speaker would turn coldly to face her accuser and ask: "How much money have you given to help these young people buy guns to free your country for you?" A deep silence. A finger was melodramatically pointed at the rash questioner: "Then you are responsible for forcing fine young men to become robbers!" This was usually greeted with great applause, more because of the discomfiture of the questioner than because of the noble phraseology of the speaker. As for the accusation that the IZL extorted money—this I dismissed with the cutting contempt which it deserved.

My questioners very often emulated the vaunted month of March—they came in like lions and went out like lambs.

The Jewish Agency propaganda in South Africa against the "terrorists" was cynically subtle. They took advantage of the general color-phobia amongst the whites and the particular Polish-phobia amongst the Jews, the majority of whom had emigrated from Lithuania, to condemn the underground out of hand by dubbing its members "Yemenites and Poles." And the Jewish Agency flogged that horse to death, adding, as a malicious afterthought, with a shrewd eye on the provincial snobbishness of most of the Jews, that they were also uneducated, uncultured barbarians. Now I, to my regret, am not a Yemenite; I am descended from good Lithuanian Jewish stock and have had a University education. So, whenever I was asked whether that description really fitted all the "terrorists," I would gravely turn to the questioner, give a courtly bow, and say "Madam (or Sir), I am a terrorist. You may judge for yourself."

*   *   *   *   *

We had no difficulty whatsoever in sending the money which we collected to Palestine, as both that country and South Africa were at that time in the sterling area. Avraham had provided me with a number of addresses of people who acted as receiving agents for him. All I had to do was to go into any bank and transfer the money quite legally and openly to one of Avraham's agents, who then passed it on to the right source.

Our difficulties arose over the question of receipts. We wanted the people who gave us money to know that one hundred percent of it went to the IZL in Palestine; but we could hardly have individual receipts sent from there—a process which would have necessitated our sending lists, obviously an impossibility in the circumstances. We never solved this problem—which was entirely one of our own making as none of our donors

26

ever raised the question. Those who knew me and my family accepted my verbal receipt unquestioningly. I never approached anyone whom I did not know, without being accompanied by a common acquaintance, in the halo of whose reflected honesty I basked. This complete and implicit trust in the emissary of the IZL on the part of the South African Jews was both touching and encouraging.

One man, however, did get a receipt. I had received an urgent cable from Avraham asking me to send £2000 immediately. This I did within a few days with the help of one very large donation and a few smaller ones. Two weeks later, the IZL blew up the British Army Officers' Club in Goldschmidt House, Jerusalem, in a brilliantly-executed operation. As soon as the news reached the Johannesburg newspapers, the man who had given the very generous donation phoned me and thanked me for his "receipt."

A weekly ordeal was my letter in code to Palestine reporting on my activities and on the various sums of money transmitted to them. The code was a very simple one to understand but very difficult to use; and somehow or other it seemed to lend itself most easily to love-letters. My weekly outpourings of ardor left me as completely drained of energy and feelings as if I had really been consumed by the flames of passion. I subsequently heard that my correspondent had to do a lot of explaining to his wife, who accidently came upon one of my letters.

He played up, and replied in terms of endearment considerably restricted by his limited knowledge of English. His knowledge of the proprieties, too, was somewhat deficient as, on one occasion, after a particularly successful venture into the fields of amorous elegaics, he ended his letter with a request that I convey his respects to my husband. The Palestine censor must have shaken his head dolefully over that one.

*　*　*　*　*

In spite of the fact that we took a certain amount of care, it soon became public knowledge that the IZL were receiving money from South Africa. Questions were asked about this in Parliament and on the day that Mrs. Bertha Solomon, a Jewish member, hotly denied the libellous accusation that the British-loving Jewish community had contributed to the terrorists in Palestine, I had the supreme satisfaction of receiving a £1000 donation.

Two officers of the Palestine Intelligence Service came out specially to try and trace the source and the method of transfer of South African

Jewry's financial contributions to the underground forces. We heard that they had discovered how the money was sent—first to London and from there to Tel Aviv. At this we breathed normally again and continued sending money directly to Tel Aviv without any qualms for the feelings of the sadly misinformed "Intelligence" officers.

While I was in Johannesburg, some IZL and LHI detainees escaped from the British detention camp in Kenya and were reported to have entered the Union of South Africa illegally and to have been given refuge there by sympathisers. We knew that this was not true, but the Union police did not; and this report, coupled with their certain knowledge of the existence of a strong core of supporters of the IZL in the Union served to put them on the alert.

The South African Government would probably not have been much concerned over whether her Jews supported the "terrorists" or not, were it not for the fact that the British Royal Family were just about due to arrive on an official visit. The Government probably felt they had quite enough on their hands without having a royal assassination thrust upon them. The police consequently approached the Jewish Board of Deputies and asked them to use their influence to secure the Royal family against terrorist attacks. Instead of ridiculing the idea, the Board of Deputies flew into a panic, approached the local committees of the New Zionist Organisation (which was considered to be hand in glove with the IZL) and set up a great wail about the dire consequences to South African Jewry should any harm come to the King. One local New Zionist chairman, with a sense of humor, sent his personal guarantee to the head of the police for the safety of the Royal Family. In spite of this, the police precautions were numerous and elaborate. And while posses of police patrolled the streets and plain-clothes detectives mingled with the crowds, the "dangerous terrorists" watched the Royal procession—from very much less than a bomb's throw.

I actually got my look at the Royal Family in my birth-place in the Orange Free State. I found myself standing next to someone almost as dangerous as myself—Mr. R., a teacher at my High School, a rabid follower of Malan, anti-British, anti-Jewish, anti-native—in fact, just plain "anti." We fell on each other's necks, exchanged some nasty remarks about the British and taunted each other with lacking the courage of our convictions by coming out to stand in the sun for an hour in order to watch a British king and queen ride by.

Our conversation drifted naturally to Palestine and he started explaining to me how the Jewish claim to the country on Biblical grounds was based on a false premise. Then followed some very involved interpretation, liberally scattered with quotations, and a somewhat original theory based on the division of ancient Palestine into Israel and Judah—all of which boiled down to the argument that Palestine really belonged to the Arabs. And, at any rate, said Mr. R., it is only fair to let the majority in a country decide to whom that country should belong. I asked him, very innocently, whether he thought that principle should apply to South Africa also, where the blacks outnumber the whites by four to one. At this he looked rather startled and withdrew his suggestion. We parted on the most amiable of terms.

*   *   *   *   *

By March, 1947, Shmuel wrote that he was on his way back to Palestine, and I began to think of getting back to the yoke of domesticity. Once more I started a hunt for transportation. I eventually managed to get a first-class berth on the Windsor Castle which was sailing to England via Port Said. The ship was under charter to the British Ministry of Transport, whose representatives made all the arrangements.

When I arrived in Durban to take up my "first-class berth," I discovered I was sharing a cabin on C deck with twenty-seven other women. It was just at this time that the British Government was carrying out a pious, sanctimonious campaign against overcrowding on the "illegal" refugee ships to Palestine. Oceans of crocodile tears were shed over the cruel plight of those miserable, human animals forced by the Jewish authorities to sail to Palestine in hell-ships. These "miserable, human animals" were falling over themselves to get away from the memory and the perpetuation of the concentration camps of Europe. They welcomed a short boat-trip in very much better conditions than they had experienced for years, albeit those conditions did not conform with so-called civilized conceptions of modern comfort.

But I and a thousand other people on the hell-ship that was the Windsor Castle were not fleeing from terror and persecution and on top of it were paying first-class fares for the privilege of travelling in slightly less discomfort than the "illegal" immigrants. The British might have been a little less raucous about other peoples' hell-ships while they themselves were making a nice little profit out of their own line of Stygian sea-craft.

29

My cabin consisted mostly of Lebanese, Egyptian and Syrian women—all disembarking at Port Said. They jabbered incessantly, each trying to over-shout the other. When they started quarrelling amongst themselves after the second day at sea, I had enough and made a timid appeal to the Purser. When I told him what cabin I was in, he threw his hands up in horror, exclaiming: "How in heaven's name did *you* get there!" and immediately arranged to transfer me to another cabin—on A Deck. A dark suspicion began forming in my mind. This ship was evidently more hellish for some people than for others, and the distinction was not one of price, as we had all paid first-class fares. My suspicions were fully confirmed when I saw my new cabin-mates. All of them were going to England and each one had at least four Aryan grandparents. The distinction was evidently one of race. For Semites of any description, crowded conditions of C-deck were sufficient, but the true-blue Anglo-Saxons had to have something better. I should, of course, have refused the change, in solidarity with my fellow-Semites; but I suffer from occasional lapses of character and this lapse was considerably helped on by the sight of a Syrian woman breast-feeding a four-year-old child in my original cabin. I partially calmed my conscience when the conversation in my new cabin turned to Palestine, by getting in some very effective blows at British policy—blows which were all the more telling as they came ostensibly from "one of us."

Before arriving in Port Said I received a cable from Shmuel saying that he had arranged an air-passage for me from Port Said to Lydda. I silently blessed him for saving me the awful train journey from Egypt to Tel Aviv.

Anyone landing in Egypt at that time had to declare his religion. An irate official revealed the purpose of this declaration when, on one occasion, a fellow-traveller, whom the Americans would picturesquely call a "wise guy," started explaining that his father was a Methodist, his mother a Catholic and that he had not made up his mind yet. The Egyptian official interrupted him impatiently: "I don't care what your religion is! Are you a Jew or aren't you?"

When I came through Egypt the first time with Shmuel, he declared that his religion was Jewish and I had, perforce, in solidarity to do the same. When I came there the second time, alone, I revolted and answered a good deal more truthfully: "Atheist." The puzzled official wrote down "religion unknown." This third and last time I was given no choice. The official was a burly, suave Egyptian with a horrible leer. He looked at me,

30

wrote down "Christian" in spite of my feeble protestations, and got me off the ship in five minutes in order to make my plane to Cairo.

I had an afternoon and evening to kill in Cairo. During the afternoon I took a stroll down the main street and was almost immediately stopped by a young Egyptian boy. He told me it was not safe for an English woman to be walking alone in the streets as there was an anti-British demonstration going on, and offered to accompany me back to my hotel. I thought it would be just like Fate to play a silly trick on me and get me murdered in Egypt for being an English woman, so I decided to beat a hasty retreat.

In the evening my great stand-by in Cairo took me to a dinner-party to inaugurate a new air-company. There were a number of British businessmen and diplomats there, as well as a sprinkling of high Egyptian officials, one of whom had a white-slave-traffic look in his eye which made me shudder. At our table were four Britishers who, on hearing I was returning to Palestine, immediately began bombarding me with questions. They first wanted to know how I was able to return to Palestine when all British women and children were being evacuated. (It was just at this time that the Mandatory Government, as a first indication of the complete disintegration of their administration, had evacuated the families of officials and all British subjects who were not on essential work. This, of course, did not apply to Jews with British passports.) I assured them gravely that my husband was on essential work and that I was considered good for his morale. During the conversation, Mr. W., the manager of a large British Company, leaned over and told me confidentially that he was sure more Englishmen were shot every day in Cairo than in Palestine, but it was not politic to make a fuss about that in the newspapers. We all parted on very cordial terms about 2 a.m., giving me just enough time to catch an hour's sleep and be at the aerodrome at 6 a.m.

When we arrived over Lydda, there was an unprecedented fog and we were forced to land first at Akir aerodrome, where passengers and plane were jealously guarded by RAF police, until we could take off again for Lydda. I felt a little nervous as I passed through the security officials at the Lydda airport. But no one took much notice of me and I slipped away unobstrusively to join Shmuel in Tel Aviv and start life in the underground.

CHAPTER IV

LIFE IN THE UNDERGROUND

LIFE in the underground sounds very romantic, or at least exciting. Actually, for most people, it alternated between the day to day struggle against financial and physical hardships with its concomitant tedium and monotony, and the constant worry and anxiety about the safety of friends and acquaintances in general and those nearest and dearest to them in particular.

For the handful of young men and women who took part in actual operations, there was the ephemeral thrill of adventure while the attacks were being planned and executed. And then anti-climax, if you were still alive and whole. Back to the incessant grind of training and the nerve-wracking precautions, the iron control over tongue and action, the strict attitude of caution towards even one's closest friends.

As for being romantic in the sentimental meaning of the word—nothing killed romance quite as effectively as membership of the IZL. The young men, who regarded themselves either as potential corpses to be buried for all time, or as potential prisoners to be buried in detention camps for years without end, would, for the most part, not even consider the question of marriage. And to have passing love affairs and flirtations with their fellow-members was not considered to be quite the thing. So they sought out other fields for their amorous excursions.

The girls, on the other hand, had neither the time nor the opportunity to meet young men outside the IZL and many of them suffered deeply from the pangs of unrequited love, and, still more, from the natural horror that young women have of becoming old maids. So romance was sadly lacking in the ranks of the IZL.

My first real introduction to the underground came with my meeting Menachem Begin soon after my return to Tel Aviv. Shmuel and Avraham took me to see him. We entered a ground-floor flat in a new, modern building, in a fashionable area of Tel Aviv. In one of the rooms, furnished as an office, sat Begin. There were no bodyguards, no precautions, no dramatics. I expected him to have a beard and be dressed in the long black coat favoured by the fanatically religious. This had been his form of disguise when we first arrived in Palestine. By the time I got to hear about it he was already safely accoutred in another role.

Begin had not been out of doors in the daytime since he had shaved off his beard, and the part of his face which had once been hirsute was consequently deathly pale. He is slight, baldish, and ugly, with an ascetic and refined ugliness. In his sports-coat and grey flannel trousers he looked like the Diaspora version of a Hebrew teacher. His mild and gentle manners were hardly in keeping with even my educated conception of a "terrorist." I found later that these manners were deceptive. He could, when necessary, be as hard as a rock. But a rock with a soft sub-stratum which may endanger the security of the upper strata, however firm and solid they may be. Begin's soft sub-stratum is his incurable sentimentality, which prevents him from being a truly great man. He has the brain and strength of character to make him one of the outstanding figures of our age but for his one weakness—a weakness liable to prove fatal in the ruthless, cruel game of politics.

The one fear of every member of the underground was that of being caught by the British and forced to spend years of idleness in prisons or detention camps. The fear of death in an operation took second place in the hearts of the young men. But not so with their parents or wives. There were women who fervently prayed that their sons or husbands might be sent to Latrun and Eritrea where they would at least be safe from the daily peril of death which hovered like Damocles' sword over their heads. They felt that the pain of separation from their loved ones would be fully compensated for by the respite from the constant, sickening agony of fear and worry under which they lived.

The young men, themselves, did not appreciate the advantages of sitting safely, but somewhat too securely, in enforced exile, and they contrived all manner and means of conspiracy to avoid being captured. These methods of conspiracy fell roughly into three categories: those practised by Avraham, Shmuel and Begin respectively. The choice of method depended on circumstances, the need of the hour and, to some extent, on the temperaments of the people concerned.

The Avraham method consisted broadly of changing one's name and address from time to time and avoiding former acquaintances like the plague. Avraham favoured this method by necessity. His home had been in Haifa, from where he had been forced to run away as the police had got onto his tracks. When they found their bird flown, the police arrested Avraham's wife instead, in the hope of using her as bait to trap her husband. But Ollie, his wife, who had herself never been associated with the IZL, had other ideas and sent him word that he was on no account to hand himself over to the police in a burst of chivalry. She was eventually allowed to return to her baby after a few days in prison.

In Tel Aviv Avraham, whose real name is Haim Landau, assumed the name of Haim Grossman, the identity of a German Jew, and disappeared completely as far as the British were concerned. He saw his wife secretly two or three times a year and hardly knew his son. He was the arch-conspirator. Only one or two members of the underground knew that he went under the name of Grossman and no one knew where he lived. His wife knew that he had had to leave Haifa because he was suspected of being connected with the IZL, but for years she thought he was practising his profession as an architect in Tel Aviv and did not know that, after practically every other member of the High Command had been betrayed to the British, Avraham had become the right-hand man of Menachem Begin and Chief-of-Staff of the IZL.

Although he moved around freely, disguised only by coloured sunglasses, Avraham's life was restricted as if he were behind prison bars. It consisted of work and work and then more work. He never visited friends, never went to a cinema or theatre. His only social life was the occasional exchange of pleasantries with the wives of his fellow-workers whom he met at the Begin's flat. The people who worked under him considered him inhuman—a man who had no thought for family, for rest, for relaxation; who was completely consumed by one over-riding passion—the IZL. But they respected him for his unsparing self-flagellation and worked all the harder for his good example.

Shmuel, who had now become a member of the IZL High Command had a different conception of conspiracy. We lived in a flat in Ramat Gan, which is about five kilometres from Tel Aviv, under our own name. We met our friends, had frequent visitors and generally lived a life whose very normality belied Shmuel's occupation. Very few of our friends knew of Shmuel's connection with the IZL (even though some did vaguely suspect it), and no member of the IZL, except those at the very top, knew where Shmuel lived. To the neighbors and to our acquaintances, Shmuel was a newspaperman. This accounted for the odd hours which he kept and also for his frequent trips abroad. When I was pressed to say exactly

34

on what newspaper he worked, I would declare with a grand gesture: "Oh, all kinds of papers, American, South African and . . ." and I hoped my questioner was satisfied. As we lived in a rather compact little community, our neighbours took a great deal of interest in us. However, no one ever suspected our nefarious connections, mainly because I spoke such an Anglicised Hebrew and because Shmuel always wore a suit. Who had ever heard of a terrorist who wore a suit! It was notorious that they wore khaki shorts and shirts—as most of them did, anyhow, in company with at least 80 percent of the male population of Palestine.

I was in charge of disposing of or hiding all incriminating documents. Shmuel had given me strict instructions to burn any unnecessary papers and to put documents that he needed in a secret niche in his writing-desk. I soon discovered that burning papers in a country where there are no incinerators and no open fires was a major operation and one likely to attract a good deal too much attention. So I simply tore them up and put them in the dust-bin—a fact which I did not think it necessary to worry Shmuel with. As for putting documents into the desk—I had a much better hiding-place which the male mind could not possibly be expected to appreciate. Instead of going through the laborious process of opening up the desk to find the secret spring and then closing it again, as Shmuel fondly imagined I did, I used to slip all discriminating documents amongst my underclothing. No British policeman with a proper upbringing would have descended into prying into a lady's lingerie drawer!

Shmuel did his work, which consisted mostly of writing, in an office in Tel Aviv; but he very often worked at home, too. This necessitated his travelling to and from Tel Aviv with papers in his briefcase which could have incriminated him beyond any shadow of a doubt if he had ever been searched by the British. While the taxis and buses in which he travelled were searched on innumerable occasions, he, himself, was never touched. The very respectability of his appearance ensured him a safe conduct.

The third and most extreme method of underground conspiracy was, as far as I know, practised only by Menachem Begin. He lived with his family under a false name and never left his home during the day. For a year he did not see the sun. When he had to meet anyone he was fetched in a car by night and brought back the same night, or else he spent the following day at the flat where the meeting had taken place and returned only when darkness had fallen.

The Begins lived in a secluded and select part of Tel Aviv under the name of Konigshoffer. The selection of their residence was entrusted to Meir, one of the oldest members of the IZL and the universal "uncle," in whose capable hands the general management of the Begin household was placed. He based his choice of a flat on its two-fold advantage: it was on the ground floor and had a separate entrance so that none of the family had to use the communal staircase; and it had five exits, in case of emergency.

Ala, Begin's wife, hardly left the house at all in those days. She could not visit or be visited by her friends. Her sole companions were the members of the IZL High Command who came to confer with her husband, and the wives of those who were married—rather a hit-or-miss arrangement as far as she was concerned. Household supplies were provided by Meir, at whose flat Begin very often met people or simply sat and worked in greater convenience than in his own home. Ala's own personal purchases were made by the wives or by Rukhama (Begin's and Avraham's secretary and one of the few other people allowed to visit at the Begin flat). Her only relaxation was sitting on the secluded porch and knitting.

At this time the Begins had two children—Benny and Chasya. Ala could have no domestic help whatsoever because of the peculiar, inexplicable habits of her husband; so Begin helped her. I got a middle class shock of surprise the first time I saw Menachem Begin, notorious rebel-leader and Public Enemy No. 1 of the British, washing the baby's napkins. But he said he liked house-work as it gave him some means of exercise and relaxation, and I very soon got used to seeing him wash the floors without wanting to rush up and take the mop away from him and do the job myself.

He would wash, dress and feed the children while at the same time discussing matters of high policy with one or more members of the High Command. Shmuel was somewhat taken aback at first, but he, too, soon learnt to disregard these domestic activities in the midst of taking life and death decisions.

Chasya at this time was a baby of six months, but Benny, who was four, was a problem. He was a very intelligent child and conversation had to be considerably camouflaged. He felt there was something peculiar about his household but he never said a word to his playmates at the kindergarten. Nevertheless, it was thought safer not to rely entirely on Benny's discretion, and everything discussed in the house had a code-name, while everyone who visited there had a pseudonym with uncle or aunt attached to it. Shmuel was "Dod Yaacov" and I was "Dodah Rivka." In the comparative safety of the domestic atmosphere we sometimes grew a little lax so that Benny, in whose honor the whole performance was staged, used to call me "Dodah Rivka whom father calls Doris" and Shmuel was "Dod Yaacov whom Dodah Rivka calls Mooky" (which is Shmuel's nickname.)

Begin himself was called "Ben David" after David Raziel. His lieutenants shortened this to "Bad"—the name generally applied to him except in his own home where everyone called him "Aba" (father). Neither the name "Menachem" or "Begin" was ever mentioned, even in the strictest privacy. I disgraced myself considerably at my first meeting with him when I addressed him as "Mr. Begin." Shmuel and Avraham looked horrified and the former whispered fiercely to me: "Don't you know you mustn't use that name!" I did not know, but I accepted the rebuke meekly.

Shmuel had a veritable forest of pseudonyms. He was first known in Palestine as Emanuel, but when a note in his handwriting and signed with that name fell into the hands of the Rome police, he changed his name to Karni. In Europe he was known first as Perkin and later, after the British CID had got possession of a list of code-names which they found amongst the papers of an IZL representative, as Parker.

Amongst the journalists, whom Shmuel met frequently, he was known as David or Haerlinger, according to whom he saw. To visitors from abroad he was Feldman. The wonder is that he never got entangled in his own conspiratorial nets: but I suppose he could, if necessary, always have laughed off any mistake with the good old Cockney music hall chestnut: "I'll forget me own name next!" I felt rather like a polyandrist with none of the advantages.

This very necessary practice of pseudonyms sometimes resulted in rather amusing comedies of errors. Shmuel and I, for example, used to call Begin by the English version of his pseudonym—Davidson—when we discussed him between ourselves at home. This habit caused me a great deal of confusion at a time when Shmuel was meeting Carter Davidson of the Associated Press rather frequently. When he came home and told me that Davidson had said this and that or had done this or that, I often found it difficult to reconcile the information with my knowledge and conception of Begin. Then I would realise that he meant the other Davidson. Very often in sheer desperation I would cry out wildly: "For

37

God's sake, which Davidson are you talking about." As if life was not sufficiently complicated.

We had a rich overseas supporter of the IZL whom we called Wallace. On one occasion, on returning from Paris, I was greeted by one of our American friends with the important announcement that Wallace was in Palestine. She was referring to Henry Wallace, but I have a one-track mind and naturally took it to mean that our Wallace, our rich Wallace, was here. I immediately passed the information to Shmuel and he and Avraham set the wheels in motion in order to find him.

A few days later at the breakfast table Shmuel took a few seconds off from his absorption in the newspaper to tell me that Dr. Altman had had an interview with Wallace. I snorted disdainfully and said: "What's so important about that, that they've got to print it in the newspaper." Shmuel looked at me with new respect. After all, this disdain of celebrities was rather admirable. A few minutes later I realised that this was *Henry* Wallace he was talking about and that it had been *Henry Wallace,* and not our rich Wallace, whom my American friend had been talking about. I kept a discreet silence until the time came when Shmuel remarked wearily that he and Avraham had been unable to trace our Wallace. Then I broke down and confessed to my parochialism.

* * * * *

The IZL High Command at that time consisted of eight young men, amongst whom the 34-year old Begin, the Commander-in-Chief, was the oldest. Avraham was Chief of Staff, Amitzur was in charge of training. He is Russian-born, short, thick-set, with flashing eyes and a brilliant smile. He was the toughest-looking member of the High Command and certainly the nearest approach to a "terrorist" in appearance.

Joel was the head of the intelligence service. Tall and fair, he could pass anywhere as an Englishman as long as he did not open his mouth. He cloaks some pretty sharp claws beneath a bland and courteous exterior. He had been a policeman, and must have been a very good one as there was no information he could not, and did not, get hold of.

Gideon was Chief of Operations. Immensely tall and immensely clever, this quiet, shy young man was, at 24, the military genius of the IZL. He planned all the operations against the British and often led them personally when he could wheedle the consent of Begin.

Reuven, in charge of stores and arms-production, was the Beau

Brummel of the High Command. He always looked natty, whether he wore the Palestinian national costume—khaki shorts and shirt—or whether he appeared in a well-cut lounge suit. He invariably exuded an air of prosperity and well-being, than which there could be no finer disguise for a member of the underground.

Yitschak was in charge of the treasury. The onerous occupation of trying to balance the IZL budget had prematurely aged him. His greying hair, weary stoop and languid long-lashed eyelids, belied the number of his years.

Then there was Shmuel who ran the foreign press and propaganda department. Quiet, studious, with a fine and an excellent sense of humour —the very antithesis of the British conception of a "terrorist."

I always felt it was somehow not fair on the British that so few "terrorists" had horns, wild unruly hair and gleaming fanatical eyes. It was really too much to expect them to recognize in these respectable, quiet, young men the bogeys which they had conjured up for themselves.

The High Command worked together smoothly and harmoniously in spite of their widely divergent characters. The common cause bound them closely together and mutual respect helped them to gloss over differences of opinion and clashes of temperament. Begin's patience and tact played a large and necessary role too. All major decisions had to receive the approval of the majority of the High Command. Discussion was free and untrammelled and no one was overborne or overwhelmed by the presence and personality of Begin.

The meetings of the High Command usually took place in the Begin's flat, and it was just sheer luck that all these very fragile eggs in one basket were not turned into one large savory omelette for the delection of the British. By some miracle, no member of the last IZL High Command was ever arrested or detained by the British, in contrast to the previous one where everyone, except Begin was captured and sent to the Eritrean Detention Camp. Or perhaps it was not so much a miracle as the combination of improved security technique among the IZL and the passing of the phase of betrayals on the part of the Haganah.

While I liked and respected the young men of the IZL, it was the women who won my greatest admiration: and foremost amongst these were the "forgotten men" of the underground—the wives. These were the women who ran their homes and brought up children on the not very magnificent salary which full-time members of the IZL, irrespective of

39

their rank, received. These were the women who trembled at every knock on the door lest the dreaded hour had come, who spent days and nights of loneliness, waiting—and worrying when a husband was hours overdue. Women who never knew, as they bade goodbye to their husbands each morning, whether that was the last time they would do so—for years or maybe for ever. Women who, forcibly parted for years from their husbands, struggled to educate and bring up children on the pitiful allowances which the IZL could afford to give them; who sacrificed and slaved uncomplainingly to send food and gifts to the fathers of their children whom, in turn, they fiercely protected from the coldness of want and privation which those fathers' courage and idealism had innocently brought on their heads, and who, because of the need for perpetual vigilance and secrecy, could not even seek the slight comfort and solace of pouring out their troubles into sympathetic ears.

Two women, amongst the hundreds whom I did not know, typified for me the courage and steadfastness of the wives. The first was Ala Begin and the second Zipporah Meridor.

Ala is small, thin and stooped from long, endless days and nights of knitting and reading to tide over the interminable solitude of life in the underground. She wears glasses, having been eventually persuaded to that by her husband when the toll of cups and plates which she just missed putting on the table, rose too high.

Ala's courage is of the quiet, steady kind, without flamboyance and without heroics It manifested itself in her amazing cheerfulness in all circumstances. For most women the act of childbirth is both a frightening and a solemn occasion, which merits the sympathy and appreciation of an attentive husband, and the petting and pampering of relatives and friends. Ala gave birth to two children in the days of the underground. No loving husband brought her flowers and gifts, no friends helped to while away the days. She lay alone, unvisited, unknown—and she returned home each time to tackle the additional burden smilingly and cheerfully.

Ala's delightful sense of humor stood her in good stead in coping with the small difficulties of life which annoy and irritate in inverse proportion to their size. Her worry for Begin's safety and for the success of the revolt was a great and difficult burden—but a noble one. On the other hand, her inability to go out and buy what she needed when she needed it, to relax occasionally in a cinema or a theatre, to stretch her legs and breathe in fresh air, were niggling irritations which required all the patience and humor which she could muster. When, in addition to these burdens, one adds the painful suffering and terrible debilitating effect of chronic asthma, then truly Ala's gaiety and fortitude were such as to command both the amazement and admiration of her friends.

Zipporah Meridor was the faithful Penelope patiently awaiting the return of her husband, Yaacov, whose adventures, though unbrightened by the charms of sirens and sorceresses, were no less spectacular than those of Odysseus. Yaacov had been second-in-command to Begin and the military brain of the High Command before his betrayal to the British in 1945 and subsequent deportation to Eritrea, and then Kenya. Barbed wire and guards held no terrors for Yaacov. Five times he escaped from detention and four times he was recaptured. On the fifth occasion he got to France—too late to take any further part in the revolt against the British who, by that time, had already given up their Mandate in Palestine and were evacuating their troops from the country.

Zipporah struggled against financial hardship and continual ill-health as she brought up her two children. Yaacov's adventures kept her in a continual state of anxiety and nervousness. When she had reconciled herself to a long separation, tempered by the thought that he was at least physically safe, she was once more thrown into a tumult of hope and fears when she heard that he had escaped—hope that they would once more be together, and fear lest he should be shot or wounded in the efforts to recapture him. Each time he was recaptured, would come anti-climax, and relief at his safety, to be shattered once more by a fresh attempt on his part to break the chains of bondage.

There were other women in the IZL besides those who merely sat and waited. There were those who took an active part in the struggle: young girls who went out on actual operations; others who pasted up the wall newspaper and the frequent declarations and warnings; and yet others who worked on the radio, who typed, who acted as messengers. Some were unsung heroines, others were sung heroines.

I had the privilege of knowing intimately one of the unsung heroines of the IZL—Ruhama, secretary both to Avraham and to Begin, and general factotum of the High Command.

We first met Ruhama soon after we arrived in Palestine. She was with Israel Epstein, a young school-teacher who acted as general secretary for the IZL High Command. They seemed to mean a great deal to each other. Two months later Israel was sent on an IZL mission to Rome.

41

There he was arrested by the Italian police on suspicion of being connected with the blowing up of the British Embassy in Rome. In an attempt to escape from confinement, Israel was shot and killed.

Ruhama took this on the chin and went on quietly with her work. She lived in a room in Tel Aviv away from her family, as the British had got onto her tracks and constantly watched her home. She is a person who is very much attached to her family, but she saw her young brother, Arye, only occasionally, and had infrequent, secret meetings with her mother. Her elder brother was in the detention camp in Kenya.

I met Ruhama frequently at the Begin's flat, but got to know her really well only when she came to stay with us to recuperate after breaking her thigh. She was on a mission for the IZL when the car in which she was travelling overturned. For three long months she lay in a hospital suffering the tortures of hell. When the pains had abated and she was beginning to recover, the attack on the Acre Fortress took place. At the head of the attackers fought, and fell, Dov Cohen—a dearly-beloved friend of Ruhama's.

A week later she came to stay with us. She was deathly pale, as thin as a wraith and could not walk a step. With supreme courage and willpower she set herself the task of recovering her strength and ability to walk. Within a fortnight, she walked unaided, albeit with a limp which she cheerfully refused to notice.

Her brother, Arye, visited her daily, but she refused to allow her mother to come for fear of attracting attention to our flat. Between the brother and sister there existed an unusually strong bond of affection. They were happy in each other's company and looked forward eagerly to the daily hour spent together.

A year later a third intimate friend of Ruhama's was killed in the battle of Jaffa. This blow preceded by a few days the hardest and cruellest of all Ruhama's bereavements—Arye, her beloved brother, was also killed in the fight in Jaffa.

Ruhama steeled herself once more and went on quietly and efficiently with her work, only the paleness of her face and the dark rings under her eyes revealing the tragedy beneath the mask. She will always be to me the personification of that strength and idealism which turned ordinary boys and girls into fearless fighters for the liberation of their people. She received no medals and no official praise, but, to me, she will always remain the bravest woman I know.

Of the sung heroines of the IZL, Esther Raziel is a shining example. She was both wife and mother, and active participant in the struggle of the underground. She joined the organisation in its early years when her brother, David, was just building it up. She was imprisoned several times by the British, spending many weary months in the women's prison at Bethlehem where she set a fine example of fortitude and cheerfulness to her fellow-prisoners who loved and revered her.

Esther later worked as the IZL broadcaster. When the British found a radio-transmitter in her home, both she and her husband were arrested. He was exiled to the detention camps in 'Africa, where he remained for years, while she was sent to Bethlehem Goal—leaving behind two young sons in the care of her aged parents. She was released from Bethlehem a few months later, in time to give birth to her third child—a daughter. A few months of freedom, then again to Bethlehem, this time leaving her old mother with an extra baby on her hands. After a short time in Bethlehem, Esther was released again. She now had the burden of supporting her three children alone and unaided. She went back to teach school in the mornings, to care for the children in the afternoons—and to continue writing and reading broadcasts for IZL in the evenings. Her poverty, her frequent imprisonments, her hard life, did not dim her ardor for the cause of freedom. Without fear of the consequences, fully aware of the risks which she took, she continued her work for the IZL till the day the British left and the "Voice of Fighting Zion" spoke its last message and was silent.

*　　*　　*　　*　　*

My first taste of tragedy at close quarters came with the Dov Gruner case. Dov Gruner had been captured by the British after an attack on a police station. He was badly wounded and lingered on the threshold of death for months. Afetr nine months in hospital he was considered fit enough to be tried. He was sentenced to death by hanging. In an effort to prevent this, the IZL kidnapped a British Magistrate, Mr. Wyndham. The British then postponed the execution and Wyndham was released. They tried to persuade Gruner to appeal but he refused, saying that as he did not accept the legality of the court, he did not recognise the sentence imposed on him and so could not appeal against it. Dov Gruner's sister, who was in America, appealed to the Privy Council on his behalf. The case aroused considerable interest throughout the world and the quiet, unassuming Gruner became a national hero overnight. His calm courage under the

43

strain of so great an ordeal filled everyone in Palestine with admiration—even the bitterest enemies of the IZL.

After Gruner's case had been submitted to the Privy Council, another three young men were sentenced to death. They were Kashani, Alkoshi and Rosenbaum, two of whom had been found guilty of the enormity of having in their possession thong whips. They had been caught after the flogging of a British Major by the IZL in retaliation for a flogging sentence against two young Jews. This flogging had set the whole world laughing and the British smarted more over this blow to their prestige than they did over the numerous deaths amongst their ranks. So what more fitting punishment could be dealt to the defilers of the British escutcheon in the Middle East than hanging by the neck until death!

The third boy sentenced to death had committed the heinous crime of being found in possession of fire-arms.

The IZL made plans to release Dov Gruner and his comrades from the Jerusalem prison where they were confined. Each night as Shmuel came home, I would greet him with the laconic, but meaningful query: "Well?" And each time he would shake his head sadly and say: "Not ready yet." At last Shmuel could say: "The plans are all cut and dried. The break will take place the day after tomorrow." But fate dealt a cruel blow. On the morrow, the four were suddenly transferred to the Acre Fortress.

No one, not even the IZL who had sufficient reason to distrust the British, ever dreamt that they would carry out the death sentence while the Gruner case was still under consideration by the Privy Council. Plans were made for releasing the four from Acre Fortress.

Dov Gruner's sister came from America to see her brother and try to save his life. She saw him once and was promised a second interview. In the early morning of the day of his promised interview, and while his case was still under consideration by the Privy Council, Dov Gruner and his three companions were secretly hanged. They were not given the privilege accorded to the basest criminal of having a minister of religion give them his last blessing. They were not given the privilege afforded to the foulest murderer of taking leave of their loved ones.

They were hanged in a cowardly, furtive way by an administration which vented its spite on four defenceless young men, because it was incapable of putting out the flame of rebellion against its repressive and cruel government. But Dov Gruner and his fellow-victims went to the gallows singing "Hatikvah" and the echo of their voices resounded throughout Palestine. There was not a man, woman or child in Palestine, friend or enemy, who was not shocked and horrified at this cowardly act. British prestige sank to an ever lower level and hate began smouldering in the hearts of even those who decried the acts of the IZL.

We first heard about the hanging on the early morning radio broadcast. Shmuel and I were completely stunned. I had still had a last lingering spark of faith in British sense of justice. This was violently and finally doused that dreadful morning.

The British gallows had forestalled the intrepid young men of the IZL; but, nevertheless, the High Command decided to carry on with the planned attack against Acre. A fortnight after the hanging of Dov Gruner and his comrades, British prestige received another terrific blow in Palestine. Acre Fortress, which had resisted the onslaught on Napoleon, was penetrated by the Irgun Zvai Leumi. They sent the guards fleeing, panic-stricken, to seek safety, with the result that over 200 of the Arab prisoners walked out of the gaol too. Although all the Jewish prisoners could have escaped, only twenty-seven did so, and only a specially selected twenty-seven. The rest knew that no preparations had been made to receive them and did not wish to embarrass the operation by over-loading the lorries and over-burdening the rescuers with the additional responsibility of disposing safely of extra unplanned-for, escapees. They remained behind in a supreme exercise of discipline.

The operation went off smoothly and would have been even more than the brilliant success that it was, if not for a stroke of the most ill-fated bad luck. The retreating attackers and escapees ran into a party of soldiers returning from a bath, accompanied by a tank for their greater protection. But for this entirely unexpected and unplanned-for event, the fortress of Acre would have been stormed without any loss of life. As it was, eight young men lost their lives that day—seven of the attackers including the officer-in-charge, and one of the escapees, Ashbel—that same Ashbel who, a year previously, had been sentenced to death, and whose sentence had ben commuted to life imprisonment after the IZL arrest of the British officers.

A drag-net was immediately sent out after the Acre break but, except for a few Arab prisoners, no one was recaptured.

This exploit aroused the admiration of all freedom-loving people. Even the British, to give credit where it is due, expressed grudging respect. Only our political opponents saw in it a deliberate and malicious manoeuvre

45

to liberate Arabs imprisoned for anti-Jewish activities. This propaganda did at least raise a laugh if it did not succeed in anything else.

The Acre gaol-break added immensely to the prestige of the IZL and did a little towards allaying the grief and despair caused by the Gruner tragedy. Triumph was, however, tempered by sorrow. Eight young men had fallen—eight of the best, who could be ill-spared by their own families or by the large family which was the Irgun Zvai Leumi.

* * * * *

On the 1st May, 1947, the United Nations Commission arrived in Palestine. This was to be the Commission to end all Commissions. The Jews were already somewhat blasé about commissions. They did not expect this one to achieve any more than the Anglo-American Commission from whose burnt-out embers this new Phoenix had arisen; but, still, it was quite exciting to see the fleets of UNO cars, and to meet all the celebrities—a not inconsiderable consideration in a country where "lions" are feverishly hunted.

Judge Sandstrom, the Swedish Chairman of the Commission, expressed a wish to see the leaders of the IZL, and Carter Davidson of the Associated Press arranged a meeting. Begin, Shmuel and Avraham were present at the meeting.

Two weeks later Begin, Shmuel and Meir met Dr. Granados of Guatemala and Professor Febregat of Urugay, another two members of the Commission. Following on this latter meeting, the IZL High Command thought it advisable to have someone on hand in Geneva, where the Committee had decided to write its report, in order to act as a channel of information between them and the sympathetic members of the Commission. For want of anyone who could be easily spared they decided to send me there. I did not think their choice a very wise one, but nevertheless agreed to go.

In order to make the acquaintance of Dr. Granados, I travelled up to Jerusalem after Joel had forewarned him that some one would be coming to see him. Dr. Granados asked that the visitor be provided with passwords so that there should be no change of mistaken identities. He suggested Bolivar, Juarez and Lincoln.

I came up to Dr. Granados' hotel room and gave my password rather shamefacedly. He murmured his, even more shamefacedly, at which I made a feeble attempt at giving my counter-password. We both burst out

46

laughing instead and I said: "Silly, isn't it?" He agreed wholeheartedly. After thus establishing good relations, I arranged to meet him in Geneva.

* * * * *

The arrival of the UN Commission and their appeal for restraint on the part of all contending parties in Palestine was heralded, by the British, with the passing of the death sentence on three young men who had taken part in the attack on the Acre Fortress and had subsequently been captured.

In response to a dramatic and heart-rending appeal from the parents and relatives of the three condemned men, Haviv, Nakar and Weiss, the UN Commission made a half-hearted attempt to dissuade the British authorities from carrying out this sentence. This attempt was met by a cold and contemptuous slap-in-the-face from Sir Henry Gurney, the Chief Secretary, who practically told the Commission to mind their own business. Whether this matter came within the scope of the Commission or not is a debatable point, but what was quite indisputable was that it certainly was the business of the IZL.

After the treacherous behaviour of the British in the case of Dov Gruner, the IZL did not take any chances with the three victims. There were only two practical alternatives: either to rescue the three boys or to take hostages. The first alternative proved impossible as the army and police were on a day and night alert at all prisons after the Acre break. There remained only the second alternative. Now, no one of the IZL Command approved of taking hostages as a principle. But if there were any possibility of saving the lives of three young men who, by no stretching of any moral code, could possible be considered to have warranted the odium of death by hanging, then that way, however odious in itself, was justifiable. Obviously, it would have been far more just to have captured and held as hostage the man directly responsible for the death sentences, General McMillan. But General McMillan evidently had an uneasy conscience and considered it necessary to have his person well protected. All his senior officers were equally well protected when they dared venture out of their self-created ghettoes. So it fell to the lot of two sergeants, apprehended after many a vain effort and false start, to be martyred in the cause of Bevin and his henchmen.

The two sergeants were captured in Nathanya and held prisoner there. The British declared a curfew in the Nathanya area and searched it house by house, foot by foot and practically stone by stone. The Nathanya sum-

47

mer season was ruined; Nathanya's chubby little mayor grew hysterical; the calm, undemonstrative British grew even more hysterical, but the sergeants were not found.

The British then committed one of those acts of brutal stupidity for which Mr. Bevin was becoming notorious. They hanged the three boys. Perhaps the British thought this hanging justified on the grounds of saving British prestige in the eyes of the "natives." This mythical prestige, which had received a severe kick in the pants when a British major was flogged by a couple of "Jew-boys" had actually been laughed out of existence after the Acre gaol-break. But if Bevin could not have it, he was determined to resurrect it. So he hanged three boys—and with their dying gasps flickered out the last dying embers of British prestige.

The whole country was thrown into a turmoil. Would the sergeants be hanged or wouldn't they? I was sick at heart. It seemed to me that many of my fellow-Jews had become intoxicated with that same brutish bloodlust as must grip the audience at a bull-fight, and those who cried for blood today would be the first to turn upon the executor tomorrow and revile him for "bringing disaster upon the Jewish people."

For me the important thing was that three young men had been brutally and senselessly deprived of their lives and that three families had been steeped in tragedy. I hated the thought of further horror and bloodshed and with my whole being wished that some means could be found of freeing the two sergants. I know now that many of my friends in the IZL felt the same as I. It was a very difficult time for the IZL High Command. None of them was in the least blood-thirsty, and I felt sure they too would have welcomed a chance to take some other decision. But they decided to hang the two British sergeants—and they were right. They were right because they considered the lives of young Jews as more important than the lives of British soldiers and because they knew they owed it to Nakar, Haviv and Weiss, and to Dov Gruner and his comrades, not so much to avenge their deaths as to ensure that their comrades should be protected from a similar fate. They owed it, too, to the young soldiers of the IZL whom they ordered to carry out operations which would have meant sure death by hanging for anyone who was captured, unless the British could be forced even though brutally, to revoke a law which was both illegal and barbarous.

I see this now, and I saw it then, but my woman's heart prevailed over my head and I kept on hoping that some miracle would happen and the sergeants would not be hanged. For nights I dreaded to close my eyes and plunge into a nightmare world of gibbets and hanging figures—usually those of Shmuel and my brothers.

And this passed too. The sergeants were hanged; not, as Shmuel assured me in reply to my agonised query, by the same men who had guarded them and had surely come to have some kind of feeling for them. And in my heart was born a newer, deadlier, hatred for these British who had made hangmen out of my friends.

CHAPTER V

A TERRORIST ABROAD

SOON after the hanging of the sergeants, I was due to leave for Geneva. At the last minute, to my intense relief, it was decided that Shmuel should go to Geneva and that I should accompany him and carry out several commissions for the organisation in Europe. My chief qualification for this task was my British passport with which I could travel through practically half of the world without the nuisance and delay of getting visas.

The IZL Intelligence Service had got a copy of the CID lists for use at ports of embarkation. These lists were divided into three categories: the A list consisted of those people whose arrivals and departures were to be reported to the CID, on the B list were those who were to be searched for suspicious documents; and on the C list those who were to be arrested on attempting to leave or enter the country.

They discovered from these lists that Shmuel, who had previously been given a clean bill by the CID, had now been promoted to list B. So, on the morning of August 6th, 1947, I carried all the essential and incriminating documents in my handbag.

At Lydda, Shmuel was searched but I went unscathed. Everything passed off quietly and we breathed a hearty sigh of relief as we entered the plane. We all waited expectantly for our passports to be handed back and for the plane to take off — but nothing happened. After twenty minutes an apologetic official boarded the plane and explained that there was some delay about checking the passports and would we kindly alight once more. This looked bad. We knew that none of the other passengers were "suspicious characters" (but of course the British might not have known that) and that, to the best of our knowledge, only Shmuel had been searched. We naturally concluded that he was the nigger in the woodpile.

For two hours we sat in the airport looking as unconcerned as possible while Shmuel feverishly passed on insrtuctions and information to me so that I could carry on with the job in case he were to be arrested. I had to memorise everything as I dared not write anything down, and was in despair at the prospect facing me. I would have a difficult job to perform in Europe for which I was but ill-equipped, and all the time I would be worrying about Shmuel languishing in Latrun, or possibly Kenya. To say that I was in high spirits would be something of an exaggeration. My spirits were not improved by the information we casually elicited from an airport official that the police were awaiting telephone instructions from Jerusalem CID Headquarters.

After two hours we were told we could return to the plane. We all trooped back and were handed our passports, Shmuel's being kept until the last. When his turn came, he was solemnly told by the police officer that he could have his passport only if he stated his address in England, whither we were ostensibly headed. And that was all! Well, if it was merely to be a war of nerves, I could take it. Nevertheless, the plane rose the more easily for having got rid of some ballast which was the lump in my throat and the load on my heart.

Not until we reached Geneva did we hear that early that morning the Revisionist leaders and the Mayors of Tel Aviv, Nathanya and Ramat Gan had been arrested as being in league with the terrorists. Shmuel's Revisionist antecedents had evidently been looked into and he had been pronounced "not dangerous."

*　　*　　*　　*　　*

Geneva was a miracle of peace and beauty after the heat and heartache which was Palestine, and we revelled in the calm and normality of the country as we got down to work.

I contacted Dr. Granados and arranged to meet him over an after-dinner liqueur. Shmuel waited for us in a near-by park. Precautions seemed unnecessary in this beautiful town, so remote from the atmosphere of hate and suspicion which we had left behind, but Shmuel knew and was known by many newspapermen and we could not take any chances.

I told Dr. Granados that I was merely an intermediary and would take him to meet one of the men he had met in Palestine. So we talked of South America as we sipped our liqueurs and behaved as any two people without any missions. It was very pleasant while it lasted.

We took Dr. Granados up to our hotel room and disclosed that we were man and wife, just in case he should be distracted from the subject on hand by idle speculation on whether or not we were "living in sin."

The whole purpose of Shmuel's conversation with Dr. Granados was to continue the effort made by the IZL leaders in Tel Aviv to persuade him and Professor Fabregat to bring in a minority report in favour of a Jewish State in the whole of Palestine, in order to counter-balance a

51

possible minority report in favour of the Arabs. But his task was hopeless from the start. Dr. Granados was intent on bringing out a report which was "ecceptable" and he kept on confounding every argument with the irrefutable: "But what do you expect of me if your own leaders don't ask for more than partition?"

The next day I went up to the very impressive League of Nations building to see Dr. Bunche. The moment I sent up my name, which on this occasion was Mrs. Freeman, I was ushered into his office and given a very cordial reception. Dr. Bunche has become an internationally famous figure since his appointment by the United Nations as Acting Mediator between Israel and Arab States, but even in those days he was one of the outstanding figures on the United Nations Staff, with an international reputation as a courageous fighter for the elementary rights of colored people in the U.S.A. and throughout the world.

Consequently, I regarded it as no small compliment to the IZL that he treated me not only with cordiality, which is natural to a man of good breeding, but with respect, which is an indication of his attitude towards the people whom I represented. He readily agreed to meet me the next day, at any place appointed by me, and be taken to see Shmuel.

The meeting place was the main Geneva railway station and the time 5 P.M. I waited until nearly 5:30 and had almost given up when he hurried up in a taxi, and apologized profusely for keeping me waiting. He had been at a conference and could not get away sooner without exciting undue comment.

From there he was driven away to the flat of Rammy—the Irgun representative in Geneva—where he had a long talk with Shmuel, from whom I gathered later that Bunche maintained complete discretion as to the work of the committee but provided us with a valuable insight into the background of international interest in the Palestine problem. Bunche then told Shmuel of his belief that the United States would support the partition scheme.

Shmuel remained in Geneva for three weeks more, pursuing his conversations and keeping IZL Headquarters informed of the progress of the UN Committee's work. I flew to London. I was met at the air-terminal by Shiloni, who was at that time in charge of the IZL money-raising campaign in England.

Shiloni is a young S. African doctor who gave up a promising career to work on behalf of the underground. His energy, devotion and single-mindedness earned him the respect and regard of everyone with whom he came into contact, from the illustrious heights in which sat Menachem Begin and the High Command to the lowest plane of money collectors and payers of lip service. He is dark, spare and bespectacled, with a passion for neatness. It would take a great adept to search his rooms and belongings without his spotting it immediately, so precise and pedantic is he about the correct disposition of every article of furniture, clothing, books and papers.

His note-books and address-books are always a miracle of neatness and detail—which is very useful in the ordinary pursuits of an ordinary life but which requires yet a second miracle to preserve them from the hands of the police in the ups and downs of underground life. His fellow-workers had a wholesome distaste for those note-books and when, on suitable occasions, they tactfully suggested the advisability of destroying them, Shiloni did so with a heavy heart at so much wasted effort.

Shiloni is a great believer in book-learning. When I arrived in London I found him studying with great intensity a book which was going to solve all our problems, with a flick of the wrist. The book was Dean Carnegie's "How to Win Friends and Influence People." I still cannot decide whether the fact that a year later he was studying Dean Carnegie's "How to Keep Friends" is an indication of the success or failure of the application of Mr. Carnegie's recommendations.

It was just one year since we had left London for Palestine and England was still suffering from the war and post-war austerity. The small talk consisted mainly of food troubles and the scarcity of elecricity and gas. The people grumbled and complained as only the English know how, but whereas there had always been an element of stoicism, even of cheerfulness, in their grumbling during the war, now there was the faintest suspicion of a whine.

The newspapers were still smarting over the hanging of the two sergeants, and amongst the local Jewish inhabitants the pros and cons were fiercely and bitterly contested. Jewish public bodies had published violent denunciation but, in private, opinions were very mixed. A brave little group of young men had put up large posters in the main thoroughfares of London and the suburbs explaining the IZL point of view and blaming Bevin and the British administration for the tragic loss of Jewish and British lives in Palestine. In Hyde Park, that most remarkable of British institutions, the Jewish Legion—an ex-Servicemen's Organization—had a platform propounding the IZL doctrine. The leading lights of this group, as well as their chief orators, were Major Samuel Weiser and

Lieutenant David de Lange. These two men did a great deal towards educating the man-in-the-street who was curiously ignorant of the situation in Palestine, despite, or because of, the immense amount of publicity, for the most part hysterically un-British, which it received in the national press.

I went to Hyde Park on my first Sunday in London and heard David de Lange explaining why the two sergeants were hanged. This required a great deal of courage at a time when British public opinion, quite naturally, was not very sympathetic to the IZL. De Lange's harangue, as is usual in Hyde Park, was continually interrupted by hecklers. At one stage he asked his audience: "Why were three young Jewish boys hanged by our Administration?" A voice, which sounded genuinely surprised at the question replied: "Because they were murderers." Up piped a Cockney standing next to me: "Murderers, they wasn't murderers, they was bloomin' 'eroes." Which does show that not all the British were completely unenlightened.

In this atmosphere, I was expected to collect money for the IZL. It did not seem very propitious and I must confess that my heart failed me. Money-collecting, at the best of times, is a nauseating business. But to try and draw it out of people who are afraid for their own skins, is doubly nauseating. The Jews were, perhaps naturally, afraid of being connected with the IZL. I suppose, if it could have been proved that they were actively supporting the IZL, some kind of action could have been taken against them. And to top this, the British Board of Deputies and the local Zionist Federation intensified their campaign against the "terrorists," using all the old slogans and cliches, and not stopping short of veiled intimidation.

Then again the *Daily Express* with its usual sensation-mongering lack of taste, had printed a full page picture of the hanging sergeants, with lurid captions. This naturally upset many people and they expressed their great horror at the barbarity of the act to me. I answered them curtly that a picture of the three hanged Jewish boys would not look any less grisly.

In spite of the difficulties, we, that is Shiloni and I, did suceed in raising some money, due mostly to the former's perseverance. We were particularly successful in Manchester where a few stone-throwing incidents had persuaded the local Jewish residents that there was, after all, anti-Semitism in England and that the IZL was not completely wrong in wanting to wrest Palestine from the British for the Jews.

I was often in conflict with Shiloni and the local committee about the method of approach. They preferred wrapping their request for money in the tin-foil of charity—money for the dependents of the internees. It is true that the IZL had to divert money badly needed for arms and equipment to the dependents of their members who were held for years in detention camps by the British, and any money collected directly for these dependents naturally lessened the burden on the IZL. But my soul revolted at the thought of seeking for charity; and, from a practical point of view, I was sure that a direct request for money to buy guns and bullets would be more effective than another whine, following upon the positive caterwaul of charity wailings to which the Jews the world over were perpetually subjected. In some cases the straightforward approach brought a startled and frightened look into the eyes of our 'victim.' One man threw up his hands in horror and said: "For God's sake, don't tell me what you want the money for. Here's £100 and I don't want to know what it's going to." But for the most part people liked to be told outright what we were collecting for and felt that, in a small way, they too were taking part in the fight for their country.

In spite of the general grimness of my work in England there were some lighter moments. On one occasion I went into one of the City branches of Barclay's Bank to transfer money for the Irgun to Palestine. I filled in the necessary forms, using my London pseudonym, which was Mrs. Merriman. I also supplied some fictitious address. I had to wait for a few minutes for some formalities to be completed and sat down to read a newspaper. The clerk called out to me when he had finished but I went on blithely reading. He called again and then I suddenly jumped up, remembering that I was the "Mrs. Merriman" who was being addressed. This happened to me frequently. I simply could not remember my own name. I secretly thought the whole business of pseudonyms a bit silly, but Shiloni insisted on it, if only for Shmuel's protection. I met many of our London friends and acquaintances and passed off my presence there airily, with some vague allusion to "doing a few jobs for Shmuel who hasn't time to come over from Paris to do them himself."

I stayed in England a month, and when Shmuel telephoned asking me to go to Paris, I was very pleased to get away.

* * * * *

Paris was in the middle of a September heat-wave when I arrived, but it was Paris, and Paris seen for the first time. The contrast to London was amazing. Here too the people were poor and shabby. There were

55

THE LADY WAS A TERRORIST

frequent strikes and demonstrations. Food was expensive and hard to get. Electricity was off at all peculiar hours. But there was an air of carefree gaiety, of cheerfulness, in direct contrast to the gloom and positive morbidity of Londoners. One felt that here was a city which would overcome its troubles and survive, whereas in London one felt the cold and cutting touch of the sickle of death.

The sympathy for the IZL in France was warm and heartening. There was the traditional feeling of friendliness for anyone who opposed their age-old bete-noir—Albion—very much strengthened by the incident of the "Exodus-Europe 1947."

The "Exodus" had been intercepted by the British Navy off the coast of Palestine for which she was headed with her cargo of 4000 so-called illegal immigrants. On orders from the British Foreign Minister, every resisting passenger had been forcibly transferred to three British vessels and sent back—to Germany. En route the ship spent weeks at Port du Bouc while the British tried in vain to persuade the immigrants to avail themselves of Franco's offer of hospitality. Eventually the unfortunate men, women and children were returned to Hamburg, to the Displaced Persons camps—those symbols of their annihilation and humiliation, the memory of which they had sought to leave behind in a new life amongst friends in Palestine.

France had behaved as decently and as dignifiedly during the whole incident as Britain had been gauche and doltish. The French press had paid a great deal of attention to the affair and the French people were particularly well-informed of the reasons for the IZL's fight against the British. In general, the French, while of course paying most attention to their troubles at home, do at least seem to take a little interest in other people's affairs without confining themselves entirely to the price of beer and the tax on greyhound-racing as does the ordinary British man-in-the-street. While the French behaved as any ordinary, decent people would behave in similar circumstances during the Exodus incident, yet one felt, nevertheless, that the opportunity of vivarious retaliation for Britain's fine, Italian hand in the liquidation of French interests in Syria was not altogether absent from the thoughts of the French Authorities.

In Paris I met Benjamin and Eliezer for the first time. Benjamin was in charge of the European headquarters of the IZL. He had been detained in Eritrea from where he staged a dramatic escape to Abyssinia. After several very long months in Abyssinia, he was spirited over to France by the tortuous path of the underground. Benjamin is a Russian-born

"Chinese" from Harbin. The appellation "Sini" (the Hebrew for Chinese) is hardly in keeping with his auburn hair and very marked Russian accent. He is the sweetest and gentlest of men—a characteristic which did not help him much in dealing with some of the real tough guys of the underground movement or with the suave politicians of the "Aid Organisations" such as the Hebrew Committee for National Liberation.

The latter organisation had done an excellent job of work in putting Zionism on the American map, and in making propaganda in the United States for the IZL—for which they deserved much credit, in spite of the fact that there were not a few who felt that the actual actions of the IZL, were their own advertisement and that money might have been better spent in putting guns into the hands of the underground forces than in putting full-page advertisements in the New York Herald-Tribune. The originator and head of this group was Hillel Kook, known in America as Peter Bergson, whose acquaintance I renewed in Paris. I had met him previously in London in 1940. In those days he was a frustrated, impatient young man, capable but erratic, with unbounded energy and ideas for which he could find no outlet in the rather stodgy confines of the Revisionist Party. In America his own particular genius for propaganda and publicity found a fertile group and eventually sprouted prolifically in the framework of the Hebrew Committee of National Liberation. In Paris, in 1947, Hillel Kook had completely sumberged his identity in that of Peter Bergson, well-groomed, suave and charming, a consummate politician with the brains, opportunism and self-seeking which go to produce one.

Eliezer was in charge of organisation and operations in Europe. He came from Poland to Palestine as a youth and worked his way through the Hebrew University, receiving a degree of Philosophy. Working his way for Eliezer consisted of being at various times a tutor, a night-porter in a hotel, where he sometimes got his Plato mixed up with his entries in the register, and, most exalted and amusing of all, an inspector of "kashrut" in the local butcheries.

Epikaurus in all matters and epicurean in matters pertaining to food could sum up Eliezer succinctly. I loved eating with him. Just to watch him so obviously glorying in his food gave an edge to my own appetite. Being married to him would be a culinary pleasure. He is the only man who could have persuaded me to visit Meska's Restaurant in the Place de la Republique a second time.

Eli is a cynic with a delicious, subtle, sense of humor. He will describe a girl in glowing terms—she is attractive, intelligent, has a nice figure—and then he will shatter the vision with a malicious little twist— and she wears glasses. His air of flippancy and general well-being is, however, a snare and delusion. For, beneath the cynical, amused twinkle in Eliezer's eye, one can glimpse something dark and elemental. It is nothing other than stark fear. For Eli has a fear complex derived from the horrors of six months of torture at the hands of the Haganah in Palestine. He was strapped down in a bed for six weeks and kept alive by having liquids poured down his throat and food crammed into his mouth. The ordinary human, elementary rights of hygiene were denied him and he lay in his own excretion for six weeks until his body began to rot. This was only one of many devilish refinements which man's ingenuity can conjure to debase the very name of man.

It is no wonder that after six months Eli emerged from captivity with a bitter hatred of his torturers and all they stood for, and a subconscious terror of his fellow-men. He was immediately smuggled out of Palestine and sent to Europe to work for the IZL there and recover his physical and mental health. No-one could have staged a quicker recovery than Eli, with his intelligence, strength of character and perseverance. But the recovery could not humanly have been a total one. He has remained with this fear complex which he attempts to hide by laughing at himself in particular and the world in general, but which makes itself felt in his verging on cruelty towards anyone who attempts to get too close to him and make him vulnerable to heartache and disappointment.

Besides this fear of personal relationships, Eli has a fear of the authorities. He spent three years in Europe, working in a clandestine, illegal organisation, which necessitated his crossing borders illegally, bringing over money illegally, and being concerned with para-military "illegal" operations, such as the blowing up of the British Embassy in Rome and the derailing of the British troop-train in Italy — and he did all this while being mortally afraid. Eli is one of the bravest men I know — he does things in spite of his fear.

This fear of Eli's led him to meet people only on street-corners. There is practically no street-corners in the main thoroughfares of the capitals of Europe where Eli has not met some-one. This habit annoyed people who objected to kicking their heels at street-corners, sometimes on a bitter winter's day; but Eli insisted. This desire for secrecy, however, did not always help him. He still managed to get himself arrested twice in Italy. On one occasion he was picked up by the police for being without papers and was detained for weeks.

On another occasion, a few weeks after the blowing-up of the British Embassy in Rome, the police came to arrest him. He started running and was naturally followed and caught. He claims to have told the police that he has a nervous disorder which makes him run whenever he sees a pretty girl (after her, naturally, not from her). When this explanation made no apparent impression on the police, Eli changed his tune and became a pathetic victim of the concentration camps, who instinctivey ran whenever the menials of authority appeared on the horizon. Whether this story touched the soft hearts of the Italian police or not, I do not know; but they nevertheless released Eli after a few days' detention.

Any arrest of his fellow-workers, which occurred quite frequently, would send Eli into a frenzy of hotel-changing—one night in one hotel and then off again. When he decided he had put the police off his track (they weren't on it in any case, nor had they the faintest suspicion that they were, in all innocence, causing someone so much trouble) he would settle down in some quiet back-street place until the next volcanic eruption.

Eli had offices scattered all over Paris. Here he received telephone calls from all over Europe. In each office he had a different name. It was quite impossible for any ordinary, normal human-being to keep track of this conglomeration of names, offices, countries, telephone calls. But Eli could and did. He very, very rarely got himself mixed up with himself in some other guise.

* * * * *

I was rather exhausted after my mission in England, so Shmuel sent me off to Normandy for a few days with a friend. We stayed with the only real French people I have ever met. (All others had been either French Jews or emigrés). As my French vocabulary consists of exactly five words, of which two are "Oui" and "Non" I concentrated on the food and left the polite conversation to Dinah, who knew about 50 words. We discovered to our great horror that French country-dwellers do not set much store by hygiene and sanitary arrangements; but by the end of our stay we had worked out as ingenious and intricate a system of nocturnal bush habits as any Australian aborigine. Our custom of taking a cold shower in the moonlit garden under the spray of a well-directed hose-pipe was much talked about and laughed over in the French household and amongst the youth of the neighborhood, who on one occasion directed their bicycle lamps on us and spotlighted us in our dripping, shivering nudeness. In spite of the temporary discomfort one feels when the first ice-cold spurt hits one, I recommend this method of performing ablutions, if only for the exhilirating blood-coursing after-sensation and the rather primitive delights of splashing around in a moon-drenched sylvan glade in a real nymph and satyr atmosphere (though, alas, there were no satyrs!)

When I returned to Paris, having quite recovered from the after-effects of London, Shmuel informed me that I was going on a trip to Stockholm. The purpose of this trip was to spy out the prospects of raising money for the IZL and also to probe, very gently, the possibilities of buying arms. I was quite thrilled at the chance of seeing Scandinavia, but my ardor was considerably dampened when Shmuel informed me that because of currency restrictions, I could get only a single ticket to Stockholm and could take £5 with me. For my subsistence in Stockholm and my return fare, he informed me that I would have to rely on our Stockholm contact. In Paris this didn't sound nearly as bad as it really was, but, nevertheless, I can hardly claim to have set out in high spirits.

We left Paris in a blazing heat-wave and arrived, after a few hours of non-stop flying, in an icy-cold, dark Stockholm. My feeling of foreboding developed from an uncomfortable feeling in the abdominal region to a positive certainty of forthcoming catastrophe when I found no message from our Stockholm man awaiting me at the air terminal. Shmuel had cabled him a few days previously and had asked him to meet me.

Stockholm, like any other capital in Europe, was very full and it was only through the influence of the air company that I was fixed up in the Hotel Gillet for a couple of days only.

The next morning I started a hunt for our contact man whose telephone number I had. After a great deal of exasperation and trouble through the fault of the South African education system which did not consider it necessary to insist on the teaching of Scandinavian languages, I managed to gather that he was out of Stockholm, had been away for a week and would continue to be away for another week. I knew nobody in Stockholm, I had five pounds and no return ticket. Obviously, the first thing to do was to have a hot bath and a good breakfast which did not have to be paid for in cash, but went on the hotel bill. So I did that.

The hotel was scrupulously clean and the room accommodation included an adjoining W.C. and wash-basin, but no bath. Baths were extra and they provided the biggest, cosiest, wooliest, bath-towels I have ever seen. One of these would have made rather a bulky souvenir to take away, but I was sorely tempted.

Having reinforced myself, I set out to try my fortunes in Stockholm, amply provided with instructions and directions from the hall porter, all ending in "gatan" with a few "storts" and "bergs" thrown in. First of all I tried to change my precious five pounds into Swedish kronen. The first two banks I visited turned up thir noses at my English pounds and intimated that they had "enough of that rubbish."

The thought of what effect this attitude would have on a pukka Britisher, was the only bit of pleasure I got out of my trip to Stockholm. Eventually, at my third attempt, I managed to change my English pounds and the two thousand French francs I had tucked away in my purse. I then had approximately 60 kronen with which to get through the week. So I went and had a good lunch at the Gillet Hotel (and the Swedes certainly can eat), which cost me 7½ kronen, and was the first and last good lunch to which I treated myself in Stockholm.

In the afternoon I set about finding my secondary contacts whose addresses and telephone numbers Shmuel had given me, just in case. . . . The first was a fairly prominent business-man—Mr. K.—who had a reputation for being wealthy. He was out. The second was a young woman by the name of Esther Lerenman, who stayed somewhere in the suburbs. Her I had literally to track down. When, after much helpful gesticulating on the part of the local inhabitants, I arrived at the address I had been given, I found it to be a hospital. Nothing daunted, and in spite of the ice-cold drizzle which had started, I decided to reap some benefit from the pounds I have spent on detective stories and adopted one of the better-known methods of tracking. By the simple process of walking into one apartment house after another in the same street as the hospital and looking at the lists of the occupants, I eventually found Miss Lerenman's home. She too, however, was out. . . . I left a note for her and started the weary trek back to the hotel.

Having arrived there, wet and bedraggled and full of self-pity, I was somewhat restored to find a telephone message from Mr. K. awaiting me. Would I come and see him the next morning, which was Sunday, at his home? I most certainly would, and did. I travelled there by tram (I was still in the money then). Mr. K. lived in an apartment house in the fashionable residential district of Stockholm. His flat is large and beautifully furnished. Mrs. K., who opened the door, was large and beautifully dressed. Mr. K. did not spoil the symmetry. He had started life (in Germany evidently) with the initial advantage of a large frame, which, when filled in by Swedish food, produced a veritable mountain. His suit was so beautifully cut, however—and I strongly suspect a little judicious

61

corseting too—that the impression he conveyed was merely that of a man who over-indulges himself somewhat.

Mr. K. was very courteous. He wanted to know who had sent me, how I had got his telephone number, who I was, what I was and, most of all, what I wanted. I explained as best as I could because, by now, I was beginning to feel a little vague myself about what I wanted in Stockholm. I very gently and timidly touched on the subject of money needed in general by the IZL and in particular by me. "Oh," said Mr. K., "we have just had a campaign for the IZL and we all contributed very generously." I subsequently discovered that Mr. K. had generously donated 300 kronen, which translated into English money means £30, and into American money means 84 dollars—less than the price of one of his suits. I explained that the IZL had never seen any of the money collected in their name, which was one of the reasons why I was in Stockholm. The conversation was carried on in German on his part and a very poor imitation of Yiddish on mine. By the time I left Stockholm my Yiddish was fluent, if somewhat original.

Mr. K. went off to phone his fellow Committee-members to arrange for me to meet them, while I carried on a desultory conversation with Mrs. K.

I met the Committee for lunch. There were six or seven of them— all well-dressed and well-fed and looking extremely bulky and bear-like in their heavy overcoats and mufflers. I felt positively lost amongst them— a veritable orphan Annie. We went to a Jewish restaurant—the same gefulte fish, Kneidlach and roast chicken that one gets in any Jewish restaurant in any town in the world. Only here, the liberality of the portions and the cleanliness of everything supplied the Swedish touch.

Over lunch I had the unpleasant task of telling my hosts that the money which they had ostensibly contributed to the IZL had never reached its destination. Nor was there ever any intention on the part of the people represented by the collector that it should. People who have just parted with their money (and in this case parted with great reluctance) do not like being told they were deceived and, still less, do they like the teller. So by the time we had eaten our fill, I was none too popular with our worthy Swedish revolutionaries. Only one member of the Committee, a certain Mr. H. seemed to see my difficulties and remained friendly throughout my visit to Stockholm.

In the afternoon Esther Lerenman came to see me. She was blond, intelligent, fairly attractive, Latvian. She told me of how she and her mother had escaped to Russia when the Germans occupied Latvia. The Russians had sent them to Siberia. There Esther had married a Polish Jew, fictitiously, in order to become a Polish citizen and so fall into the category of those who were allowed to leave Russia under the Soviet-Polish agreement. Esther, her mother and "husband" were permitted to come to Stockholm. Her husband refused to give Esther a divorce and was pestering her to come and live with him. But she did not like him and bitterly regretted the marriage. Neither of us could foresee then how her life, tragic as it was, was to end so soon in the ultimate of tragedies. Two years later she and her mother came to Israel and Esther found work in an office in Tel Aviv. A few months later they were followed by the importunate lover. Having found out where Esther worked, he waited for her in the street at lunch-time one day, and started begging and pleading once more that she should come to live with him. When she refused yet again, he drew a revolver and killed her.

Esther told me about the activities of the Jewish youth in Stockholm and of the attitude of the Stockholm Jews to the refugees. The entrenched Jews feared that the influx of more Jews would endanger their comfort and safety. In fact, the great help accorded to the miserable victims of Hitler's concentration camps by the Swedish government had been given in spite of the local Jewish population, rather than because of them. I later met a few Swedish Jews who boasted to me of their long line of Swedish ancestors and complained bitterly about the "foreign" Jews who were lowering their prestige. One might still have had some sympathy, if in tolerant mood, for the complaints of the Swedish "aristocracy"; but what irked me was to hear similar complaints from Jews who had themselves immigrated from Germany or the Baltic States fifteen or twenty years previously.

The next day, which was Monday, the hotel manager informed me that they needed my room. I had perforce to settle my bill, which left me with 2 or 3 kronen in my pocket. The porter very kindly tried to get me a room in another hotel, but they were all crowded. Eventually I found accommadation in a kind of rooming-house, patronised by visiting Anglo-Saxon students and other impecunious travellers. Its one advantage was that it was cheap and clean. But it was cold. That started my cold-feet period in Scandinavia. From that day until I left for Paris ten days later, I hardly slept at night because of my sheer inability to get warm.

Then followed three of the most miserable days of my life. I had no money and was too proud to mention again to Mr. K. and his friends that I needed some, after my first hint had not been taken up. I had a scanty breakfast in my boarding-house and that ended my gastronomic programme for the day. I explored all the districts of Stockholm within walking distance of my boarding-house and quite a few which were a good deal farther than walking distance.

When I got tired of walking I sat in my room and re-read the few books I had with me and waited for the telephone to ring. There is nothing more nerve- and heart-rending than waiting for a telephone call. Every time the bell rang my heart started beating wildly and then, for a few seconds, I was in an agony of suspense lest the call should be for me and the house-keeper should say I was out. But each time, somebody else was called to the 'phone and I could have wept with disappointment.

When the strain of waiting and the boredom of reading the same detective story for the third time got my spirits down, I went out—and walked. The beauties of Stockholm and of its fashionably-dressed women have been extolled ad nauseam. And undoubtedly it is a lovely city graced by magnificent goddesses. But I hated the place intensely.

At night I went to bed early and rested my weary limbs. But, unfortunately, those weary limbs were also very cold and, without any artificial means of heating, they continued to remain very cold, sending constant biting messages to my brain to do something about it. The net result was that my brain became overheated and feverish and my feet remained cold and I spent most of the night tossing restlessly in my bed. The arrival of morning and, most important of all, of breakfast, was a sheer release.

On Wednesday afternoon, by which time I was pretty hungry, Leo arrived post haste, having received an urgent message from his wife to return immediately to Stockholm, and my period of purgatory was over.

Immediately upon Leo's return we set about planning a campaign of action. We agreed between ourselves that we would not draw on Leo's very slender funds, established for the purpose of organizing members of the IZL in Sweden. So we simply had to raise money by a snap collection. Leo drew up a list of probable donors whom he would contact and I, as I had to get to Helsinki somehow or other before returning to Paris, set about getting myself a visa for Finland. My job was by far the easier.

I went along to the Finnish Consulate where I found one other aspirant for a visa—an American newspaperman. Neither of us had any difficulty about getting our visas—I as a tourist and he as a journalist. We struck up an acquaintance and he gave me a lift back to town. I felt that in my attempt to camouflage the real purpose of my visit, my replies to the usual friendly questions were somewhat misleading. I myself got the definite impression that my relations with my husband were somewhat strained and that, therefore, I was holidaying by myself in Scandinavia at a most inappropriate time of the year—ostensibly to forget or forgive or something equally melodramatic. My American friend and I met again the next day at the Finnish Consulate in order to pick up our passports, duly visa-ed, and discovered we were travelling to Finland on the same boat. I eventually went by plane and, except for a fleeting glimpse in Helsinki, did not come across him again, which, perhaps, was all to the good. Conspiracy and flirtations are not very good stable companions.

Leo's task was not so easy. Most of the people on his list were not in Stockholm and those that were felt that they had already contributed their share to the gallant struggle of the IZL by donating their £15 or £20 to my predecessor. Nevertheless, after super-human efforts, Leo managed to raise enough money for a ticket to Helsinki and to cover the expenses of my room until the end of the week.

As I stepped into the plane on Friday morning, my spirits soared so much that I decided to risk writing to Shmuel. A few days previously I would not have dared write for fear of giving such vitriolic and splenetic vent to my feelings as would have turned the writing paper to ashes. As my pen was useless, I borrowed one from my neighbour. It happened to be one of those advertised as being capable of writing under water. Unfortunately, that is the only place where they do write, and unless one puts on diving gear and esconces oneself at the bottom of a swimming pool, one is likely to dislocate one's wrist trying to achieve a whole letter. Nevertheless, my spirits were not to be dampened.

Leo had telephoned his father to meet me at the air terminal and when I arrived, there was a veritable deputation awaiting me. I was given so warm a welcome that I hardly felt the cold weather—and the temperature was 4 degrees below zero. We all went to Leo's father's flat where I explained the purpose of my visit. I found their enthusiasm and admiration for the IZL very heartwarming after the rather cold appreciation of the Swedish Jews. They asked for a little time to discuss the matter amongst themselves and meanwhile undertook to make my few days' stay in Helsinki as pleasant as possible. This they did with a right good will. I was wined and dined until I felt positively bloated, and all this in a Helsinki which was still suffering from the after-effects of a crippling war. The rations were very scanty, but the restaurants were amply stocked with every variety of food—at a price.

A very good example of the austerity conditions in Helsinki at that time was the hotel in which I stayed. It had just been evacuated by the Russians, and had still not been properly equipped for visitors. There were only two or three rooms which were habitable. My hosts apologized profusely for the lack of comfort, but Helsinki was full of foreign correspondents and trade deputations who had monopolised the very scanty accommodation. I had a huge room and bathroom. There was, however, no heating whatsoever and not the faintest sign of hot water. And any attempt at extracting any out of the maid or porter was simply hopeless. They just did not understand anything except Finnish and no-one who has not heard Finnish can possibly imagine how outlandish it sounds to anyone not born and bred in the country. During my four days in Helsinki I did not manage to separate even one word from the jumble of sound.

So, having given up any hope of getting hot water, I had to make do with cold. By breakfast time the morning after my arrival I had even solved the problem of hot water. I was given the austerity, standard breakfast which consisted of "silver tea," a lovely name for something as prosaic as hot water, a little milk and sugar and some dry bread. I "bathed" in the silver tea, drank the little milk together with the dry bread and licked up the sugar. Fortunately my Finnish friends believed in "second breakfasts."

There were at the time about 1,200 Jews in Finland, mostly of Russian origin, and as warmhearted and hospitable as the Swedish Jews are cold and stingy. I remarked very mildly to my friends that I thought the people in Stockholm were not very generous. They laughed uproariously and told me tales about their notorious tight-fistedness. There was the story of my money-collecting predecessor who was given a fixed daily allowance and when, by dint of scraping and pinching he was able to save enough to buy a much-needed shirt, the Committee were very indignant and said he should have told them that the allowance was larger than he needed.

Helsinki is a very clean and spacious town—a queer mixture of provincialism and modern architecture. The people are stolid and lumpy, suitably, rather than well-dressed, in striking contrast to the almost Parisian elegance of Stockholm. I felt very much as though I were in Bloemfontein, the capital of my native province in South Africa; and would hardly have been surprised if the worthy burghers of Helsinki had suddenly started speaking Afrikans, so much do they resemble the typical Boer of the Orange Free State. But all comparison ceases the moment one enters the countryside. Unlike the Orange Free State where the sight of a tree is a great event and where people have been known to fall into rivers and get out and dust themselves off, Finland is one riotous mass of forests and lakes. Although it was so very cold when I visited there, it was nevertheless only autumn and the forests were a miracle of beauty in their russet and gold, with a bright blue sky as background and the cold, breathlessly blue lakes mirroring the preenings and titivatings of the beautifully clad, majestically dignified trees.

On the Sunday we drove out into the countryside and lunched in a fashionable restaurant beside one of the numerous lakes. I suppose one needs to eat as much as the Finns do in order to keep warm in their climate; or, maybe, the magnificence of the scenery adds zest to the appetite. I didn't do too badly myself, but then I had a few days of semi-starvation behind me.

On one of my evenings in Helsinki I went with Leo's parents to see "Odd Man Out." The Jewish population of Helsinki was greatly excited over this film as they had heard it was about the underground; and for them there was only one underground—the IZL. I did not have the heart to disillusion them and tell them it was about Ireland and not Palestine.

The day I was due to leave, my friends explained to me that they very much wanted to help the IZL, but however much money they collected in Finland—and in a population of 1,200 it wasn't possible to collect over-much—when taken out of the country and converted into terms of dollars or pounds would amount to very little. So they suggested we should send out a young man to collect money, but that it should be converted into goods—either timber or arms—and, in this guise, taken out of the country. I promised to convey this to our headquarters in Paris. Eventually, nothing came of the scheme as it was thought too much of an undertaking to ship arms all the way from Finland when there were some available a good deal nearer home. But, nevertheless, the good intentions and the warmth of feeling towards the IZL on the part of our friends in Helsinki was greatly encouraging.

I returned to Stockholm by ship which I boarded at a port called Abo. At least it's written "Abo," but I dread to think how it is pronounced. The short train journey to Abo through the Finnish countryside was a delight. What particularly fascinated me were the dainty, picturesque, little wooden houses with which the country is liberally dotted. I made a mental note to try and transplant one of these houses to Palestine if we

67

should ever become respectable enough to live above ground, literally and figuratively.

When I boarded the boat I found I had a two-berth cabin to myself. As always in these Northern countries it was scrupulously clean, it was warm and there was plenty of hot water. I went out on deck for some air before dinner and was "picked up" by the ship's engineer—not very surprisingly a Finn. We got on famously in German, of which I know very little and not more than about five words. But I understood him well enough to know he was making a date with me for 9 that evening. The simplest thing was to say "yes" instead of breaking my teeth and trying his patience, so I said "yes" and, of course, did not turn up. No doubt he found someone to console him.

Then I went down to look for dinner. I offer the following solemn invocation to the Finnish Merchant Navy: "For heaven's sake write instructions to passengers in any European language, mind any, in addition to Finnish, which is quite meaningless to ignorant travellers like myself." I wandered around helplessly for half-an-hour looking for the dining salon. The trouble was that in every nook and cranny there were people eating and I was completely at at loss to find which nook would suit my requirements. Eventually, a young Norwegian, seeing my plight, asked in tolerably good English whether he could help. I practically embraced him with relief and explained my difficulties. He looked a little askance at such abysmal ignorance but, nevertheless, took me under his wing and undertook to escort me to dinner as soon as the first session was over. My new friend, whose name was Nils, had escaped to England from Norway after the Narvik disaster and had served in the British Army—hence his very welcome knowledge of English.

When we eventually got in to dinner, Nils piled up my plate with a gorgeous selection of mixed foods. I finished this with difficulty to find, to my horror, that it had merely been an hors d'oevre and the meal proper was yet to follow. I retired gracefully and spent the rest of the meal in wide-eyed astonishment watching Nils eat. And he was so slight too.

After spending a pleasant hour in the cocktail bar, I retired to my cabin and slept properly for the first time in days, as my feet were actually warm.

We arrived in Stockholm very early in the morning. It was drizzling and Leo was not there to meet me. He apparently had not received my cable. I just had no luck in Stockholm. Fortunately, Nils was still attentive. He took me to breakfast and then we tried to phone Leo. Just in case one hasn't enough troubles in Stockholm, the public telephone booths are so built that one's legs are completely exposed to the curious gaze of the passers-by and, what is a good deal more serious, to the elements. I was told, in all good faith, that the reason for this was so that the Stockholm authorities, who are great sticklers for the conventionalities, could observe whether any unseemly conduct was being practiced in the telephone booths. I must say that any couple who could manage to make love in a Stockholm telephone booth ought to have earned respect and admiration for their perseverance and ingenuity, rather than the opprobrium of the authorities.

Nils and I spent an hour trying to 'phone Leo, taking it in turns to enter the telephone booth so as not to shock the local populace unduly. Nils, of course, was at a distinct advantage as he was, most sensibly, wearing trousers. Skirts may be quite the thing for the well-dressed woman-about-town, but they are hardly suitable protection against the bullying nor'-westers (or sou'westers, or what you will) which came blustering in under the partitions of the Stockholm telephone booths. When I had emulated Lot's wife to the extent of having been turned into a pillar of ice from the thighs downwards, we eventually located Leo. To my eternal disgrace, as soon as Leo said he would pick me up in ten minutes, I despatched Nils quite unceremoniously, in spite of his long-standing kindness.

Leo and I went off to look for an hotel room and once more I landed up in one of the lesser-known rooming-houses. This time my room was a huge, cold, old-fashioned drawing-room, literally bedecked with 19th century knick-knacks, with a bed tucked away as unobtrusively as possible in a corner. My feet turned cold at the very thought of sleeping there. Adjoining my room was a bathroom which had a second door leading out into the passage. I was always scrupulous about locking *both* doors when I used the bathroom, which is more than could be said of the other occupants of this most gloomy of houses, to my continual embarrassment.

Leo and I had a council of war and I impressed on him the dire necessity of my getting back to Paris and out of Stockholm as soon as possible. There was only one slight hitch—the price of a plane ticket. Leo had a short, a very short, list of people who had promised to give him donations. They were mostly Jews born in Sweden who sympathised with the IZL. We visited them, and, after much sweating of blood, came away with a total sum of 500 kronen, leaving us still short of 100 kronen (short £10) for a ticket and expenses. This we borrowed from Mr. H. who behaved quite handsomely, even taking me to dinner at the posh Stockholm

Restaurant on a cople of occasions. I have often wondered why Mr. H., who has a family, did not ever take me home to meet his wife. I presume that, like all stolid and respectable citizens, he does not believe in worrying his wife about business matters; or maybe there is, after all, something of the adventuress about me, which only the exceptionally acute eye of Mr. H. could spot. Nevertheless, I bear him no grudge. On the contrary, he and Leo were the only two beings in Stockholm who appeared human to my somewhat billious and prejudiced wisdom.

At last, after another couple of days of tramping and chocolate lunches, I took the plane to Paris on Friday morning, exactly two weeks after I had set out on my ill-fated journey. And even my leaving was not without incident. At the airport the Authorities demanded 10 kronen overweight for my luggage. I very firmly offered to pay in English pounds and they just as firmly turned my offer down—very fortunately, as I had no English pounds to pay with. Eventually, with the judicious use of my sweetest smile, we reached a compromise. I gave them Leo's address and they said they would collect the money from him. I have never found out whether they did or not.

In Paris I proceeded to the hotel where Shmuel was staying, tearfully reprimanded him for not coming to meet me (which was not surprising since I had written that I was returning on Saturday) and then soaked away all the bad memories of Stockholm in the hottest of hot baths.

CHAPTER VI

PRELUDE TO WAR

SHMUEL had to stay on in Paris for another two weeks, but he decided to send me back to Palestine immediately as there were no other commissions to be done in Europe. I went by train to Amsterdam and had my first experience of travelling by wagons-lits. We passed through Rotterdam where the sight of cows grazing peacefully in the middle of what must once have been the shopping-centre of the town was all that remained to remind one of the brutal havoc and disaster which Hitler's planes had hurled down on a peace-loving kindly community.

I had a day and night to myself in Amsterdam and went on a sight-seeing trip. The luxurious feeling of being a tourist with a couple of pounds in my pocket quite outweighed what must otherwise have been a sense of utter loneliness in this strange town. And, also, I was delighted at being able to understand, more or less, what the people were talking about, since Afrikaans, one of the national languages of South Africa, originates from Dutch. It is, however, a very much simpler and less guttural tongue, and I was abashed to find, when I tried out my Afrikaans on the hotel staff, that they thought I was indulging in baby-talk.

The next morning I took the plane to Lydda and found myself seated next to a prominent member of the Tel Aviv community who had been on a mission to Holland for the Jewish Agency. We soon struck up an acquaintance and he, perhaps naturally, concluded that I was a regular member of the highly respectable South African community in Palestine. The talk in the plane was about the Partition plan and its pros and cons. I opposed partition, whereas my neighbor, as was to be expected, was in favor of it. He turned to me and asked: "Why is it that all the South Africans oppose partition?" While not betraying my pleasant surprise at this revelation of anti-partition solidarity on the part of my fellow-counrtymen, I replied: "Maybe, it is because they are afraid that by the time they want to, or have to, come to Palestine, there won't be any room left for them."

In spite of our disagreements, my neighbor and I remained on ex-

71

tremely friendly terms; so much so that when a violent atmospheric storm broke out and the lights failed, he very tenderly held my hand—presumably to prevent me from being frightened, or maybe to fortify himself. When we parted at Lydda he gave me his card and told me to be sure to call on him whenever I needed help. The only other time I ever met him he was with his wife, so I tactfully did not recognise him. But I still have his card!

In Lydda I went through the formalities of security and customs, receiving the unfailing courtesy which my British passport always earned me. In the main hall there was a terrific din going on. The police had arrested two suspected "terrorists" who were very loudly and volubly protesting their innocence. They were two young men from a religious colony who had come to meet their mother, arriving from abroad. Unfortunately for them, they had not had the foresight to change from their workaday khaki clothes and hats to the irrefutable respectability of lounge suits. So they were detained as suspected terrorists and only after a lot of gesticulating and explaining on their part, and weeping and beatings of the breast on the part of the poor bewildered mother, were they eventually escorted out of the airport and released.

I returned to our flat in Ramat Gan, which had been faithfully cared for by Yael, a Jerusalem-born American-educated girl, who was the mainstay of the IZL public relations department.

The next day I took Shmuel's report to Menachem Begin and that night he and I went out for a walk in the streets of Tel Aviv—the first time he had walked in Tel Aviv since he had gone underground. We avoided all street-lights and spoke English for greater security. Nevertheless we were both a little nervous and did not stay out too long. But this walk whetted Begin's appetite for the outside world and we made plans for the whole family to spend a Saturday at our flat in Ramat Gan.

Any arrangements that Begin and I might have made for a family outing were purely academic and theoretical. They had first to have the official sanction of Avraham, who was the final arbiter on the question of security, before it came within the bounds of feasibility. And Avraham was not in the least enamored of the idea. His reluctance was eminently understandable. The expedition necessitated Begin's going out in broad daylight, and in the company of his family. Even if he, himself, were not recognised, there was always the danger that Ala might be recognised and the fact that they had two children and that Ala was about to have a third, would be divulged. The British never knew that Begin had more than one child and consequently in all their searches they looked for a man with a wife and small boy. Chasya was thus a vital part of the conspiracy and the revelation of her existence would naturally increase the danger of discovery.

Nevertheless, after a little pressure from everyone concerned, we finally succeeded in wringing a very hesitant "yes" from Avraham—on condition that everyone was as careful as possible.

Meanwhile Shmuel returned from Paris, having once more got past the security officials at Lydda with nothing worse than a search of his baggage. The fact that Shmuel was never detained during the years of his active participation in the underground remains one of those miracles in which the history of the revolt abounded. He was continually leaving the country and so exposing himself to the scrutiny of the security officials; he was known to have been one of the leaders of the Revisionist Party, and he was always meeting foreign correspondents who had an unfortunate habit of mixing with the local correspondents, many of whom knew Shmuel by name, if not by occupation. I think it is as much to the credit of the discretion of the correspondents as to the apparent inability of the authorities to reconcile his studious, "civilised" appearance and South African passport, with their own conception of a "terrorist" that Shmuel owed his immunity. The fact that he featured on the CID B list did indicate that he was not entirely above suspicion, but, fortunately, the seeds of distrust had no chance to germinate into fully-grown conviction of guilt, before the British withdrew their administration.

*   *   *   *   *

On the momentous Saturday morning, Shmuel went into Tel Aviv early to pick up the Begin family. Avraham waited in a taxi a few corners away from the Begin flat and Shmuel then escorted them to the taxi, walking behind with Menachem, while Ala and the children went ahead. For Bennie and Chasya this was a most wonderful adventure. Not only were they going out with their father for the first time in their short lives, but, most wonderful of all wonders, they were going in a motor-car! The excitement was terrific.

There were no British barriers out that day and inter-urban cars were not stopped and searched as very frequently happened. So the Begin family arrived without any mishap to spend the first of many Saturdays with us in Ramat Gan.

Menachem was in "disguise"—he was wearing a hat and had taken off his glasses. Contrary to reports from the most authentic sources that Begin had had numerous plastic operations and that his face was altered beyond recognition, he had never done anything more drastic than grow a beard to conceal some of his more prominent features. At this period he had only a moustache and relied on this and on the removal of his glasses as a means of camouflage.

This first Saturday of many was a lovely day, so Begin donned his disguise and we all went for a walk to the Yarkon River. We looked a very ordinary party of Sabbath strollers. Bennie ran along ahead, Menachem wheeled the pram with Chasya in it and talked earnestly to Shmuel, while Ala and I strolled leisurely along. No one could possibly have guessed that this party of children and women, pregnant and non-pregnant, included the most wanted man in Palestine, and the lorry-loads of British soldiers and police which drove by us certainly suspected this least of all. One young man did get rather a bad fright. He came riding towards us on a bicycle, looked at Menachem, turned round and looked again and gracefully fell off his bicycle. Menachem recognised him as one of the members of the IZL whom he had but lately met.

As part of Shmuel's camouflage consisted in his living an ostensibly normal life, we naturally had friends and acquaintances dropping in on us unexpectedly at all times, and particularly on Saturdays. This presented somewhat of a problem at first, when we were still a little nervous. We overcame this by having Begin spend most of the day, when he was not outside, in a back room into which our visitors did not usually penetrate. After a while, when we all became much bolder he would come out and move around freely and even take part in the conversations.

On one occasion a young friend, B, who had done an excellent job for the IZL in Europe, came to visit us. He was anxious to talk to Shmuel, but Begin was in the room. B waited and waited, chitted and chatted about mutual acquaintances, about the weather, about everyhing under the sun except what was most on his mind. Shmuel and I noticed his discomfort but did not betray our amusement by so much as a dimpling of a cheek. Eventually B could stand the strain no longer. He leaned over and whispered to Shmuel in English that he would like to speak to him privately. With his face completely devoid of any expression, Shmuel got up and left the room with B. If the fact of his refusing to divulge information of the IZL before Menachem Begin were not sufficient proof of B's caution, then the fact that he succeeded in hiding his connections with the IZL so effectively as to enable him today to hold a very high position in the Israeli Army, (in which IZL members have deliberately been kept down), certainly is proof positive of the very highest degree of discretion.

Our neighbors, as well as friends and acquaintances, got used to seeing the Begin family around. None of them had any suspicion whatsoever. In fact, when the Arabs later began their attacks, one of our acquaintances was quite convinced that they were a family from the Jaffa-Tel Aviv border to whom we were giving temporary refuge from the danger of Arab snipers. I did not disillusion him.

These Saturday excursions did both Begin and Ala a lot of good. He began to get some color into the pallor of his face and she could escape, at least for the day, from the cares of domesticity and from her semi-imprisonment in their apartment. Neither of them gave a second thought to the palpable risk they were taking in walking abroad in daylight, Begin because he was quite unperturbed about his own personal safety and Ala because the long years of anxiety had bred in her a philosophical fatalism which, added to her own natural cheerfulness, enabled her to take in her stride all danger and discomfort.

* * * * *

At the beginning of November, 1947, my mother arrived from South Africa. I immediately went out and bought Shmuel khaki shorts and shirts in preparation for his impeding exile to the detention camp in Gilgil, Kenya, so positive was I that his camouflage would go up in smoke the moment my mother arrived. For she is a great politician and she does not believe in hiding her light, or her opinions, under a bushel—a characteristic which does not fit in very well with life in the underground.

All her life my mother has been a passionate Zionist. She came to South Africa with her family from Lithuania in 1905, instead of going to Palestine as she had planned because, at the last minute, my grandmother sat down on her luggage and refused to budge unless my mother accompanied her to South Africa. My grandmother's motives were two-fold: first of all, she felt she could not cope with all the children, the baggage, the barrels of salt herring and the feather mattresses on her own (my grandfather had preceded her by a couple of years); and, secondly, she could not bear to part with her eldest daughter and have her murdered by Arabs or Turks in Palestine. She insisted that she would rather they were all murdered together by the Kaffirs in South Africa. Then at least there would be a greater chance of a family re-union in the next world. (My grandmother remained pleasantly surprised by the ostensible tameness of the South African black people till the day she died.) So my mother had to give up her dream of draining the marshes in Palestine and instead helped shepherd the brats and the salt herrings across Europe and over the seas to South Africa.

But all the time her heart remained in Zion. When she married my father she made a Zionist out of him too and we children were naturally brought up to consider Palestine our real home-land and South Africa as merely the place where we were born. I had my first lesson in Zionism when I was four years old. For the first time I noticed a picture on our breakfast-room wall. It was one of the less successful efforts of some quite unknown artist and depicted a young Jewish girl being burnt at the stake during the days of the Spanish Inquisition. With childish curiosity I asked my mother about the picture and heard, for the first time, of racial and religious persecution. That picture haunted me for years and probably did much to keep me on the beaten track than did all the Zionist history and propaganda which was pumped into us.

In 1930, Vladimir Jabotinsky came to South Africa and my mother and eldest brother, Michael, became his ardent supporters. Michael was at the University in Johannesburg at the time and came home one vacation and told us younger children that we, too, should be supporters of Jabotinsky. As, in those days, Michael was our great hero and wielded an immense amount of power and influence over us, we unquestionably became Revisionists (as members of Jabotinsky's party were called) too.

My father was chairman of the local Zionist Society and had been so for the previous twenty years. He stuck to his guns and remained a General Zionist.

Then, in 1935, Jabotinsky broke away from the World Zionist Organization and formed the New Zionist Organization. This breakaway cleft the Zionist movement in two and set the opposing parties into snarling and howling at each other for years.

My mother, with the same enthusiasm and fanaticism that she had put into working for Zionism in general, now turned her attention to the New Zionist Organization. Our small town was split in two as surely as if some venomous giant had carved a yawning chasm through its middle.

My mother quarreled with her opponents with great gusto. Her best friend, shocked by what she considered sheer betrayal on my mother's part spread invidious rumors that my mother had lost her reason. This moved my mother to flights of fancy which could hardly be called ladylike and are certainly unprintable. My father, who I have always been convinced was really still a General Zionist and wanted to remain in the Old Zionist Organization, finally gave in (probably in sheer self-defence) and joined the Revisionists, resigning his 25-year old chairmanship of the local branch—to the great delight of his rivals who had grown old and decrepit waiting for a chance to oust him.

When I came home at vacation time from the University, I had to be supplied with a list of the people with whom we were on friendly terms. Old Zionists did not visit the homes of New Zionists and vice versa. At all communal functions the opposing factions lined themselves up on opposite sides of the hall. To an objective onlooker the whole affair was quite impossibly comical, but to the parish politicians, with my mother vehemently in the forefront, it was deadly serious.

By the time the IZL came on the scene my mother had moved to Johannesburg and there she took up the cudgels for the terrorists with the same zeal and an improved power of invective.

Amongst the Jewish community she gained herself the reputation of being practically the chief bomb-thrower of the IZL and certainly one of its most vehement protagonists. She even got herself into trouble with the local general press in an escapade which was quite typical of her. She had heard that a newly-rich member of the Jewish community had given £10,000 to the Red Cross Fund. So my mother went off to get a donation for the IZL from him. She could not get to the great man, but saw his secretary instead. The secretary happened to be a gentile, and an Englishman; but my mother, who is incurably hopeless at catching names, decided that he was Jewish and so a fit receptacle for some suitable propaganda, which he could duly pass on to his boss, about whom she could hardly have been said to have minced words. The net result of her efforts was a big headline in the following day's "Star," one of the biggest dailies in South Africa, to the effect that the Palestinian terrorists had launched a big money campaign in South Africa and had sent thousands of pounds out of the counrty. My mother defended herself against the attacks of my brothers and her fellow-workers with the plea that the secretary had encouraged her and had not divulged his real sympathies—in short that he was a provocateur and a dirty dog. All of which may be quite true, but it did not enhance my mother's reputation as a conspirator and keeper of secrets.

That is why I bought the khaki shorts and shirts when my mother arrived in Palestine. But to give her her due, except for informing the whole neighborhood of what she thought of the British and of the Jewish Agency, she was remarkably discreet. Perhaps the lurid picture of all the sufferings Shmuel would have to endure at the hands of the British which I painted and embellished for her had some effect.

*   *   *   *   *

On the 29th November, 1947, the United Nations' decision to partition Palestine was announced amid wild hilarious celebrations. Throughout the night young people and old danced in the streets. Venerable chassidic rabbis danced their ritual dances amid a motley, swaying mass, drunk with ecstasy. And on the 30th November, the first Jews were killed by Arabs and the Yishuv was brutally jerked back into sobriety.

From that day, the IZL was transformed from an underground anti-British organisation into a semi-secret army. A complete British withdrawal from the Tel Aviv to Petach Tikvah area enabled the IZL to set up proper training camps for full-time courses. This change-over and complete re-orientation in training methods brought to a head the chronic shortage of arms and ammunition. In a series of daring and spectacular escapades, the British were relieved of quite a substantial amount of equipment, but this could not satisfy the growing needs of a miniature army. It was then that the plan for robbing Barclay's Bank in Tel Aviv was conceived.

Shmuel told me of the daring scheme to take away the £250,000 which was purported to be in the vaults of the Bank. We waited on tenterhooks for news. Twice, unbeknown to the authorities, the plan failed through some technical hitch. We who knew about the plans beforehand were bitterly disappointed at each failure and felt the tension and expectancy reach practically to bursting-point. At last Gideon, who was the perpetrator of all the schemes, announced that his plan was fool-proof. The date was fixed for a Monday, late in February, 1948.

The plan was as beautiful as it was simple. A squadron of British soldiers used to come regularly to Barclay's Bank in an armoured bren-gun carrier to collect the army pay. They would throw a cordon round the bank and prevent anyone from entering it until they had finished their job. This usually happened at about 8:30 on a Monday morning, a few minutes after the bank had opened.

On this particular Monday, it was planned that the bren-gun carrier, complete with "British" soldiers, would draw up at the bank, which would then be duly cordoned off. Meanwhile Gideon and a confederate, who

78

had been introduced into the vaults on Sunday night, would wait until the usual bank official had opened the vaults, would then calmly take the money, probably gagging the official so as to prevent him from giving premature alarm, and would hand it out to the waiting "soldiers." The bren-gun carrier, complete with loot and accompanying lorry-load of "Tommies" would then disappear into limbo. All this would take about 15 minutes and be completed before anyone outside the bank was aware of anything untoward.

On Sunday evening I got a message that Ala had gone into the nursing home to have her baby and would I come early the next morning to look after the other two children. I decided to drop by Barclay's Bank on my way to the Begins in order to be able to pass on the good news at first hand. I arrived at the bank a little after 8:30 and found an excited crowd milling around. This was not quite according to plan, and my heart sank. I asked one of the bystanders what was going on and was told that the bank had been robbed. My spirits soared again. While I was watching, the boys came out of the bank and started climbing the bren-gun carrier. They had sacks on their backs, but they looked rather light and empty to me. At a whistle, the soldiers forming the cordon scrambled onto the lorry and the procession moved off to the accompaniment of bullets directed at them by an over-zealous and stupidly officious Haganah squad, which had got wind of what was afoot and had hurried to the scene to protect the interests of the British. At the sound of firing, the crowd scattered precipitantly, not without many a mutter and a growl about people in the Haganah who could not mind their own business. I thought it wise to retreat too, as bullets have a nasty habit of straying from their intended direction, and a dead messenger could hardly be a harbinger of tidings, whether good or bad.

I hastened to the Begins and told Menachem what I had seen, being able to assure him only that the boys had all got safely away.

We waited that morning for news from Gideon and news from Ala. The hours went and Gideon did not turn up. I made a feeble attempt to explain this away by the fact that he was probably busy counting the money. But we both knew that in the event of success, Gideon would have arrived as soon as possible, bursting with excitement.

At one o'clock I heard the secret ring and let Gideon in. His first words dispelled any last vestiges of hope which we may still have entertained. "Did you hear of the terrible catastrophe in Jerusalem?" he asked Begin. That day a British "special squad" had blown up half of Ben

79

Yehuda Street in Jerusalem, killing over fifty people and causing millions of pounds of damages.

Disaster was added to disappointment, and just to put the finishing touch for Menachem, Ala gave birth to another daughter.

What had happened to the plan which was as simple as it was beautiful? It was one of those incalculable imponderables which inspired Hamlet to quote Shakespeare on "the divinity which shapes our ends" or, on a lower plane, wrung from the Burns the heart-rending admission that "the best laid schemes, of mice and men gang aft'agly." The official in charge of opening the vaults had unfortunately just that morning had to visit the synagogue to offer up a prayer for the soul of his dead father. In consequence, he had arrived a little late at the bank, only to find himself kept out by the cordon of Tommies, in spite of all his protestations. Gideon and companion waited inside ten minutes longer than the appointed time and then decided to withdraw. Prolonging their stay would not have helped at all, as their very presence in the bank meant the maintenance of the cordon and the concomitant holdup of the relevant clerk.

A few months later, the LHI pulled off the same trick—but successfully. They took the precaution of picking up the clerk at his home and accompanying him to the bank.

*   *   *   *   *

Soon after the Barclay's Bank fiasco, it was decided that Shmuel should go to America. He had applied a few months previously for visas for himself and me. Early in March, we received information from the American Consul in Jerusalem that our visas had been granted and that we should come to Jerusalem to receive them.

Jerusalem is only 1½ hours from Tel Aviv ordinarily, but in March, 1948, the trip was a hazardous military operation. Tens of people had already been murdered on the road by Arab snipers and guerilla bands. Cars had been overturned and set alight with their occupants inside, and generally the prospects were a little grim. My mother took tearful leave of us, quite convinced that she would never see us again.

The journey was made in convoy by armored buses or steel-plated taxis. We did not succeed in getting into a bus so we travelled by armored taxi. There were seven of us and our suitcases crushed into a space large enough for four. On the way we picked up a Haganah man with a bren-gun, just to complicate matters. Fortunately, the bren-gun protruded through a hole in the roof, so we were at least spared the indignity of one of those slapstick comedy ladder scenes, where everyone either ducks quickly or gets knocked over every time the fellow carrying the ladder swivels round. The armour-plating of the car was rather ominously full of bullet holes, which did not reflect very well on the thickness of the steel and did not augur too well for our futures.

The journey was quite uneventful until we arrived at Bab El Wad, a spot well-beloved of Arab snipers and just about the most treacherous part of the road. At this psychological moment one of the foremost buses broke down. The whole convoy was halted while hasty repairs were effected — an operation calling for considerable courage from the drivers and mechanics in the expectation of being greeted at any minute by a hail of bullets from the wooded heights on either side of the road.

Our taxi was an idyllic haven for anyone with claustrophobia. It was pitch dark, except for a chink of light coming through the bren-gun peep-hole. The little bit of air was inhaled in great gusts by the somewhat nervous, fidgety occupants of this modern black hole of Calcutta. There was no room to stretch out an arm or leg and we had to reconcile ourselves to losing, by slow degrees, the feel of each limb in turn. There was just no question of getting out of the car and breathing in some air and stretching our legs. We would have been too easy a target for any Arabs perched on the crags above us. We whiled away the time with feeble jokes and feebler stories, our wits seeming to become as atrophied as our legs. After a while we had to choose between being suffocated alive or presenting a few more peepholes for the penetration of enemy bullets. We chose the latter, and opened the slits in the armor plating, which served as windows.

The Arabs must have been busy elsewhere that day, or perhaps they had knocked off for morning coffee, an amiable practice with which Lawrence of Arabia had found it so difficult to cope during World War I. Anyhow, they spared us their attentions during that week-long half-an-hour that we spent at Bab-El-Wad.

Three-quarters of an hour after the convoy re-started, we reached Jerusalem and had practically to be pried out of the taxi with a lever, so stiff and numb were we.

The strife-torn city was an ugly and depressing sight with its maze of barricades and road-blocks erected by the British for the double purpose of protecting themselves against the underground and isolating themselves from the Jewish-Arab conflict. To the ugliness of the road-blocks was added the tragic sight of the fresh piles of rubble which had once been hotels, shops and blocks of flats in the wrecked Ben Yehuda Street.

The Arabs exacted a daily toil of Jewish lives. People were killed by snipers; many had been brutally murdered when passing through Arab quarters; and the bloody slaughter and incineration of a convoy of professors, doctors and nurses, ambushed on their way to the University and the Hadassah Hospital on Mount Scopus, had horrified the whole country. The Jewish population felt frustrated and desperate. They were prevented by the British from defending themselves, but were not defended by the so-called administration. The Ben Yehuda massacre had served to inflame the hatred of the Jews for the British Army and the latter, in turn, exacted spiteful revenge for the drubbing they had received from the undeground by giving the Arabs practical carte blanche to do as they pleased with the Jews.

There was an ominous tension and gloom in the city. At night the streets were desolate and deserted as the Jewish population hardly ventured out. All night long the sounds of shooting filled the air, a deadly portent of what was to come when the war started in earnest.

Getting to the American Consulate was by no means a simple operation. It was in one of the ghettoes in which the British had enclosed themselves and, in order to get there, we had to get military passes at the ghetto gate. These passes were issued between 8:30 and 9 A.M. only, so we had to wait until the next morning.

That evening Shmuel and I were invited by the IZL Commander, Raanan, to a unique little ceremony. We entered an old house in a typical Jerusalem back-street, scrambled up some rickety, tortuous stairs and arrived at the headquarters of the IZL. There, by candle-light, we drank a toast in beer to the first thirteen IZL-manufactured sten-guns which had arrived in Jerusalem that day—an event not to be underestimated in the light of the desperate shortage of arms. For the first time in my experience of underground activities I really felt like a conspirator. We could have been a gang of Jacobins plotting the overthrow of the dynasty, so perfect was the cloak and dagger atmosphere—candle-light, shadowy figures flitting in and out and holding whispered colloquoy with Raanan; a tough-looking woman with a bandana round her head passing round the cups of beer and chunks of cheese; the toast delivered in subdued tones with equally subdued responses; in a dark corner the sten-guns being lovingly caressed and cooed over by unseen enthusiasts.

The tough-looking woman—who was incidentally the lady of the

82

house—was the "mother" of the IZL in Jerusalem and was as kind and generous in nature as she was tough in appearance. She and her husband—known in the underground as Gandhi, probably because of his most unsylphlike figure—were two of the mainstays of the organization in Jerusalem throughout some of its most difficult and troublous times.

The next morning Shmuel and I were at the ghetto gates punctually at 8.30. We had no trouble about getting passes, and Shmuel went off to the American Consulate while I retraced my steps a few yards to the corner of the Jewish Agency building where I had to meet Dan, at 9 a.m., prior to my going to the Consulate.

While waiting at the corner I remembered I had a message to deliver in the Agency building for a friend in Tel Aviv. The guard at the barricade was polite but firm—no one was allowed into the Agency building without a pass. He advised me to phone from the cafe across the road. As I returned from carrying out his advice, an American Consulate car driven by an Arab chauffeur drew up and was allowed to enter without any difficulty. Dan arrived punctually at nine. I spent a few minutes with him and then started off for the Consulate which was five minutes from the Jewish Agency building. I had gone a few hundred yards when there was a terrific explosion behind me. I did not wait to see what was happening, but hurried to get to the Consulate with most unheroic precipitancy. I found Shmuel in the waiting-room, deathly pale and quite touchingly pleased to see me whole. The blast of the explosion had brought down bits of the Consulate ceiling. After the first few minutes of shocked silence, everyone in the waiting room started babbling at once, with that animation which comes from relief at having been spared the fate of others less fortunate. Phones started ringing and rumors started flying. Out of the conglomeration of fantastic stories, one pattern appeared constantly—the explosion had occurred in the Jewish Agency building and the explosives had been introduced in an American Consulate car.

When the handful of people in the waiting room, with whom we had suddenly become bosom pals, heard that Shmuel and I intended going from the American Consulate to the French Consulate, there were cries of horror and protest. And not without reason. The French Consulate was in the Arab part of the New City and to get there from where we were meant traversing quite a few unhealthy streets from the Jewish point of view. An intrepid Jewish newspaperman had been stabbed and severely hurt in that neighborhood a few days previously. Our original plan had been to refrain from mock heroics and go there by taxi, but this was thwarted as the whole area was closed to vehicles immediately after the explosion. So we had perforce to walk to the French Consulate as Shmuel needed a French transit visa on his South African passport. With my British passport I did not need any French visa, but I insisted on accompanying Shmuel for two reasons: firstly, I thought my un-Jewish appearance might be some kind of safeguard for him, and, secondly, I was dead scared to go back to town alone. Everything appears to be so much less dangerous when there are two of you.

We set off on our perilous path with complete nonchalance outwardly and with a good deal of inward trepidation. We were the only two lunatics in the streets, except for some of the most villainous-looking Arabs I have ever seen, sitting on the pavement outside their shops. As we passed them I felt the hair rising at the back of my head and a cold shiver went down my spine. Our overcoats seemed very flimsy protection for our vulnerable backs and I swear I felt the knife between my shoulder blades as surely as if it had been plunged there by murderous figures.

Whether my light hair proved a talisman or whether the Arabs had had enough blood-letting for one day we'll never know; but we did arrive safely at the French Consulate to the great surprise of Benjamin Cohen, the Secretary of the Consulate and a good friend of ours. We both presented a very bold front and laughed the matter off with sang froid. Benjamin very kindly undertook to deliver Shmuel's passport, duly visa'ed, that afternoon at the Vienna Cafe. He was the only Jew in the French Consulate and, in fact, one of the very few Jews who still came to work in that part of town. He risked his life every day getting to and from work and sometimes, when the tension was high, was virtually marooned in the Consulate for days on end. But he carried on steadfastly, typifying the Jews of Jerusalem who went about their daily tasks calmly and courageously in the face of terrific day-to-day strain and tension.

We decided that we had drawn sufficiently on our good luck account for one day and, on the way back from the French Consulate, took a circuitous route which, for part of the way at least, led past a British encampment. It is true that the British troops in Jerusalem had been more effective in blowing up the "Palestine Post" building and Ben Yehuda Street rather than in protecting unarmed Jews against the attacks of cutthroat Arabs, as was their ostensible task. Nevertheless, we thought that if confronted by an actual attempt at slaughter on their doorstep, they might lift a hand to prevent it, if only out of sheer sportsmanship. Their presence could not, of course, be any guarantee against the ill-effects of sniper's bullets, but death by a bullet seemed rather a clean, civilised way of departing from this world in comparison with some of the exquisite refinements which the Arabs had invented.

We once again got safely through the danger zone, passed through the gates out of the British ghetto and came to a barricade hastily erected by the Haganah at the Jewish Agency building after the damage had already been done. At the barricade was a squad of black-bereted Haganah boys in charge of a cocky, bumptious little officer modelled to a T in the stlyle of a British army "type"—from the little, fair, moustache to the jaunty cane. He stuck his nose in everywhere, interfering with the efficient execution of his men's duties and generally pushing everyone around, especially old women and men with long grey beards. I am generally quite mild-tempered, but any attempts at bullying me or pushing me around make me wild. So, not unnaturally, I took an intsant dislike to this officer. This dislike was considerably enhanced when our turn came to be identified and passed through the barrier. I produced my British passport and was immediately fawned upon and slobbered over in English, until he saw the obviously Jewish name, when his attentions cooled off considerably. Then came Schmuel's turn—and Shmuel had no passport and was very obviously Jewish. He explained very politely and apologetically that he had to leave his passport at the French Consulate and had come out without an identity card, not anticipating such a contretemps. The officer replied as rudely as possible that Shmuel could then spend the rest of the day at the barrier until someone turned up to identify him. I offered at once to identify him as my husband and asked rather caustically whether all these elaborate precautions weren't somewhat belated. The officer bridled and said aggressively that I was at liberty to pass on through the barrier. I replied equally aggressively that I was remaining with my husband, and challenged him to have me removed. At that stage Shmuel lost his temper too and demanded to know, in his very fluent Hebrew, why the officer was speaking English instead of his own tongue. The quarrel then continued in Hebrew with biting interjections in English from me, as my Hebrew fails me completely in times of stress. At this stage a British officer walked up from the ghetto to the barrier. Our boy-friend almost fell over himself in his rush to jump to attention and salute. When I heard the British officer addressed as "Sir," I said very loudly and clearly to the general assembly: "Now what connection could a Haganah officer possibly have with that man to make him lick his boots like that?" The British officer had the good grace to blush for his less sensitive counterpart who, nevertheless, felt he had had enough of us and of me in particular. He dismissed us haughtily, with the sneering advice to Shmuel to stay in Tel Aviv in future.

I felt that we had had enough of Jerusalem at one go and suggested that we leave as soon as possible. There were all kinds of rumors afloat to the effect that Fawzi Kaukji, who was in charge of the Arab irregulars in the Jerusalem area, had cut off the road to Tel-Aviv or had threatened to cut it off. Consequently, there was a wild rush on the Tel Aviv buses. Through the system of knowing someone who knows someone or, to use that delightful Israel expression, "protektsia" (a system which is universally abhorred and decried by those who haven't got it, until they acquire it), we managed to get into an armored bus and started our return journey.

The discussion in the bus naturally centered on the destruction of the Agency building. Each one had a story to tell of how he, or his uncle, or his grandfather's third cousin, had been refused entrance to the Agency building by the guard while free access was given to non-Jews. Feelings ran high against the bullying and boorish behaviour of the Haganah guards at the Agency barricade towards their fellow-Jews, especially the old and timid, as opposed to their servile grovelling before the Gentile. Human grief, bitterness and determination in a bullet-proof container, could perhaps fittingly describe that bus-load of intrepid travellers. The dangers of the road were completely forgotten in the grief at the death of our fellow-Jews, blown up by the enemy, bitterness at the Gentile-complex which allowed our enemy to stalk abroad untrammelled, and determination to resist that enemy to the last.

Fawzi Kaukji had not cut off the road (it was cut off a month later) and we arrived safely in Tel Aviv, to be greeted by my mother with grateful surprise. She had succeeded in convicing herself that we were both buried beneath the ruins of the Agency building, unbeknown to God or man.

In spite of the general concensus of opinion in our bus that the destruction of the wing of the Agency building could be mainly ascribed to the Haganah's Gentile complex, the facts were otherwise. The story as we heard it is that the Agency had been in the habit of buying arms from the Arab driver of the American Embassy car and actually bought and paid for the load of explosives which was delivered to them at their heavily-protected headquarters, duly equipped with an appropriate time-gadget. We shall have to leave it to history to decide whether it is better to be a fool or a knave.

CHAPTER VII

I AM BECOMING A SOLDIER

IN March, 1948, Shmuel went to America, alone, as it was decided not to send me, after all. I was very pleased at this decision as the situation in Palestine looked as if it were becoming decidedly interesting, and the one and only characteristic which I have inherited from my mother is my intense dislike of missing anything exciting.

The purpose of Shmuel's trip was to speed up the collecting of money with which to buy arms, and to finalize the arrangements for the despatching of a ship containing arms, ammunition and potential soldiers for the IZL. This ship was the Altalena.

Shmuel left on one of the last—if not the last—'plane to take off from Lydda airport which was immediately afterwards encircled by the Arabs. His car was fired on several times during the journey without suffering any direct hit.

A month before this I had decided that it was time I stopped being a tame terrorist and learned how to be a soldier. As a result of my "proteksia" in high quarters, my request to be put into a training group bore immediate results. A day later a young woman, fully a head taller than I and correspondingly broader, arrived at our flat. She introduced herself as Rachel, a pseudonym, and said she was my instructress-to-be. I had been assigned to a group of young women who were starting a course in the handling and use of fire-arms. One of my jobs was to be the "contact-man" of the group. That meant that Rachel would let me know when and where we were to meet and I had to pass on the information to every member of the group. Rachel suggested that I start my career immediately and very kindly volunteered to take me on a tour of the houses of my fellow-adventurers so as to acquaint me with their addresses. I looked obviously at my semi-high-heeled shoes and suggested changing them, but she assured me heartily that we didn't have far to go.

We set off, Rachel with great gusto and greater strides, and I trotting obediently behind her. The first house we had to visit was on a hill-top in Bne Brak—about two miles from our flat as the crow flies. To my horror, I discovered that Rachel intended taking the same route as the mythical crow, except that ours would be on a lower and much more uncomfortable plane. We started off across country, climbed through barbed-wire fences, ploughed through cow-infested fields, traversed murky-looking lanes and, in a final spurt, climbed a steep hill to our destination. The crowning indignity was by being left outside to kick my heels and stub my toes while Rachel went in to transact some secret business. By this time I had worn down my high heels, torn my nylon stockings, ripped my narrow skirt and was now thoroughly equipped for the rest of our journey. We tramped around for another hour and I began to have some inkling of the trials and tribulations of the infantry. I made a mental note to recommend myself as a tank-driver to anybody who was really seriously thinking of using me.

We had our first lesson in ballistics at our flat. My mother wanted to join in also, but I managed to dissuade her tactfully on the ground that the instruction was in Hebrew, of which she does not know one word. After the first lesson we moved over to a less conspicuous flat. We learned everything there is to know about the revolver—the precautions, the types, how to take them apart and re-assemble them, how to load, how to unload, with eyes open, with eyes closed—until we all shuddered with distaste at the very sight of a revolver. But we still had not had a chance to shoot anything until Yechiela, one of our classmates, during a lesson with live bullets, pulled the trigger. She swore it was in error but I suspected then, and still suspect, that it was sheer curiosity to see if the things really shot. Fortunately, none of us were within range and, except for a chip in the floor and a neat hole in the door made by the ricocheting bullet, no harm was done. That discounts, of course, the partial shattering of our nerves and the temporary damage to our ear-drums. The neighbours showed no apparent interest in the noise of the explosion probably because in those days revolver and rifle shots were as common as street cries.

From revolvers we went on to Sten-guns (this time without live bullets) and hand grenades. I found it difficult to lift a hand-grenade, let alone to throw one (not that anyone let me try). I made another mental note: if the need ever arose I would drop the grenade and run like mad in the opposite direction.

After Shmuel left for America I suggested to Amitsur, who was in charge of training, that I would like to go to a camp for a week or two really to learn how to shoot instead of fooling around. He promised to arrange this for me and, sure enough, a couple of days later, Geulah, an officer in the IZL, arrived up at our flat and told me she was delighted at the idea of my going to a camp for a week or two—to cook. Geulah's enthusiasm was understandable. She was in charge of the commissariat for the district and had also to provide the cooks. This was an extremely difficult undertaking as every young girl wanted to be in the front line and no one wanted to do anything as dull and prosaic as cooking. I did not think this a very appropriate means of improving my knowledge of fire-arms, although of course I might in the process have found some substitutes for dynamite and hand-grenades; nevertheless, I agreed to go and cook, consoling myself philosophically with the though that "they also serve who only cook and wait."

I sent my mother off to my brother, Michael, in Haifa and Geulah took me to the camp. It was housed in an abandoned Arab farmhouse set in the midst of an orange grove. There was no water on the premises and the nearest tap was a mile away. The "kitchen" consisted of a few shelves, three primus stoves and a sink—a very precious item of furniture as I discovered later.

The camp was known as Base 6 and was used as an officers' training school. One course had just been completed and a new one was due to start the next day. Yehuda, the officer-in-charge of the school was in despair. He had forty men coming the next day and the two young Yemenite girls who had been cooking were completely hopeless. He did not have to tell us that. The smell from the kitchen hit us hard as we came up the avenue of orange trees. Geulah introduced me to Yehuda as the new cook. He looked at me blankly and then drew her aside and started a fierce whis-pered conversation. The purport of this, as she subsequently told me, was, that she had completely lost her senses; that this was no place for ladies; that she had better send me home and bring somebody a little less genteel. Geulah listened unperturbedly, told him not to worry and took me to the kitchen. My heart sank somewhat when I saw that kitchen. It was a veritable pig-sty. There were puddles of water on the floor, bits of food and dirty tins and bottles lay scattered all over the place, and in a corner was a barrel of stale fish from which arose a sicken-ing stench. I had a hurried colloquy with Geulah. The next day one of the other young women from our course, Chana, was due to join me. We were to spend a week in the camp and then be relieved by two other women from the same course. I suggested to Geulah that the two Yemenite girls stay on that day to help me clean up, but that she should send them back to their base the next day when Chana arrived. She was a bit dubious about whether the two of us would manage alone but agreed, nevertheless, to do as I asked.

The first thing I did was to have that barrel of fish removed as far away as possible. Then we set to work to scrub the floors and the shelves and some old cupboards which I found thrown out in the yard. When everything was scrubbed I sent one of the girls into Petach Tikva to buy oil cloth with money which I wheedled out of Yehudah. We covered everything possible with clean oil-cloth and the kitchen began to look almost presentable. Then I had a look at the cooking utensils. There were two large saucepans and a frying pan. With these we had to cook three-course meals for over forty people, and boil water for tea and washing up. I set to and found some clean petrol tins. (By the time we left at the end of our week the food had already stopped tasting of paraffin). In addition, we had forty tin plates, forty mugs, forty forks and spoons and three knives.

Yehuda set the guards to work to clean up the dining room and the yard and by the next morning when Chana and the forty young men arrived the camp was almost habitable.

Yehuda gave Chana and me a lecture on the necessity of punctuality in meal time. We listened very seriously but all the time an imp in my brain kept asking: I wonder how he managed with the young Yemenite girls? He must have suffered the pangs of hell. He is very precise and orderly, an excellent instructor, according to reports from his pupils, and a keen disciplinarian. But I am sure our two young Yemenites were not in the least impressed.

Chana and I agreed to try our best to have the meals ready in time: breakfast at 7.30 a.m., lunch at 1 p.m., supper at 6.30 p.m.

We were supposed to serve fish for lunch as a substitute for meat on two or three days of the week, but all the time I was at the camp I refused to look a fish in the face after my inadvertent contact with some decaying remnants of the species in that notorious barrel. So Geulah very kindly sent us meat when she sent anything at all. Although the Jewish population of Palestine was already beginning to feel the first pinch of the impending meat famine, there was no shortage of meat whatsoever in the IZL base camps. The commissariat had been provided with a few hundred head of cattle by an enterprising posse which had rustled them from a decidedly unfriendly Arab village.

91

But the worst problem was that of washing-up. The first day we took the dirty crockery down to the water; but after that we had the water brought to the dirty crockery. Even then the process was a nightmare. We had to boil water and then use all kinds of ingenius devices to over-come the deficiency of bowls in which to wash up and racks for drying the dishes. But human ingenuity rises to great heights when put to severe tests and we overcame these difficulties. Our greatest boon was the sink with a run-away pipe which gave us an outlet for our dirty water and slops. As we discovered on another occasion life would have been impos-sibly difficult without that. Yehuda allocated orderlies to keep the two large drums in the kitchen filled with water and other orderlies to cut the bread at meal-times. Anyone who has ever tried cutting bread with a blunt knife for fifty hungry men has tasted a bit of Dante's Inferno. Chana and I tried it once and then demanded five orderlies to take over from us.

To the camp guards we handed over the job of peeling potatoes while they guarded in the mornings, and scouring the saucepans in the afternoons. In spite of this distribution of labor we worked from 5.30 in the morning till 10 at night with a few minutes snatched off for meals and a precious half-an-hour in the afternoon for getting ourselves cleaned up.

We rose at 5.30, cleaned our room, dressed, washed, laid the tables, made the breakfast and served it at 7.30. After breakfast we washed up and prepared the lunch, which we served at one o'clock sharp. After that we washed up again and scrubbed the kitchen and cleaned the dining room. By then it was 4.30 and time for our "relaxation." This consisted of taking a cold shower—a privilege afforded only to the two females by the officer-in-charge of a LHI camp near the water tap. They had tapped the water and rigged up a temporary shower which we, as an extra-special favor, were allowed to use. It was still early April and quite nippy at 4.30 in the afternoon especially in an open-air cold shower-bath, but we did not once forego the pleasure of getting rid of some of the kitchen grease and dirt. We made a point of changing every afternoon from our kitchen dungarees into clean slacks, brushing our hair and making up our faces. We emerged from the shower bath like butterflies from their chrysalis to the never-tiring jeers and cat-calls of the LHI boys. But our own boys appreciated our efforts. Our neat and well-groomed appearance at supper seemed to enhance their appetites and gave the grim, barnlike dining room the faintest touch of festivity.

After supper came that perpetual housewife's headache—the washing up, for the third and last time, and after tidying up the kitchen and the dining room, Chana and I crawled into our sheetless beds at 10 o'clock and were asleep ten seconds later.

During our whole week at the camp it happened only once that we served a meal late. And this was on a day which we waited in vain until 12 noon for the food-lorry to put in an appearance and then had to concoct an ersatz meal at the last minute. And on this occasion we were only ten minutes late.

Chana and I took our meals after everyone had finished, occasionally eating with the guards and occasionally by ourselves. The first time we sat down to eat with the guards we both ate very little and struggled against our rising nausea. First of all, we found it difficult to accommodate ourselves to barrack-room eating. There were no knives and we had to manage with spoons and forks. Each person plunged his own spoon into the serving dishes; in no time the table was covered with olive stones, orange peel, bits of discarded bread and cheese wrappings. And to crown all this, the guards vied with one another in telling blood-curdling stories of how they had decapitated cats, dismembered dogs and disembowlled mules. I felt myself getting greener and greener in the face and had perforce to leave the table. But by the end of the week we were quite cheerfully spitting out olive stones with the best of them and were no longer making excuses to sneak off and eat quietly by ourselves in a secluded corner.

The tallest story-teller was a very dark Yemenite boy, appropriately called "Blondie" who, besides entertaining us with his vivisectionary activities, also gave us a vivid, if lurid, picture of what he was going to do to the Arabs when he got hold of them. He was very annoyed at being kept on guard duty instead of being allowed to go out and do a bit of shooting-up. Poor Blondie paid dearly for his enthusiasm. When the IZL attacked Jaffa, Blondie, who was still on guard duty, decided to spend his day-off profitably by helping to conquer the Arab city. So he got off to do some free-lance fighting and got blown to bits by a mortar.

Many boys of this course became top-rank officers in the IZL. There was 'Chanky,' so-called because of his resemblance to a Chinese as typified, presumably, by Chiang Kai Shek. He was in charge of the IZL mortars and was reputed to have sent over thousands of shells into Jaffa and later into the Old City of Jerusalem before an Arab shell effectively incapacitated him. Then there was Yishai who led the IZL troops to victory in Yehudiah and Malcha, took part in the attack on Jaffa and in the second attack on the Old City of Jerusalem and came out unscathed, only to be thrown from his jeep and killed in an accident in the Judean Hills after the cessation of hostilities. But then, each and every boy in that course had a history of heroism and daring-do which it would be inappropriate to recount in detail here.

The equipment used in the training camp was somewhat conspicuously marked "WD"—the stamp of the British War Department which was imprinted on all British Army equipment. A lot of it had been in British hands only a few weeks previously and had been ingeniously seized from the military camp at Pardess Hanna.

The Sten-guns, however, were home-produced in the IZL workshops and were conspicuous by their wooden butts in contrast to the iron of the usual makes.

On our last day in the camp Chana and I were rewarded by Yehuda for our efforts, and compensated for our thwarted ambition to become fighters by being allowed to shoot a couple of rounds each on a rifle and Sten-gun. I proved to be a tolerably good shot, especially with a rifle. I had no qualms about shooting at the tin target with a Sten-gun but I am positive I could never have shot at a human target, unless of course it was a question of who got in first. After having actually handled the fire-arms and having convinced myself that I could really shoot if the occasion arose, I had no further compunction about retiring back into a meek and mild civilian-like soldier rather than a rip-roaring sharp-shooter.

Being actually allowed to shoot was a great privilege in those days of bullet starvation and Chana and I were very proud of the honor which had been bestowed on us. When, in addition, the boys formally presented us with a token of their appreciation, we couldn't have been more pleased than if we had been given Victoria Crosses.

We left the camp that day with the feeling that we really had done something to help, if only to avert the wholesale poisoning of some of the IZL's most promising young officers.

I returned from the camp a few days before the Passover which I intended to spend in Haifa. The Arabs from Tireh village had started to make the Tel Aviv-Haifa road almost as unpleasant as the Jerusalem highway, so here too a service of armored buses was instituted. We travelled as far as Zichron Yaacov by ordinary bus, and then changed into an armored bus. In the bus were a few members of the Haganah with

Sten-guns, just in case. As we approached Haifa, the Haganah boys dismantled their Sten-guns and stuffed them into sacks which they hid from the prying eyes of the British police, who had received instructions to disarm and arrest any Jews who carried some means of self-protection. The Haganah boy who had been sitting near me decided that the safest place for his Sten-gun was right under me. I have had more comfortable seats in my time. Fortunately the British policeman who put his head into the bus to see if everything was all right did not notice the look of extreme discomfort on my face, or perhaps I underrate my powers of dissimulation. On arrival in Haifa I did a very stupid thing—I took a bus going to the town instead of to the Carmel. As soon as I realised my error I got off the bus, to find myself a lone and solitary figure in Kingsway—the Main thoroughfare in the town. There was not another living soul to be seen. All the shops were closed, as they had been for weeks. In spite of the state of utter desertion and desolation in the street, I could feel the presence of people and, mainly, of eyes staring at me. Perhaps this was merely my fevered imagination, but it felt real enough. I did not like the idea of standing and waiting for a bus with all those eyes staring at me and started walking forlornly back towards the Carmel, dragging my suitcase and glancing nervously up at the roofs of the flanking buildings in the hope I presume, of dodging if I spotted a sniper aiming at me.

Suddenly a taxi came tearing out of a side-street. I hailed the driver frantically and as he pulled up I hurtled up to him scarcely noticing the weight of my suitcase, and jumped into his car, without stopping to look whether he was an Arab or a Jew. He was Jewish, fortunately, and somewhat surprised to see a solitary female roaming the streets. After I had recovered my breath, I was rather ashamed at this panicky divergence from my usual cool, calm and collected state. As the driver drove me up the Carmel, the first shots in the Battle of Haifa rang out, and by the time we reached the top Kingsway was under constant fire. This, of course, gave me an excellent opportunity of demonstrating graphically how with the aid of a Sten-gun, I could have conquered Kingsway single-handed. It was very pleasant to be heroic while sitting safely on top of the mountain.

The Battle of Haifa started with the withdrawal of the British force and finished two days later with the complete withdrawal of practically every single Arab from Haifa. Rumours were rife about the reason for the British withdrawal. One story had it that a General in charge had been bribed by the Haganah to withdraw his forces and leave the road

95

clear for them, while others maintained that the British were certain that the Arabs would wipe out the Jews if they withdrew and they wanted to give them a chance.

Whatever the reason, the British withdrew and after two days the whole Moslem Arab population was in full flight toward Acre.

The IZL had been in charge of the Wadi Nisnas sector of the front and when the Arabs there heard that the IZL was taking part in the battle, they dropped their arms and ran, with cries of "Dir Yassin, DirYassin." Dir Yassin is an Arab village near Jerusalem which the IZL had conquered rather too thoroughly, giving rise to exaggerated reports of massacres of women and children and general brutality.

There is no doubt that some of the IZL soldiers, temporarily crazed with rage and horror at the brutality of the deaths meted to some of their comrades, a number of whom had been mutilated by the Arabs, had exacted retribution and slain without mercy. But not women and children. Nevertheless, the atrocity stories were spread far and wide, and resulted in the Arabs fleeing, panic-stricken, instead of staying to give battle, thus saving many Jewish lives both in Haifa and later in Jaffa.

A day after the end of the battle in Haifa I was taken on a tour of inspection of the battle-fields by a very good friend, one of the very few people who had continued coming down to the town throughout the period of sniping and dynamiting prior to its conquest. His office had actually been badly wrecked in one heavy explosion and the outside wall was pitted with sniper's bullets. There wasn't very much doing in his office in those days but he felt honor-bound not to be frightened off by the Arabs and carried on a single-handed war of nerves with the snipers. He was, in fact, much more afraid of being thought afraid than of the practical consequences of his bravado on his span of life. He, therefore, regarded himself as having some small share in the victory (a claim which no one could possibly deny) and took all the more pride in showing visitors round what had been the danger-spots of Haifa.

When we arrived at the Wadi Nisnas I got a tremendous thrill out of seeing soldiers with IZL armbands patrolling the streets. As we were standing and chatting to a sentry, a middle-aged Christian Arab came up to him and started complaining tearfully that some one had taken his refrigerator out of his flat. The IZL sentry shook his head sadly, took out a pencil and paper, noted down the address of the Town Commander and very gravely instructed the Arab to go there and register his complaint and his loss.

CHAPTER VIII

JAFFA AND YEHUDIEH

DURING Passover we were all suddenly electrified by a news-flash on the radio—the IZL had launched an attack on Jaffa, the largest Arab city in Palestine.

For months Jaffa had been a vampire on the neck of Tel Aviv—a vampire which took its daily quota of blood in the form of innocent men, women and children suddenly snatched from life by the sniper's bullet. Every day five or six people in Tel Aviv fell victim to the geographical disposition of Jaffa and its highest minaret, which served as an excellent snipers' nest for those menials of Allah who were zealously waging their holy Moslem War against the predatory, infidel Jews. And Allah evidently did not counsel discrimination. All non-believers were fair meat for his zealots: the baby who, as its mother lifted the feeding-spoon to its mouth, toppled over lifelessly with a bullet through its head; the hard-working mother hanging up the week's washing on the roof; the boy and girl walking along the sea-shore, completely absorbed in their love for each other. These and many others fell victim to the vampire.

At night, residents of Tel Aviv were treated to volley upon volley of rifle shots and repeated explosions—shattering the peaceful, sleeping city with their hideous reverberations and sickening aftermath.

In the border districts between Tel Aviv and Jaffa a regular reign of terror prevailed. The Jewish residents, most people with large families, fled in panic towards the north of Tel Aviv. Every day streams of them, with their few belongings piled on hand-carts, dragged wearily from street to street looking for garages, washhouses, foyers, which had not already been commandeered by previous roof-hungry refugees. There was not a block of flats in Tel Aviv which did not have two or three refugee families established in its entrance hall and another two or three families in its wash-house on the roof. Every empty space in a building was immediately turned into a dwelling. The problem of sanitation became a serious one for the Tel Aviv Municipality, as well as for the more fortunate, and more discriminating, flat-dwellers. Trim, well-kept gardens were turned into forests of washing on lines. Fashionable, modern blocks of flats looked like tenement houses, with hordes of grimy children clinging to the bannisters, milling up and down the stairs, using the gardens both as football pitches and as public conveniences.

Tel Avivian tempers, which are sorely tried at the best of times by the heat and over-crowding, were now tried almost to breaking point by the invasion of the refugees, the nightly nerve-wracking cacophony of noise and the daily fear of sudden and violent death or maiming.

We who lived in Ramat Gan were spared some of the anxieties and irritations suffered by the Tel Avivians. We met with sniping only when we went to Tel Aviv—which most adults did in any case every day. My only direct contact with bullets came during a visit to my dentist—a woman—who lived near the Tel Aviv-Jaffa border.

On this occasion I was in the process of having a tooth drilled when the daily fusillade started up. My dentist was in an extreme state of jitters. Each time a shot rang out, her hand jerked and the drill found its insidious way into the tooth next door or played a devil's tattoo on an exposed nerve. Each time a bullet pinged on the wall of her house, my dentist's hand developed a positive ague and that drill quivered and squirmed all over my gums and seemed to be perforating my tongue. I groaned, grunted and squirmed in protest and prayed for merciful release by a sniper's bullet—whether through my brain or the dentist's, I could not care less. In thinking back on this macabre experience, I still cannot decide why my dentist insisted on going through with the whole process, unless it was some sixth sense that told her that, unless she finished the filling that day, she would never be allowed to do so. Nor would she have been. I have never again darkened her doorway. A dentist's drill, since then, has been for me just one more proof that the end does not always jusitfy the means.

We Ramat Gannians were also given a small taste of the refugee problem when we were asked by the Local Council to give temporary homes to children who had fled the reign of terror on the border together with their families, and were living in conditions of indescribable filth and over-crowding.

I readily agreed to take a child and asked for a girl of five or six. I was given a little Yemenite boy of barely three. His name was Mordecai Sharabi. He was small, but perfectly formed, with big, beautiful black eyes, a mischievous, intelligent little face and the most cuddlesome of cholocate-brown bodies.

98

The very first thing I did with Mordecai was to give him a hot bath. His yells were blood-curdling, but it was not the water he objected to so much as being undressed to the skin. To such an indignity he had never before been exposed in his short life. After a week of violent protestations, however, he suddenly submitted to his nightly bath without so much as a squeak—until I tried to give him a shower bath. Then his native stubbornness re-asserted itself and he refused point-blank to go under "the rain."

He developed a very fine taste in clothes, too, and would forcibly prevent my dressing him in anything of which he did not approve. His method was that of passive resistance—he simply refused to put his arms into sleeves or his legs into the appropriate holes, and unless I used actual physical force I could not budge him from his decision. The clash of wills usually ended in my cursing volubly in English, which Mordecai could not understand, and submitting to his judgment.

Every morning when he opened his eyes and saw his newly-polished, brightly-shining boots, his delight was unabounding. As these impeccable, glistening diurnal beauties could not possibly be the same kicked-about, dusty, shabby monstrosities of the night before, little Mordecai was quite convinced that I bought him a new pair of shoes every night. And if nothing else endeared me to him, it was this astonishing generosity (or whatever corresponded to that in his baby-reasoning) which did.

Feeding him was a racial problem. I consulted all the authorities in the neighborhood on the feeding habits of the Yemenite; and if I had persisted in acting on their advice poor Mordechai would have starved to death. By a process of elimination I discovered that he favored biscuits, omelettes, oranges, bananas, and soup, in that order of preference.

Mordecai's Hebrew was made somewhat incomprehensible by his use of Yemen-accented baby-talk. It took me quite a long time to realise what he was getting at and my mother, who knows very little Hebrew in any case, simply did not try to unravel the Hebrew from the Mordecai-ese. She always returned a polite but consistent "alright" to anything Mordecai said to her, with the result that Mordecai eventually replied to anything she attempted to say to him with a correspondingly polite and consistent "aw lite."

We both became terribly attached to our little ward and he paid me the supreme compliment of calling me alternately "mummy" or "Sarah" (which I subsequently discovered was the name of his favorite sister).

99

When I took him out walking, this habit of calling me mother excited many an inquisitive stare and raising of eye-brows. If there were any anthropologists or geneticists amongst the passers-by, they must have been hard put to it to reconcile this remarkable physical phenomenon with the theories which they had for years accepted as gospel.

In one respect I failed Mordecai completely—I did not succeed in getting him house-trained. He had to have clean sheets every night and a couple of changes of clothing every day. Unfortunately I, unlike his mother, was not a professional washer-woman and there were days when I thought bitterly that if men had had to look after children they would long since have discovered some dehydrating agent for such cases.

When Mordecai had been with us for two weeks, his mother came to visit him and I was most acutely embarrassed by his complete refusal to go to her. Instead, he buried his head in my lap and would not even look at her, let alone accept the gifts of fruit and sweets which she must have bought for him at great sacrifice.

She looked sadly around at the clean, white bed in which he slept, alone; at the cupboard in which his clothes hung, at the scrubbed shining face and plastered-down hair of her neatly-dressed baby, thanked me with quiet dignity for looking after her child and went back to some noisome hole-in-the-ground which served her as a temporary home. I felt hot with shame that I could give Mordecai more than this quiet, hard-working woman with her beautifully-carved face and native pride and dignity.

When the time came to part with Mordecai, my mother and I shed quite a few furtive tears. I dressed him up in perfectly-pressed trousers, a spotless white shirt and a genuinely new pair of gleaming white boots. The neighbors gathered round to admire and say farewell.

At the school where all the foster-mothers were congregated with their charges we exchanged views on our experiences. Some of the women were genuinely relieved to be rid of their foster-children, but the majority of us were sad at heart. As I said goodbye to Mordecai he must have felt from the unaccustomed violence of my embrace that something unusual was afoot. He clung to me and refused to let go. One of the teachers tore him away forcibly and I left with the sound of his sobs in my ears.

The children were returned to their parents, who had been given temporary homes in a safer area. I managed to find out the address of Mordechai's "home" and, after giving him two weeks to acclimate him-

100

self to his own mother and family once more, my mother and I went to visit him.

The address was somewhere in the Hatikvah Quarter of Tel Aviv. This is a slum quarter on the border of Jaffa. After wandering around for an hour and being continually yelled at by the local inhabitants not to go here because of the snipers or there because of collapsing houses or somewhere else for some other equally good reason, we eventually stumbled on a young girl who said she knew Mordecai and would take us to him.

We arrived at a one-story, barn-like building and went in. It consisted of one large room with no flooring and very little roofing. In this room there were no less than ten families—sleeping, eating, cooking, washing and what, for lack of a better term, I have to call living.

Our guide pointed out a baby-cot in one corner of the room and indicated that this was the "home" of the Sharabis. We timidly edged towards the cot and a pile of ragged blankets and clothes suddenly came to life in the shape of a young girl. There was a quick exchange of beautiful Yemenite Hebrew—and we had been introduced by our guide to Mordecai's sister and nurse, Sarah. I asked where Mordecai was and Sarah pointed to the bed. In a far corner we saw a frightened little face peeping out beneath a pile of dirty rags and dirtier clothing. The face was the face of Mordecai, but there all resemblance ended. He was dressed in exactly the same clothes as he had worn on the day he left me, with the addition of two weeks' accumulation of mud, food-particles and God knows what else. He was thin and pale again—and frightened to death that we had come to take him away. My mother spent some of the hardest twenty minutes of her life in Mordecai's home. I had seen poverty and dirt at close quarters before and was merely saddened by it. But she was seeing it for the first time in its naked reality, and she felt physically ill.

We left after twenty minutes in a triumphal procession, followed by all the children of the neighborhood, after having succeeded in extracting a shy smile from Mordecai in response to the gift of a ball and chocolate. I begged his sister to bring him to see us sometimes. She never came and somehow or other I did not manage to visit him again until Jaffa was conquered. In the upheaval and general transplantation of people, Mordecai went out of our lives, probably forever.

*   *   *   *   *

But, to return to the attack on Jaffa. We were quite a mixed com-

101

pany that day in my brother's flat as the news of the attack came through. Those of us who were in the IZL were jubilant; the somewhat wishy-washy "sympathisers" were wishy-washy about this also—perhaps the attack was premature, perhaps it would have been better to have waited for the Haganah, perhaps this and perhaps that; while the outright opponents of the IZL saw in this action a Machiavellian political move to divert attention from the Haganah's magnificent conquest of Haifa.

The latter, true to type, came out with a scathing radio attack on the IZL for "endangering the Yishuv" and "stabbing the authorities in the back"—in fact denunciation No. 3 (I am positive they had their Phillipics catalogued and merely told their readers to produce No. 1, 2 or 3 as the case may be, so uniform and repetitive were they.) However, the attack on Jaffa proved to be so popular in Tel Aviv that the Haganah diatribes began to look a little foolish and with a magnificent, face-saving, gesture they suddenly found it necessary to come to the rescue of the IZL, who, they declared, were unable to cope with the magnitude of the task.

So, suddenly, it was the Haganah who was conquering Jaffa, according to some of the local newspapers, and the IZL were merely lending a little assistance.

In the completely mistaken, if zealous, belief that nothing could be done without me, I hastened back to Tel Aviv to be in on the battle. I went straight to the Begin's house. Ala told me that she hadn't seen Begin for days, except for a fleeting glimpse now and again when he rushed in to change his clothes. I asked how I could get to the war, and she advised me to try the Freund Hospital, where the IZL had established its battle headquarters. I found the Freund Hospital fairly easily but did not find the guard too kindly disposed to stray, inquisitive females. Fortunately, Yael arrived a little later and took me in under his wing.

The Hospital was being used both for its original purpose, with an efficient staff of IZL doctors and nurses, and as the army headquarters. The whole IZL High Command were there. Menachem Begin, still unbeknown to most of his soldiers, had come out of the underground and was moving around quite freely. The place was buzzing with activity. Everyone had a job and every job had been snatched up by eager first-comers. They were managing quite well without me and I was about to go home, sadly disillusioned, when Yael came to the rescue again and asked me to drive her to a few places. I was delighted to be of some use and gladly consented.

Yael was acting as Begin's secretary and general right-hand woman. She translated statements from Hebrew to English for the foreign press, arranged press conferences, acted as public relations officer, typed, telephoned, rushed about the town and remained always smiling, cheerful and obliging—which endeared her considerably to the harassed, nervous and over-worked members of the High Command.

I never got anywhere near to the fighting in Jaffa and with justice—there really wasn't very much I could do there. Instead, I was appointed Menachem Begin's occasional driver.

I took him for long drives in the country away from the heat and noise of Tel Aviv, where it was impossible to think anything out to a clear conclusoin.

The IZL were in "occupation" of the whole area from Petach Tikvah to Tel Aviv. They patrolled the roads, controlled the traffic, guarded the settlements against possible Arab attacks. The blue armband with the IZL emblem was a familiar sight in these districts.

On one of our drives Begin and I were stopped by an armed IZL man. He apologized politely for troubling us, got into the back of the car and ordered us to take him to a spot well out of our way. I turned the car round obediently and the IZL commander was taken for a forced ride at the polite, but firm, insistence of one of his sergeants, who would undoubtedly have been acutely embarrassed had he recognised his travelling companion.

Although Begin had come out of the underground in Tel Aviv, to the extent that he left his house in broad daylight and was known to be constantly at the Freund Hospital, yet he had still not made any public appearances and was unknown to the vast majority of IZL members. This was still a very necessary precaution as the British were still in the country even if they had moved out of the Tel Aviv district.

*   *   *   *   *

About a week after the conquest of Jaffa, Geulah suddenly descended on me again at about 8 o'clock one evening. She needed helpers urgently to provide a meal for a battalion which was setting out at dawn to attack Yehudieh, a large Arab village in the neighborhood of Petach Tikvah. We immediately set out for the base camp at Kfar Ona. Arrived there at about nine, we plunged into the thick of the hustle and bustle of an army preparing for action.

The base consisted of a deserted Arab house with a large courtyard and surrounding out-houses. The house was used as army headquarters and kitchen.

In the courtyard were clustered groups of men numbering about 200 in all, getting last-minute instructions from their sergeants, cleaning their weapons, laughing and joking—and all by the light of the stars. So have men throughout the ages prepared for battle and only the absence of the champing of horses and rattling of spurs served to distinguish this moonlit army encampment from that of Caesar or Judas Maccabeus. There was also one other distinguishing feature—the women, from the First Aiders who went into the front-line with their male comrades, to the humble cooks who stayed ignominiously behind.

Our instructions from the commissariat were to provide a midnight meal of sandwiches, hard-boiled eggs and cocoa for 200 people, and a packet of sandwiches for each soldier to take along with him to tide him over the initial period of disorganisation, until the field kitchens were set up.

Our equipment consisted of two primus stoves, two large saucepans, a few knives, fifty cups, and a tank of water. The furniture consisted of one large table. Light was provided by a hurricane lamp which was being continually borrowed by the first-aiders and forcibly recovered by the cooks to the detriment of tempers already frayed. We eventually had to take the matter to arbitration. We rounded up one of the officers in charge and each side presented its case vociferously: was it more important that the men should be fed or that the First Aid equipment should be in order? Even Solomon would have been hard put to it to decide. But our modern Solomon settled the problem simply: he ordered a hurricane lamp to be taken away from somewhere else and given to the first-aiders. The centre of strife was thus transferred to another quarter.

Having successfully outmanoeuvered the harpies we next fell into the clutches of the furies—our two antiquated primus stoves. They either belched out smoke and flames with terrific verves and gusto, roaring boisterously all the time, or else they obstinately shut up like clams, refusing to be cajoled or threatened by the local Prometheans.

We struggled manfully with them, which was a supreme act of courage on my part, for if there is anything I am afraid of it is a primus stove. But eventually we realised that we couldn't possibly get the eggs boiled and the cocoa ready by midnight with our recalcitrant equipment.

It was a point of honor to have everything ready in time, so I found a solution for which I now beg our soldiers' pardon: we boiled the eggs in the cocoa! There is a saying in Afrikaans: "What doesn't kill, fattens." the soldiers of the IZL must certainly have put on a lot of weight during the period of their active service.

Our "kitchen" had no sink and no drainage system whatsoever, with the result that the water we spilled in the dark and the water which leaked from the tank, combined with the dregs of the cocoa and the water from the cups which we were continuously rinsing to make up for the deficiency in quantity, soon formed into a pool on the stone kitchen floor. By the end of the night we were standing up to our ankles in water and wadding through it with that horrible squelching sound which wet shoes make.

At two in the morning a bugle call brought the men in the courtyard to attention. The sergeants yelled out commands and in a few magical minutes there stood in perfect array, row after row of well-disciplined soldiers, light artillery, infantry, pioneers and first-aiders. There was a last hurried colloquy of officers and then Yishai, who was in charge of the operation, addressed the men by the light of the moon. This last Caesarean touch perfected the illusion I had had all night. Here truly was an ancient Roman Army about to hurl itself against the cruel, ruthless Huns and Vandals.

Yishai's speech was caesarean in content too. He started with a brief survey of the plan of campaign, then exhorted his men to be courageous and steadfast in face of the enemy, and ended in fine oratorical style on the duties of a man towards his country and his people.

I had always been extremely sceptical of the practicality of Caesar's stopping all proceedings to harangue vast hordes of soldiers no more than a few minutes before they plunged into the heart of a battle. But Yishai that night dispelled all my doubts and cynicism. Not only is it possible to deliver an eve-of-battle speech, it is even possible to make the occasion a very solemn and impressive one.

When Yishai had finished, the soldiers filed quietly and thoughtfully to the waiting lorries. In the moonlight pale faces were strained and set, young eyes betrayed the fear of the unknown—both in this world and the next. Then suddenly the solemnity of the moment was over as with instincitive unanimity the IZL soldiers burst out into "Allei Barricadot" (To the Barricades)—the favorite IZL song of the moment—and lorry-load after lorry-load of singing, high-spirited men and women pulled off,

105

leaving the camp deserted except for the weary cooks and the handful of older men, who were on part-time duty as guards and orderlies. We remained listening to the dying echoes of the fresh, young voices and then turned sadly back to our unheroic and unacclaimed chores.

*   *   *   *   *

By the afternoon of the next day Yehudieh was completely occupied by the IZL and it was safe for the "volunteers" to move in and start cooking. My turn came on Thursday, two days after the conquest.

Geulah picked me up and we travelled by car to Kfar Ona, from there transferring to an "ambulance" for the rest of the journey. Our vehicle earned the dignified name of ambulance by virtue of the red Magen David painted on its side. But that is where all comparison with the sleek, white, immaculate, well-equipped limousines that the magic word usually conjures up in one's imagination, began and ended. It was merely a converted tender with a canvas hood and two narrow rails for taking a stretcher.

The road to Yehudieh is a rough, pitted cart-track; the driver drove like a hell-fiend and the ambulance had no seats, so that we were compelled to sit on the floor. By the time we reached the end of our half-hour journey I was a mass of bumps and bruises, from my head, which continually hit the roof, to some of my better-upholstered but equally tender parts. I sat down with difficulty for days afterwards.

When we were half-way to Yehudieh we met some of the IZL lorries returning from there. We stopped and were told that the Arab Legions were attacking with heavy artillery from Wilhelma, a large village in the neighborhood. Geulah was a little dubious about the advisability of letting me go on, but I was not going to miss the one and only chance I might ever have of becoming a heroine. So despite Geulah's misgivings, we continued on our journey and arrived at army headquarters without anything worse than extremely battered behinds. During the 24 hours I spent in Yehudieh I didn't even hear a shell, let alone come face to face with one, and my heroic aspirations were once again frustrated.

The army headquarters and cook-house were situated in the Public Health Department of Yehudieh. The young officers in charge of the operation, by a quite natural process of reasoning, had decided that this must, by virtue of its function, be the cleanest building in the village—and quite probably it was! When we weren't chasing the flies off the food we were waging a fixed battle against a battalion of stray cats. And when we rested from these exertions we took care to keep a safe distance from the walls so as not to have too many unwelcome bed-companions. On account of other manifestations of primitive hygienic conditions in Yehudieh, there was a bonfire going perpetually in the courtyard, and a steady stream of men and boys, from young "generals" to even younger privates, filed past this bonfire and dropped into it their lice-infested clothes.

The problem of feeding the men was two-fold. We had to provide a proper three-course meal for those who could come and get their food, and we had to send food to about 100 men at the front-line who could not leave their posts. Again we came up against that perpetual nightmare in the IZL catering department—the chronic lack of utensils. We managed to provide a meal for the base soldiers with what amounted to consummate ease in comparison with our second problem. We simply did not have any available means of sending soup and hot drinks to the front line for 100 people. So we sent out scouts to scour the Arab shops. They came back with an amazing assortment of kitchen and bedroom ware. We first used the various species of jugs, then the wash-basins and bowls and, in the last resort, we had recourse to chamber-pots. In the latter instance we confined ourselves strictly to new ware only. Nevertheless I suspect that our thoughtfulness did not receive due recognition from the recipients of its fruits.

As the cooks were on 24-hour periods of duty, I had to spend the night in Yehudieh. The other women lay down to sleep on camp-beds in the first-aid room. I waited to see what the consequences would be, and the moment I saw first one, then another, surreptitiously scratching, I beat a hasty retreat. I found myself a comparatively clean deck-chair, placed it in the middle of the officers' duty room and settled down to get some sleep. Each time I managed to doze off, there was another interruption. Once it was the sentry to say the cats had got in through an open kitchen window and were devouring the next day's meat. This necessitated a quick but boisterous sortie into the kitchen to disperse the marauders. Then it was a burst of ribald laughter from the duty officers in the corner or a hearty greeting to someone just in from the front-line.

At one in the morning I was cordially invited to join in a meal of chicken prepared by the sentries. I prudently refrained from enquiring how the chicken had been cleaned and in what kind of vessel it had been cooked. I chose a drumstick. Never have I lingered so long over a morsel of chicken. It must have belonged to the oldest rooster in the village and one whose muscles had been toughened and developed by decades of cock-fighting. The young men attacked their chicken with gusto and looked at me in great surprise when I suggested timidly that perhaps another hour or two in the "pot" would have improved it considerably. Evidently the Palestinian youth grew teeth in keeping with their characters.

After the chicken everybody else was in such high spirits that I gave up any further attempt at sleep and, after resting my jaw-muscles for a while, joined in the general merriment.

My period of duty was over after breakfast and while waiting for transport back to Tel Aviv I betook myself on a tour of inspection through Yehudieh. The village was one of the largest and richest in the country, by Arab standards. By European standards it was nothing more than a cluster of mud-baked hovels, set unevenly in rough-hewn, steep, winding streets, with here and there a stone house belonging to some local notable. Some of these notables must have had tidy-sized stockings stuck away somewhere. Their houses were furnished with magnificent carpets and drapes and excellent furniture. They obviously made up for their lack of toilet and washing facilities by the liberal use of expensive perfumes which they bought by the litre, or even by the gallon, if the size of their perfume bottles was any gauge. In nearly every house hung a picture of Haj Amin El Husseini—the ex-Mufti of Jerusalem and organiser of all the anti-Jewish riots in the previous two decades. In quite a number he shared honors with Hitler whom he had assisted in exterminating the Jews of Europe.

The local inhabitants had left in a great hurry and had clearly taken very little with them in their precipitate flight. Not that the houses bore that peaceful look of being lived in and merely temporarily deserted by their owners. On the contrary, some of them had received a severe drubbing in the house-to-house fighting and others showed signs of having been invaded by a conquering army. And it was just these signs which indicated the precipitancy of the flight of the owners of the house: a few pitiful articles of clothing thrown out into a courtyard, a child's shoe lying on a dust-heap, a baby's doll kicked into a corner. These little things would have taken away any "conquering hero" feeling if I had ever been disposed to have any. In spite of our victory and the very small loss of life amongst our forces, I felt rather sad about Yehudieh and the babies and children and women who were innocent victims in this war as in all other wars. But whenever I begin to feel sad and sentimental about the "innocent" Arabs, the thought of the 70 doctors, nurses and university lecturers brutally murdered and incinerated on their way to the Hadassah Hospital, or the raped, mutilated remains of Jewish women fighters discovered by their sorrowing comrades, jerks me back to reality. And in Yehudieh, too, the eventual toll of Jewish blood effectively counteracted any false sentimentality for the "poor Arabs."

Every village in Palestine has a water-tower which is its highest building and consequently its best look-out point. Yehudieh is no exception. One day, shortly after the proclamation of the State of Israel on May 14th, two young IZL women were on look-out duty on the water-tower in Yehudieh. For days the small detachment in Yehudieh were anxiously expecting a strong Arab counter-attack from Wilhelma. They had sent frantic messages to the Haganah for reinforcements. They received promises, re-assurances and finally abuse. But no reinforcements. On this lovely day in late spring the expected counter-attack took place. Before the two girls could join their comrades, the water-tower was surrounded and they were cut off, together with a small unit defending the tower.

This small group of tired and dispirited soldiers fought like tigers against overwhelming odds. In bitter, hand-to-hand battles they fell, one by one, until they were all wiped out. Only the two girls remained on top of the water-tower. They were first-aiders, not soldiers—they had no revolvers, no knives. They knew only too well what horror awaits them if they were to fall into the hands of the Arabs alive. The air and gravity were their only allies, and entrusting their souls to their God they plunged off the tower to shatter their bodies to pieces at the feet of the enemy.

CHAPTER IX

A MOMENTOUS SABBATH

O N Friday, May 14, 1948, twenty-four hours before the time they had previously announced, the British declared the end of their Mandate in Palestine and their remaining officials were withdrawn that day. The Army, which had already been withdrawn from all the towns and was concentrated in a coastal strip near Haifa was to be evacuated gradually, the last troops leaving in August 1948. On the afternoon of May 14th, Ben Gurion proclaimed the formation of the new State of Israel, with a Provisional Government composed of all the large parties, except the Revisionists.

Early on Saturday morning the residents of Tel Aviv and Ramat Gan were awakened by the noise of explosions — the Egyptians had launched their first air-attack on the new State.

Intrinsically the Egyptian air-raids were on a small insignificant scale, and in comparison with air-raids in London, or Berlin, where tens of thousands of tons of death were hurled on the heads of a defenceless population during the course of one night, they could almost be described as puerile. They used three Spitfires at a time and the bombs they dropped were 25 pounders, or at most, 50 pounders.

But the fact that they had an absolutely clear run with no anti-aircraft or fighter opposition, was rather discouraging, and even frightening, to the civilian population; and even a 25-pounder can cause rather drastic results if it falls on one's head.

The Egyptian air-raids on Tel Aviv continued for some weeks and caused many casualties, the majority of whom were killed when a bomb fell on queues of waiting passengers at the Central Bus Station.

After the first two days the Israeli "Air Force" took up the cudgels. The mainstay of the Air Force was a handful of training-planes affectionately called "primus stoves" by their pilots. These planes and their crews had done sterling service in bringing supplies to isolated and cut-off settlements and in patrol-work, but they were hardly a match for the Egyptian fighter-bombers, despite the willingness and stout-heartedness of their intrepid crews.

However, in a few short weeks, the Air Force was sending their own Spitfires into the air manned by Jewish airmen from all over the world who flocked to the tiny State to help her out of her difficulties, and the Egyptians were chased out of the skies. The air-raids had one salutary effect: they compelled the Jewish refugees from Jaffa to go back to their homes. Even after that town had been liberated and most of the refugees from the border had returned from their temporary foyer-and-roof homes in Tel Aviv to comparatively comfortable dwellings in Jaffa, some had, nevertheless, refused to budge, preferring their laundry rooms in a fashionable northern suburb to tenements in the unfashionable Hatikvah quarter. The first air-raid soon sent them scurrying helter-skelter back to the safety of Jaffa and dwellings a little less exposed to the heavens and the little missiles which fell from them.

*   *   *   *   *

On that Saturday of the birth of the State of Israel the Begins were at our flat as usual. In the afternoon I drove them over to visit Zipporah Merridor. We sat down to tea with Zipporah and her two children—Rachel aged 11 and "Doodie" aged 6. Suddenly Rachel, who had walked over to the window, announced in the calmest of voices: "Mother, there's father." We all laughed at the joke. It was true that Jaacov Meridor had succeeded at last in escaping from the British detention camp in Kenya after four unsuccessful attempts, but we all knew that he was in Paris and couldn't possibly take the risk of travelling at this juncture even in his anxiety to be reunited with his family whom he had not seen for four years. So we laughed at the joke, but Rachel was insistent. Zipporah rose to look out of the window and burst out: "It is Yaacov!" Then we all rushed to the window. Down the path, all wreathed in smiles, walked Yaacov and Shmuel. They could not have timed their arrival more dramatically.

When the shouting laughing and crying were over we heard the story of their trip from Paris from Shmuel. They had chartered a special plane to take them to Palestine, and arrive there on May 15th. The plane was British with a British crew who had been given instructions by their firm to land in Cyprus. When they heard that their clients insisted on being landed in Palestine they protested volubly. The British Government had forbidden British planes to fly to Palestine and, in any case, the date was very unpropitious as no one knew just exactly what would happen in

Palestine after the 14th of May. After a great deal of arguing and tele-
phoning to London the British business instinct evidently won the day
and the captain agreed to fly to Tel Aviv. (Lydda was in the hands of
the Arabs.)

The passengers in the plane were decidedly nervous all the way. There
was every chance that it might prove impossible to land in Tel Aviv and
that they might perforce have to go to Cyprus or that Cyprus would
instruct the crew to land there in any event. The prospect of landing in
Cyprus, in the very den of the lions, was not a cheerful one either for
Meridor, even though he was travelling on a false passport, or for his
travelling companions, among whom were two more who had escaped
with him from Kenya. Indeed the whole planeload would have been an
interesting catch for the British.

While the tension in the plane grew steadily greater and greater, Tel
Aviv was suddenly sighted below, and the plane began making preparations
to land. The Tel Aviv aerodrome was never intended for large aircraft
and the plane pitched up right at the end of the run-way just short of
taking a header into the sea. The passengers disembarked to a ghost airport. The place seemed completely deserted except for a plane which had
suffered recent damage. As they glanced around curiously, human forms
began cautiously detaching themselves from the nearby buildings until all
at once they were surrounded by excited members of the Haganah who
had come out from where they had been sheltering against possible bombs
from the approaching plane. A short while previously they had been
bombed by Egyptian planes and quite naturally suspected that this plane
too might very possibly have been up to no good.

So Yaacov Meridor, Hillel Kook, Shmuel and company were the first
air-passengers to land in the State of Israel. The British crew were at one
and the same time relieved at their safe arrival and on tenterhooks as to
their own fate and that of their plane, at which the Haganah men were
casting overt looks of desire. A Haganah officer actually took one of the
passengers aside and asked him if it would not be possible to persuade the
crew to sell the plane. Eventually, to the considerable relief of both
passengers and crew, the plane was ordered to take off for Cyprus, and
pick up its passengers for the return trip on the following Tuesday, at
the Haifa airport.

*   *   *   *   *

On the evening of that momentous Saturday Menachem Begin was

112

due to broadcast for the first time on the IZL radio. I drove him to the block of flats in a quiet side street where the IZL transmitter had been operating during the time of the British. This was the first time I had seen a secret transmitter in operation. I am not quite sure what I expected, and I ought to have become attuned to the conspiratorial atmosphere of the underground, nevertheless I was somewhat disappointed to find that the much-sought after and much-cursed IZL secret radio-station was housed in a comfortably furnished, "bourgeois" flat and was operated by ordinary-looking, pleasant, well-dressed young men and women.

The lack of "atmosphere" was fully compensated for by the impressiveness of the occasion. This was the first time since he had taken over the command of the IZL in 1943 that Menachem Begin's voice would be heard by the people of Eretz Israel. Whether for or against the activities of the IZL none would deny that its commander had captured the imagination of the people, that he was a mysterious and glamorous figure wrapped in legend and romance. Every radio in the country was tuned in to the "Voice of Fighting Zion."

The crowded little room was stiffingly hot. Not a breath of wind penetrated the shutters which were tightly closed in accordance with the black-out regulations. Begin was nervous—this was his first public speech in years and he had lost his composure and poise. The radio operators sweated in the heat and the strained atmosphere. Eight-thirty struck and a dead silence fell over the room. We were on the air. The first few bars of Hatikvah, a short introduction by the announcer and Menachem Begin was talking to the people of Israel. He made the speech of his life. In every home in Israel, men, women and children listened raptly, with tears in their eyes.

After 2000 years of exile and political slavery the Jewish people had regained their national independence as a nation among other nations, as a free, dignified people among other free peoples. And Menachem Begin, leader of the small band of revolutionaries who had chased out the British Goliath, who had freed their people from the yoke of the oppressor, spoke to the people, told them that one struggle had ended to be superseded by an even greater, more dangerous battle—the battle to maintain their fragile State against the attacks of their vicious enemies whose combined armies were hammering at its gates. He spoke to the sons of Israel and to the mothers of Israel, adjuring them to be of good heart and to finish their monumental task with the same magnificent spirit

113

as they had started it. And he spoke to the future Government of Israel, exhorting it to be wise in its dealings with other states, energetic in bringing the exiles back to Zion, just and righteous in its rule over the people, and steadfast in safeguarding the independence bought with the blood of heroes and martyrs.

If this had been his last, as well as his first, message to the people of Israel, Menachem Begin would have become a great legendary figure in Jewish history. He will still feature prominently in any objective story of the liberation of Israel as the great commander of the great army of revolution, but the aura of glamor and mystery will have been rudely plucked away by the cruel fingers of Madam Politics and her faithful henchmen—Spite, Prejudice and Intrigue.

CHAPTER X

BIRTH-PANGS OF THE ALTALENA

YAACOV MERIDOR and Shmuel had come to Israel to explain why the Altalena with its load of soldiers and arms had not arrived in Tel Aviv port at midnight of May the 14th, 1948, as had been planned. Already in December 1947, after the publication of the partition decision with its concomitant declaration that the British must leave the country by 15th May, 1948, the IZL High Command had foreseen that this latter date would mark the beginning of a concerted attack by all the Arab States on the infant Jewish State. They knew of the disastrous shortage of arms even in the Haganah despite the millions of pounds that had been collected ostensibly for the very purpose; they knew, too, that while the British were still in the country no appreciable number of arms would be allowed into the ports and any ship suspected of arms-running would be confiscated. So they planned to bring in a shipload of arms one minute past midnight on May the 15th.

If this plan had succeeded, the whole course of the war against the Arabs would have been drastically altered, but fate and the wealthy Jews of the world decreed otherwise. The ship, the Altalena, had been purchased by Avraham Stavsky in America on behalf of the Hebrew Committee for National Liberation and was available in France at the end of 1947. But the money for buying the arms trickled in with deadly slowness. Shmuel's trip to America and a lightning visit he paid to South Africa in January had been for the purpose of urging on everyone the dire need for more, and yet more, speed. In spite of the super-human efforts of the IZL representatives, the wealthy Jews did not realise the tremendous urgency of the situation and they parted slowly and lingeringly with their money, with the result that by the 15th May the arms had not yet been bought and the Altalena did not arrive.

On that evening, the IZL offered to sell the ship to the Haganah. When their offer was refused, the High Command resolved to carry on with their original plan and bring the arms at the very earliest opportunity. Contrary to the original plan whereby Yaacov was to take charge of "Operation Gun-running," it was decided that Shmuel should return to

115

Paris to supervize the operation while Yaacov would remain in Israel and lead the IZL forces against the Arabs. I was to go with Shmuel, more because of the use to which my British passport could be put than because of any personal qualifications. Thus began for me the epic of the *Altalena* and one of the maddest months I have ever spent.

Before we left, our own little colony in Ramat Gan had tumbled to our affiliations and to the seat of our sympathies. The disseminator of the news was the local grocer, himself an enthusiastic supporter of the IZL and, since that day, one of Shmuel's most devoted admirers. He had gotten the news from one of our women neighbors. Sarah, the sister of this neighbor, had been imprisoned by the British in Bethlehem and then transferred to Athlit from where she escaped. Her fiance, Eytan, one of the leaders of the IZL, had been one of the 27 who had escaped from Acre. He had been spirited away to France and had returned on the 'plane with Yaacov and Shmuel. Two days after the declaration of the State, Sarah and Eytan were married. Menachem Begin attended the wedding and I accompanied him. The first person I saw as I entered Eytan's house was Sarah's sister, my neighbor.

The next day she rushed in to Motye, the grocer, bursting with excitement: "Do you know who was at Sarah's wedding? Menachem Begin! And you'll never guess who came in with him. Why none other than the English 'shiksah' (gentile woman), Mrs. Katz. You could have knocked me over with a feather." This story was too good for the kind but garrulous Motye to keep to himself, and soon the whole neighborhood knew just exactly who and what we were. It did not matter any more. The British Administration had left the country.

* * * * *

We left for Haifa on Tuesday, the 17th May, to pick up the chartered 'plane for Paris. On our way to the airport we dropped in at my brother's flat and informed my long-suffering mother that we were off to Europe for a short spell. She accepted the news philosophically. After all, she said, she hadn't come to Palestine for a quiet life and if she didn't do much rushing around herself, she did at least get some vicarious excitement out of our fevered existence.

The Haifa Airport was a British-Jewish mixture. The guards were British soldiers, as the airport was being used for evacuation purposes, while the civil authorities were Jewish, who had taken over two days previously and were still considerably bewildered by their newly-found powers.

Shmuel suddenly uttered an exclamation of surprise and darted forward to greet an elderly Pickwickian-looking man who was sitting and drinking tea amid the hubbub and the bustle, as calmly as though he always took his afternoon tea within sight of a battle front. Shmuel introduced me to Mr. M., a prominent Johannesburg lawyer and a very old acquaintance of his. A visitor from overseas was so rare a phenomenon in those days that when Shmuel expressed his great surprise at seeing him so far from his own particular battle field, Mr. M. had perforce to explain the purpose of his visit. He had come from England to arrange a transport of meat, to bring letters and to offer the Jewish Agency some 'planes which they could buy at a ridiculously low price. Shmuel pricked up his ears at this. After all, he was also in the arms-buying market now. M. remarked, very sadly, that the Agency had dillied and dallied, dithered and dathered and that nothing had come of the whole scheme. The implication was that the fault lay entirely with the Agency. To give the latter due credit, we subsequently discovered that this was not the case, but Mr. M., who was merely a go-between, did in all earnestness and sincerity think that they were throwing away an excellent opportunity by their dilatoriness.

Shmuel immediately jumped at a chance of getting the 'planes for the IZL and we eagerly absorbed all the details: what 'planes were available, whom to contact, where to contact him, what financial arrangements could be made and all the other ramifications of international arms-running. I was jubilant at this first step in our great adventure—this ripe plum which was going to fall so easily into our accommodating and expectant laps. Shmuel maintained his customary cautious scepticism which sometimes irritated me considerably by its wet-blanketing effect but invariably proved an excellent aid to softening the cruel blows of disappointment.

In return for this information from M. and even more because of Shmuel's deep respect and liking for him from the "old days" we offered him a "lift" in our 'plane. He was delighted at the opportunity as his intention had been to fly to Cyprus in the hope of getting a passage to England from there—a process which might have taken at least a week.

The next day we were in Paris and at the headquarters of the IZL. The place was an absolute tower of Babel. Hundreds of people passed through the offices every day, talking every language under the sun. There were five telephones ringing continuously—calls from Switzerland, from Belgium, from Germany, from America, from North Africa; and meetings in every available corner. We had plunged into one of the queerest, shadiest and will-o-the-wispiest of all those nebulous, but sinisterly powerful cliques which control the under-currents of Europe—the international arms black-market.

Their agents and spies must be ubiquitous and omniscient. No sooner had a whisper gone out that the IZL were in the market for arms than all manner of peculiar and ordinary-looking strangers started dropping in at the IZL headquarters. Some were suave and well-dressed, their brown and white shoes betraying their Mediterranean origin, others were unkempt and exaggeratedly sinister-looking. Even an Olga Puloffsky in the form of a beautiful cabaret-singer occasionally flitted across the scene. But all had one story; they had arms to sell.

The arms ranged from .303 rifles to light tanks; the ports of embarkation ranged from London to Barcelona; the prices varied fantastically and the nationalities of the salesmen were as varied as their purpose was uniform—to get as high a percentage for themselves as was possible.

On our first evening in Paris I was present at a meeting between Shmuel, Benyamin and Alex, representing the IZL, and some "big shots" who had something really interesting to offer. I sat quietly at the meeting, blinking and pinching myself hard to assure myself that I hadn't wandered by chance into a Phillips Oppenheim story fraught with international spies and shady arms deals. The agent responsible for bringing the parties together was a Pole, one of the arms-dealers was a Spaniard, another a Swiss and the third a Frenchman. The arms in question were .303 rifles, which were somewhere near Barcelona and which would have to be paid for in Switzerland. The main question was how to get the arms from Spain to France, as the Altalena was at Port de Bouc, near Marseilles. I went to bed at about 2 a.m. by which time the arms had been shipped disguised as cattle, transported by lorries camouflaged as cows, flown by 'planes masked as eagles, or perhaps that was just the result of my wearied, over-fevered brain.

This problem of delivery cropped up hundreds of times. There were arms to be had all over Europe, but the IZL insisted on delivery in France, and the purveyors of the arms offered delivery in Spain, in England, in Germany, in Switzerland—in fact anywhere except France. In most cases the problem of getting the arms across numerous borders

118

was insuperable and projects which had been followed up for days and had necessitated numerous journeys had to be dropped.

It did not take our people in Paris too long to realise that there was a limited number of arms to be bought in Europe but that a vast army of agents was engaged in an attempt to dispose of them. At first, at the stage of initiation, Alex and Irma, the two principal "buyers," had shot across the length and breadth of Europe in one wild goose chase after another. Alex would hurry to Brussels to negotiate about some rifles only to be told on arrival that the rifles were not actually in Brussels, but in Geneva. Alas, those rifles had been sold, but they could offer him some machine-guns in Paris. Irma would get an urgent call to go and see some armored cars in the South of France. After a breathless rush across France he would arrive there only to discover that the armored cars were jeeps and that, in any case, they had to come from across the Italian border.

Time and again the same false hopes were raised and the same dulling disappointment followed. The fact was that most of the agents were selling the same arms. The differences in prices and the differences in location were mere blinds—sometimes deliberate, sometimes due to the intricacies of a system of sub-agents and sub-sub-agents who received their instructions from their own headquarters in some particular capital of Europe and were not authorized to do any more than pass the customer on to their own principals.

There was certainly no question of principle in this trade. The goods went to the customer who paid the highest price first. Undoubtedly the same wares were offered to representatives of the Arab States, whose needs, fortunately for them, were not as great as ours and, consequently, I presume they were spared many of the endless, fruitless journeys and the anti-climactic, hopeless disappointments, all the more exaggerated by eager, excited anticipation.

The most frustrating part of it all was the fact that, though it had come late, there was now money enough—to buy a substantial quantity of arms for the Altatena to take—if only they had not been quite so elusive. A strict control was kept by Benyamin to prevent the indiscriminate acceptance of the tempting offers which appeared like mushrooms from all directions. One of the firm rules was that no money was to be handed over for arms before they had been seen and examined; and then only a small deposit was to be given before the arms were safely delivered.

These precautions, though elementary, were none the less necessary. When the buyers are as feverishly anxious to get hold of the goods quickly as were our people, there would naturally be a tendency to cut all corners and take short cuts—a dangerous procedure at the best of times and one which could have cost the IZL thousands of pounds in their dealings with unscrupulous men who were not averse to selling goods which they did not possess or which the same buyers had already bought in another guise.

And, in spite of all stringent precautions, our buyers were cheated on a few occasions. After they had inspected the arms and paid the small deposits, the goods mysteriously vanished in transit. In each of these cases the monetary loss was small, but the annoyance, frustration and indignation were in inverse proportion to the spoliation.

The European munitions black-market was one source for the purchase of arms. There was another much more constructive and satisfying source— the remnants of the underground movements. The Resistance Organisations of Europe had ceased to exist with the conquest of Germany by the Allies, but some of their buried and cleverly-hidden arms dumps remained extant. As people who had suffered bitterly from the cruel regime of an occupying force, who had fought against it like tigers, they sympathised with and applauded the activities of the IZL in Palestine. Their sympathy and plaudits were expressed in concrete, material form,—they opened up their arms dumps to their fellow underground fighters. Not everything was usable or purchasable, but the IZL nevertheless got equipment there which it would have taken them months to buy elsewhere and would have cost thousands of pounds more. And *only* the IZL could have gotten this equipment, whose sale was based on *esprit de corps* and not on mundane, sordid, commercial considerations.

*   *   *   *   *

Soon after we arrived in Paris, it was decided that I should go to London and look into the aeroplane proposition which Mr. M. had passed on to Shmuel in Haifa. Once again my only qualification for the job was the fact that I was the only person with a British passport, except for Shmuel, who, however, was too busy to go himself. As we had people in London who knew something about aeroplanes, the risk of my making too much of a hash was not great. Nevertheless I was given minute and detailed instructions about everything, most of which I forgot in any case as I could not make notes and my memory had not received the kind of training necessary for secret service work. My task was three-fold. I had to negotiate about Mr. M.'s three Halifaxes, look into the question of a gift of two seaplanes which someone wanted to make us, and round up two or three air crews for the planes which were supposed to be coming from Canada any day. On the face of it this appeared a very simple operation and I was told to report back in Paris in a week's time.

I made the journey by train and cross-Channel steamer, landing in Dover early in the morning. We were the usual crowd of sleepy-eyed, bilious-looking early-morning Channel-crossers and the Customs officials did not pay any undue attention to us. After a cursory glance through my suitcase the examiner ticked it off with his white chalk and was just about to send me away when a man lounging in the doorway nodded at him almost imperceptibly, and strolled over at leisurely pace with his hands in his pockets. He wore a navy-blue raincoat and a short, grey, trilby and had plain-clothes detective practically branded on him. He whispered in the Customs' official's ear and the latter somewhat apologetically re-opened my suitcase and started going through it most methodically. Every scrap of paper which he found he passed on to his colleague who studied it carefully. The suitcase evidently did not divulge any great secrets so they turned their attention to my handbag.

This was the stage at which to apply one of the three accepted techniques usually employed by passengers subjected to the indignity of a detailed search: either you became convivial and suggested in the heartiest, hail-fellow-well-mettest manner that perhaps if the security officer, or the customs official, would hint what he was looking for you would be only too pleased to help him out; or else you stood on your constitutional rights and demanded the reasons for this travesty of personal liberty and dignity, or thirdly, you maintained a stony, dignified silence, suitably embellished with a cold, contemptuous look in your eye.

I chose the third course, at least to the extent of the silence. I am never quite sure whether what I think is supposed to be a contemptuous look may not appear as a simple leer or even a facial defect to the intended recipient.

The security officer went through my handbag very thoroughly. I had some notes written in hieroglyphics intelligible only to me, which he studied closely and at length. As he asked me no questions I maintained my attitude of indifferent silence. Then he examined my address-book and made copious notes. I had intentionally made no note of any London addresses and the only ones that were in the book were of perfectly innocent and harmless relatives and friends in France and Switzerland of our neighbors and acquaintances in Palestine to whom, there being no postal communication, I had promised to give regards and messages of re-assurance. But down they went on the British black list and probably have trouble to this day every time they want to visit the United Kingdom. If they are patriotic Jews they will surely forgive me the inconvenience they are suffering in their role of red herrings.

This little experience in the Customs shed at Dover taught me one thing: however inefficient the Brititsh Intelligence Service in Palestine might be, in their home country they were on their toes. Scotland Yard was not the Jerusalem CID and was not to be underestimated or dismissed with the contempt reserved for the latter.

This lesson was confirmed when I arrived in London to stay with Walter—the man in nominal charge of IZL affairs in England. Although in my case there was a possibility that I was searched merely because my passport indicated that I was resident in Palestine and was thus a natural object of suspicion, in the case of Walter there was no ambiguity whatsoever. He was constantly being followed and his telephone was tapped. On one occasion when he had to make a trip out of town he approached his uninvited bodyguard and suggested amicably to him that he ride with him (Walter) in order to save the taxpayer's money on petrol. The offer was politely but firmly turned down and as Walter swung into the main highway, there was the unobtrusive police car sticking as tenaciously to him as Mary's little lamb.

Peter, too, an ex-RAF pilot whom I met for the first time on this trip to London, was well-known to the CID. He was on particularly good terms with his "tail," treating him to occasional tankards of beer in the local pub and on other occasions taking him on a combination wild-goose chase and red-herring trail right across London and then losing him deliberately in the Underground. The "tail" took this with a good grace. There was a tacit understanding between them that he was doing his duty following Peter but that it was well within the rules of the game for the latter to employ evasive and confusing tactics. Up the cricket players and long live British sportsmanship.

Walter was convinced that the CID knew about the activities of practically every active member of the IZL in London and he was probably right. But therein lay another difference between Palestine and the islands of the United Kingdom. In the former, British rule had been exercized by a special type of official reserved exclusively for service in the colonies where the local inhabitants were mostly colored, semi-civilized people who, according to current superstition, had to be kept down with the jack-boot and the whip. The existence of these colonies provided the British Colonial and Foreign Offices with an excellent opportunity of getting rid of their political "remittance-men"—men whose autocratic domineering and cruel natures made them completely unfit for home consumption, but suited them perfectly for dealing with the "natives" of the Gold Coast, or Nigeria or . . . Palestine, where public opinion, if it existed at all, could be disdainfully disregarded.

Hence the complete absence of *habeas corpus*, of unbiased courts and of constitutional rights in Palestine, in direct contrast to the almost passionate worship of the rights of the individual and of personal liberty in their own country. And hence the reason why, while in Palestine any one even faintly suspected of coming into third-party contact with the "terrorists" was deported to a detention camp outside of the country without any trial at all, in London, plainclothes detectives were deputed merely to watch over the activities of suspected "terrorists," and nothing more serious was meted out to them than an occasional session at Scotland Yard where they were questioned and then released in the course of half an hour. This naturally applied to the cases where there was no concrete evidence other than that of association with suspected and suspicious characters. In the one and only case where a young man was found in possession of explosives, he was tried and given a vicious sentence out of all keeping with the magnitude of his transgression.

The only member of the IZL with whom the CID were evidently not familiar was the Palestinian representative. He had come to London as a student and combined his studies with less peaceful pursuits. In appearance he looked so much like the Hollywood version of a foreign anarchist that the CID probably felt he was too obvious a caricature to be genuine. He always wore a dark hat pulled well over his eyes and slunk through the streets with one eye peering round the corner and the other squinting over his shoulder—a feat of ocular acrobatics which was made all the more spectacular by his habit of wearing thick-lensed glasses. When both his eyes were focussed in the same direction, considerably magnified and somewhat distorted by the powerful lenses, he looked exactly like a venomous owl. Yona, as he was called all the time he was in England,

123

was very impatient of his lily-livered fellow-Jews. He was constantly threatening to "bump off" some one or other for obstructing the IZL or for being too luke-warm in his sympathies, and had to be patiently reminded by Walter that the enemy was the British Government and not the Jewish Board of Deputies or the Zionist Federation or the Revisionist Party. But Yona's bark was a good deal worse than his bite and to my certain knowledge all the time he was in England he did not assassinate even one tiny, little member of the Jewish or gentile community.

As soon as I arrived in London I set the wheels going in all three of my commissions. Peter and Yona were in charge of recruiting air-crews and I passed on the instruction that they were immediately to send over to Paris everyone on their lists. This was not quite as simple as it sounds. We had about six young men on our lists, one of whom had to write his final professional examinations in a fortnight's time, some had to close down their businesses and others had family responsibilities which they had to settle. But all agreed to abide unquestioningly by our decision as to whether they should leave immediately or not. I could merely pass on the instruction from Paris and had no authority to temporise. So they all crossed the Channel two or three days later and kicked their heels in Paris for weeks due to an unforeseen and regrettable hitch in the despatch of the long-awaited 'planes from Canada. Eventually some of them returned to England, but others found their way to Israel and joined the Israel Air Force which had by then come into existence.

I contacted the Mr. C. to whom M. had referred us about the Halifaxes, and Walter and I went to see him in his sumptuous suite of offices. We waited an hour and a half for him to finish a board meeting after which he gave us a very cordial reception. We were then entertained to a graphic description of the meteoric rise of his company and to beer and sandwiches, as our visit had extended itself into the lunch-hour. Eventually, we got down to what interested us. Mr. C. (to whom I shall in future refer as Mr. Cohen for the sake of clarity) agreed that there were Halifax 'planes available and that he would be delighted to let the IZL have them for a song. There was just one snag, however—how to get them out of England. He suggested that the best plan would be for the IZL to buy a converted Halifax tranport 'plane and two bombers for the ostensible reason of dismantling them and using them as spare parts for the transport 'plane. I got a sneaking impression during the conversation that the transport 'plane, which would also be provided by Mr. Cohen's company, was not going to be quite so cheap as the bombers and that the latter were being dangled as bait for the former. But I kept my own counsel for the moment. We started bombarding Mr. Cohen with questions—in what condition were the 'planes, how much fuel would they carry, when and where could our expert see them. Mr. Cohen was acutely embarrassed by all these questions and eventually confessed that he himself knew very little about the 'planes but that his colleague, Monsieur Jacques, was due at any minute and he would have all the answers at his fingertips. We waited another hour for Monsieur Jacques who breezed in just as we were about to leave, apologising profusely that he couldn't stay for more than two minutes.

As we weren't inclined to stay much longer ourselves we arranged that he should meet Peter, Yona and me the next day at twelve. I suggested the foyer of one of the large hotels as a suitable meeting-place, but Monsieur Jacques threw up his hands in horror at this. He couldn't possibly take the risk of meeting in a public place and suggested Hyde Park. Then it was my turn to be horrified. Hyde Park is rather a large place for a rendezvous and the chances were that it would be raining. Monsieur Jacques reassured me. He would drive past a certain specified part of the Row at exactly twelve and pick us up in his car. I was still very dubious and pressed him to give me an assurance that he wouldn't keep us loitering around Hyde Park waiting vainly for him. Monsieur Jacques drew himself up to his full five-feet-four and bristled haughtily. I had cast aspersions on his punctiliousness and besmirched the Jacques family escutcheon.

No sooner were we out of earshot than Walter burst out: "His name is Jacques as much as mine is de Gaulle. I know that little crook—he once cheated me out of £400." This was not a very good augury. But I maintained that a crook could possibly succeed in getting those 'planes out of England where an honest man would fail dismally, so we ought to take a chance on him. Only we had to make quite certain that his victims were the British authorities and not ourselves. I thought, too, that Cohen seemed quite genuinely to want to help us in spite of being handicapped by an abysmal ignorance of aircraft and their uses. So we decided to get hold of Peter and Yona and keep the appointment for the next day.

When I told Peter that the man behind the scheme was Jacques he groaned loudly and long. He had heard of this Monsieur Jacques. He had also heard about the planes which had been standing in the open exposed to rain, wind and sun for months. Peter was very dubious about the condition of these 'planes—if they were the ones in question—and introduced a new difficulty. Even if we were to succeed in purchasing these 'planes and in getting permission to take them out of England they would have to get an airworthiness certificate before they were allowed to take off.

The next day dawned bright and fine without any signs of rain. This propitious beginning was merely a snare and delusion. By the time Yona, Peter and I had foregathered at the appointed spot in Hyde Park the sky was already becoming overcast. At 12 noon we watched out eagerly for Monsieur Jacques. He did not come. By 1 p.m. we were still keeping an anxious eye on all passing motor-cars and another even more anxious eye on the heavens. At 1:30 the first few drops began to fall, so we took shelter under the trees and gave Monsieur Jacques some more grace. By 1:45 we unanimously consigned Monsieur Jacques and his soul to hell and ran for shelter.

I telephoned Mr. Cohen in high dudgeon. I accused Monsieur Jacques of having had no intention whatsoever of keeping the appointment and demanded to know why he had to make fools of us in Hyde Park when we could have waited fruitlessly in much greater comfort in some hotel lounge. When I stopped for breath Mr. C. chipped in. He was profuse in his apologies and fell over himself backwards to assure me and reassure me that something must have happened inadvertently to detain our phoney French friend who had certainly intended keeping the appointment. I received all this very coldly. In the end he pressed me to dine with him that evening in his apartment as something important had cropped up. I accepted the invitation—for the sake of the cause. As he had not included anyone else in the invitation I arrived alone. We had an excellent dinner in an intime atmosphere. But Mr. Cohen's intentions were strictly honorable and any romantic inclinations which I might have had would have necessitated a somewhat more glamorous target.

As soon as we got down to business I informed Mr. Cohen that we had no confidence whatsoever in Monsieur Jacques and that I thought nothing would come of our plans if we had to rely on him. I was privately rather curious to know how a man like Cohen who was in charge of quite a large business organisation, came to have any dealings at all with a type like Monsieur Jacques. I can only ascribe it to Gilbertian weakness of intellect.

Cohen tried to assure me that Jacques was a good man—in his own line. But he suggested that we forget about the Halifaxes for the moment as he had a much bigger scheme. He had just heard that another air charter company had been engaged by the British Government to fly three 'plane-loads of ammunition to Iraq—clearly to be used against the Jews. He knew that the other firm was short of air-crews and in this knowledge he had conceived a brilliant plan: that we should supply the air-crews who would simply take the 'planes with their precious cargo to Israel and hand them over to the new Israel Government.

This certainly was some scheme. But there were just two not entirely negligible factors: firstly, I was very much sceptical of the truth of Mr. Cohen's information. After all, the British Government did not really need to engage a private company to carry out its arms deliveries to Iraq. Secondly, we would have to provide three complete air-crews with civilian "A" certificates—something which was completely beyond our capacity in England. Nevertheless, I undertook to discuss the matter with our experts and let Cohen know the results the next day.

My colleagues were at first fired with enthusiasm at the thought of acquiring such a treasure galleon through a little legitimate piracy. But when we considered all the technical difficulties, they agreed with me that the whole adventure, even if it came within the bounds of actuality, was well beyond our limited resources of man-power. Yona was all for blowing the 'planes up if we couldn't divert them. But I suggested that the Haganah representatives in London were much more likely to be able to cope with the original scheme than we as they had been registering air-crews for months; and that we hand the information and the contact over to the Jewish Agency and see what they could do about it. To this day I don't know whether the stratagem was ever pulled off, but I suspect, due to the very fact that we never heard any more about it, that my scepticism was well-founded and that we had merely bequeathed one of our numerous headaches to the Agency.

Another headache which we, this time in mischievous mood, passed on to the Agency was a "death-ray" expert who attached himself to us. He was one of the numerous cranks and crack-pots who spring up like mushrooms wherever the drums and cymbals of war send out their reverberations. All he claimed to be able to do was to hypnotize the moon and cause it to stray from its appointed route, to the inevitable confusion of those who suddenly found themselves in the path of its rays. This pet crack-pot of ours even demonstrated how he would set about hypnotizing the moon, stopping just in time, however, before he brought death and destruction on the wrong people. This was obviously a case for the Haganah experts.

While on the subject of crack-pots I am reminded of another long-haired member of the species who came to see Yechiel, our chief air-force officer in Paris. He offered in all seriousness to sell him atomic energy sufficiently compact to be enclosed in a match-box; and he offered these match-boxes in wholesale quantities, not just one miserable box at a time. When he backed up his sales-talk with the attraction of a guarantee, Yechiel asked politely just exactly how this guarantee would be tested. The answer was as simple as it was startling. The amiable maniac suggested that Yechiel invite together a few people he was anxious to be rid of and he would then be given a practical demonstration of the efficacy of the deadly little match-boxes. This suggestion abruptly and simultaneously terminated Yechiel's patience and the interview.

But to return to the Halifaxes. I saw Cohen another ten times at least. Each time he raised a fresh problem, but was unable to confound us. There was the question of getting the 'planes out of England, then of getting them into France; there was the problem of taking crews from England, then changing them in France; there was the difficulty of getting the various licenses; there was the question of payment—where and in what currency. All these problems we solved, but we still had not seen the 'planes in spite of Peter's insistence that we couldn't decide on anything until we saw them.

Finally, weeks after I had left England, Peter was enabled to inspect the 'planes. He pronounced them unairworthy as they stood and, after making numerous enquiries, found that in order to bring them into fit state to receive an airworthiness certificate, they would cost as much money as brand-new bombers. So ended in ignominy our Halifax purchases.

I was extremely interested to read months later in the "Palestine Post" that there was a great uproar in England about some British 'planes which had been illegally transferred to Israel. The man-behind-the-scenes, according to the newspaper report, was none other than our old friend Monsieur Jacques... My feelings were mixed: a combination of incredulity at the validity of the whole sensational story and nervousness as to the fate of any of our very scarce and precious young pilots who had to risk their lives in Monsieur Jacques' watering-cans.

* * * *

While negotiating about the Halifaxes we did not forget the seaplanes which had been offered to the IZL as a gift. As the prospective donor was abroad at the time, Walter and I arranged to meet his brother.

This was to be my first meeting with a real genuine specimen of the "idle rich," and I looked forward to it with scientific interest. As usual, anticipation was a good deal more exciting than realisation. Mr. B. was rather a stout, young man with a very cultured accent and polished manners. But in spite of the yachts and polo horses, he did do some work, and hardly gave the impression of spending his days and nights in riotous, dissolute living. In short, he was rich, but not idle; and I can still look forward to the day when I meet my first "play-boy."

He received us in the sumptuous well-appointed lounge of one of the fashionable London clubs. I had had some misgivings about my presence there as all the literature I have ever read about London clubs depicted them as stuffy, conservative places where the female presence was ana- thema. This club, evidently, had missed the scrutinizing gaze of the novelists or else it was one of those "fast" places. At any rate my presence created no stir whatsoever and was in fact hardly noticed amidst the half a dozen or so other women—beautifully-groomed and tailored.

Our host was very kind and very hospitable, but the sea-planes belonged to his brother and all he could do was to take someone down to see them. This had to suffice until his brother returned from abroad and could make the final arrangements. Peter saw the sea-planes and, as in the case of the Halifaxes, the whole scheme went up in smoke. It is true that one should not look a gift-horse in the mouth but when that horse is somewhat lame and also needs false teeth, the repicient may consider himself justified at refusing, albeit with polite and profuse thanks, a gift likely to involve him in some considerable expense without cor- responding benefits. And, in any case, even if we had the money to lay out we did not have the time to wait for repairs and overhaul to be carried out. So we did not get the sea-planes either.

My trip to London was saved from complete disaster by a meeting with one of the local chairmen of the United Jewish Appeal—the Jewish Agency fund-raising machine. Mr. R. is an immensely energetic man with a quick, sharp brain, outmatched only by the quickness and sharpness of

129

his tongue. He is a natural-born comedian with a flair for turning the simplest narrative into a riotous comic act. He was simply exploding with zeal and enthusiasm for Palestine and the cause of Zionism, and found the lethargic lackadaisicalness of the British Zionist Federation irritating at first and positively exasperating at a time when the Jews in Palestine were fighting what could well be a losing battle against overwhelming Arab odds. He was all on fire to be doing something constructive—sending arms, sending men or what you will, as long as it was something. But all the response he could get from the Zionist Federation was that so-and-so would deal with the matter as soon as he got back from Paris, or New York or China or somewhere equally remote. Mr. R.'s accounts of his interviews with some of the leading British Zionists set us howling with laughter in spite of the immense seriousness of the implications.

So Mr. R. was on the warpath and just looking for an outlet for his energy and zeal in furthering the cause of the fighting Yishuv. When I met him he pressed me to tell him just how bad the Jewish situation in Palestine was. I confirmed his worst fears. But when I told him about the Altalena, his imagination was fired. Here was something concrete, something he had begged and pleaded for—a shipload of arms and men for the desperately under-equipped and under-manned Israeli forces. He immediately decided that he must help the IZL in some way and asked me whether I would come and speak to a few of his friends and tell them what I had told him. I readily agreed to this.

R. did not realise what a storm in a tea-cup he was stirring up by this invitation. The Zionist Federation soon heard that an IZL "agent" was about to trespass on their domain—was about to ask their own staunch members for money for an IZL project. If there was anything which could exasperate the Federation into feverish activity it was the horror of having any money—even so small a sum as I could possibly raise in one evening—diverted from their own funds. So they brought their big guns into play. First of all they tried to dissuade R. from having his little party, but he was obdurate and insisted it was a private party and he would not be dictated to as to how to run his social life. Then they tried to "get" at R.'s friends and persuade them not to attend. This put R. on his mettle and roused all his fighting instincts. The whole affair became a question of prestige and developed into a conflict out of all keeping with the occasion and certainly out of all proportion to the importance of the guest-of-honor.

When the momentous evening arrived, I discussed with Dinah, Walter's wife, a question which to women all over the world is one of momentous importance—the question of what I should wear. In this instance the problem was not so much sartorial as political and psychological. The only overcoat I had with me was a tailored tweed which had once been a smart coat—before it had been lugged all over Europe, sat in for hours on end in 'planes and trains and motor-cars, slept in on numerous occasions and used variously as a blanket, a pillow and a foot-rest. The most that could be said of that coat was that it had had an interesting and varied career. Dinah objected strongly to my wearing it on this occasion and generously offered to lend me her fur wrap. I turned down the offer on psychological grounds and gave her a brief lecture on my interpretation of the attitude of a victim, and especially of the victim's female relations—to a woman who is trying to wrest a contribution from him. If she is shabbily dressed he may be forgiven for suspecting that her interest in his donation is not entirely objective and altruistic—in short that she needs at least part of the money for herself. On the other hand if she is too well-dressed, the victim may be all the more forgiven for suspecting that previous donations had contributed towards her sartorial elegance.

Dinah scoffed at this cynicism and scepticism which I attributed to my fellow-men, but we nevertheless compromised on a plain black frock of mine which could not possibly offend any susceptibilities and a black coat of hers which defeated my first argument by being smart and well-cut and, at the same time, overcame my second argument by being a previous year's model.

We found fifteen men gathered at R.'s house. Only two or three of his friends had succumbed to pressure and remained at home. R. swore dire vengeance against them and I am positive he must have made their lives a misery merely through his quick wit and powers of ridicule.

R. introduced me to his friends, considerably exaggerating my activities as a member of the resistance movement and pointing dramatically to my appearance as an indication of the hardships which the IZL members were undergoing. This came as rather a shock to me. I knew I had, quite fortuitously, lost a lot of weight, so that my dress hung rather unbecomingly on me and I had also cut my hair as short as was femininely possible as a psychological reaction to the Yehudieh wild life rather than as an absolute necessity. But, nevertheless, I had not the faintest idea that I looked so much like a scare-crow as to be singled out as a prototype for the fighting, suffering resistance.

When my turn came to speak, I told my audience about the dangers of fighting a war with one weapon only, the vaunted Jewish "secret weapon"—miracles. I told them about the miracle of Haifa which the Haganah had conquered not by force of arms, but through a deliberate or unintentional miscalculation on the part of the British, coupled with the fearful reputation which the Irgun had gained amongst the Arabs. I told them of the miracle of Jaffa, captured in the nick of time before the Egyptians could move in and use it as a deadly base against Tel Aviv— and captured with arms which the IZL had taken a few days previously from a British troop-train. I told them how urgently we needed real arms so that we should not have to continue drawing on our funds of miracles which, for all we knew, might already be overdrawn. I spoke in this vein for about half-an-hour and ended up with an appeal for help in loading the Altalena to capacity. At the end of my talk there was a ring at the door-bell and a newcomer was ushered into the room. His presence created a buzz of interest amongst my hearers and produced a look of profound annoyance on R.'s face. The late-comer was a leading London Zionist especially commissioned by the Federation to attend the party and see that too much damage was not inflicted on their funds.

He immediately asked permission to put some questions to the speaker. The audience rose as a man and objected to his questioning me when he had not heard my talk. For a few minutes the dogs of chaos and confusion were loosed and barked loudly and raucously. When R. had succeeded in restoring order I whispered to him that I really had no objection to being questioned.

My would-be-questioner rose and, as I had expected, asked no questions but delivered the usual inflammatory diatribes and insults against the IZL, and R. and his friends were furious. In another age they would have torn him limb from limb. As it was they lynched him verbally. I was not given a chance to open my mouth. They did all the talking for me except on one occasion when I took advantage of a lull in the storm to say quietly in response to the usual hysterical and libellous outburst against the IZL's behavior at Dir Yassin, that even if that accusation were true, in this age when an atom bomb was used to bring horrible death to tens of thousands of defenseless men, women and children and when its use was justified as a military expedient in that it saved thousands of American and British lives, then any outcry against Dir Yassin was sheer and utter hypocrisy.

When the rumpus died down, R. called on his friends to contribute something towards the Altalena and passed round a hat. It came back with £1,500 in cash and promises of more to come.

I thought it a very satisfactory evening but R. was disappointed. He blamed the Federation's diversionary tactics for our failure to receive a great deal more money.

*   *   *   *   *

With my spirits considerably bolstered up by this success, I set out on my return journey to Paris. Walter and I thought we might succeed in putting the CID off my scent if I crossed the Channel by the Newhaven to Dieppe route instead of embarking at Dover where I had landed ten days previously. I had really no reason for attempting to avoid the CID, as I had no incriminating documents whatsoever with me, but Walter probably felt he would like to save me the discomfort and indignity of having to answer a lot of awkward questions. I think, too, that we might both have been subconsciously influenced in our assessment of the sinister ramifications of the CID by a talk we had a few days earlier with a friend we knew to be an Intelligence Agent, a Mr. L.

L. had provided the IZL with a good deal of very useful information and I had been commissioned by Shmuel to see him in London before I left and bring back, chronicled in my memory, his latest report. Walter and I spent a couple of fascinating hours with L. and, besides receiving his reports, heard a good deal about the seamier side of counter-espionage. What impressed me particularly and sent a horribly cold shiver down my spine was L.'s statement, in a simple, matter-of-fact tone, that he never, in any cirmustances, stood near the edge of a platform in an Underground station and always made sure that he had his back to a wall. I was somewhat curious, in spite of my queasiness, and, like one of those ghoul-like rubber-necks who always push themselves into a position to miss nothing of the blood and horrors of an accident, I pressed him to elaborate on this phobia of his. He told us that it was not only in novels that the espionage services availed themselves of the simple expedient of getting rid of an enemy by pushing him, unnoticed by the jostling crowds, onto the tracks in front of an oncoming train. For one very uncomfortable moment I felt that maybe we were playing a game that was very much more dangerous than we realised and that there was a good deal more in the heaven and earth of politcal and special police departments than was dreamed of in our philosophy. But that mental shudder passed over quickly as my sense of balance was restored.

Walter and I sadly underestimated the efficiency of the CID. No sooner had the customs-officer ticked off my suitcase at Newhaven than I found "him" standing next to me. His face differed from that of the man at Dover but the blue raincoat and grey trilby were identical. I presume that this is the plain-clothes "uniform" worn by the port detectives. The only other detective I had seen at close quarters, besides my Dover acquaintance, wore a bowler hat. But this had been in London and was probably the accepted attire for the well-dressed sleuth-about-town. Peter and I had spotted him following us one morning and immediately jumped into a taxi, more for the thrill of shaking off a real, live "tail" than for any strictly utilitarian purpose, as we were merely on our way to have a perfectly innocent lunch in a restaurant.

In Newhaven I adopted the same procedure as in Dover and my suit-case and hand-bag were searched in stony silence.

Having satisfied himself that I had no tanks concealed in my luggage and no machine-guns on my person, the detective speeded me on my way with a curt nod of his head and I came out of the investigation with no greater loss to my dignity than was occasioned by the curious glances of my fellow-passengers.

CHAPTER XI

JOURNEY'S END

I FOUND the Babel at IZL Paris headquarters considerably enhanced by the daily arrival of pilots, navigators and wireless-operators from the United States and Canada. Our friends in these two countries had responded magnificently to the call to send over air-crews to man the long-awaited planes from Canada. The only trouble was that in their over-enthusiasm they had promised these crews fantastic salaries, allowances for their families and compensation in the event of death or disablement. Our people in Paris were appalled when they heard this. They explained very patiently to the Americans and Canadians that all soldiers in the IZL received the same very low rate of pay and their families received a mere subsistence allowance. The organisation was too poor to pay the exorbitant salaries they claimed were promised them nor would it, in any case, depart from its fixed principles. They suggested to the fliers that arrangements could be made for the American and Canadian IZL representatives to see that their families received an adequate allowance, but that they, themselves, would have to agree to accept the same terms and conditions as all other members of the IZL. In those circumstances they would be gladly welcomed to the ranks, but only in those circumstances. Some ten accepted these terms. Those who did not were immediately sent back to their homes. No-one blamed them. They had offered their services as professionals and not because they were imbued with idealism and zeal for the cause of Israel.

Yechiel was in charge of the airmen, who numbered about fifteen, including those who had come over from England. He, himself, had been one of the few Palestinians in the RAF Bomber Command and had the reputation for being an excellent, if somewhat over-daring pilot. But handling a heavy bomber was child's play in comparison with handling a group of high-spirited young men at a loose end in Paris. He was in continual despair about the impossibility of balancing his daily budget and would come to the offices every day in the hope of hearing that the planes had arrived, and that he could get his unruly charges a few hundred metres above the temptations of gay Paree. But each day he met with the same shake of the head and went off mumbling dire threats about nervous breakdowns and apoplectic attacks. At last he hit on the expedient of sending the air-crews out of Paris to the countryside with a week's allowance of money which he gave to each individually, with the admonition that they could do as they pleased with their money, but they would not get another penny until the week was out. This gave him a chance to relax his strained nerves and let them recover their normal powers of resistance—at least till the airmen returned to Paris.

Soon after my return to Paris I met Joe Kohn, an American who had come over on the Altalena on its original trip from the United States. Joe had fought the Japanese in the Pacific and had been quite convinced that he had had enough of wars for the rest of his life until he heard of the revolt of the IZL against British rule in Palestine. Then this tough war-veteran voluntarily left his flourishing toy-shop in Los Angeles and came to New York to offer his services to the Hebrew Committee.

Joe explained to me that he thought America the most wonderful country in the world, and California the most wonderful State in America. He wanted to go back there as soon as possible. That was where he wanted to live—not Palestine. But he felt it was time the Jews had a country of their own and he was willing to give up a year or two of his life to help get that country so that those Jews who wanted to could come and settle there.

Nothing annoyed Joe so intensely as to hear anyone associating work in the IZL with glamor and thrills. "It's like the glamor of war," he would say. "Dirt, lice, disease, blood and fear—do you call them glamorous? My dear child," Joe would continue, "if you want glamor, go to a luxury hotel on the Californian coast. Bathe, sail in the sparkling sea, bedeck yourself in gorgeous clothes, dance and make love in the moonlight. That's glamor, that's excitement—not the questionable thrill of seeing your friends die or the romance of living like a hunted animal."

When Joe was not driving people round the countryside to inspect arms and ammunition, he attached himself to Benyamin, for whom he had an immense admiration. He acted as his chauffeur, his memory-jogger, his aide-de-camp. There was nothing too menial or too exalted for Joe. He would work uncomplainingly into the small hours of the morning and be up bright and early to give to a new day all the energy and devotion which he had stored up in his spare, wiry frame.

I drove out with Joe one afternoon to a deserted chateau whose owner, a wealthy American Jew, had given the IZL the use of it as a radio receiving station. Joe was taking out some equipment to the two IZL radio experts who lived on the premises in a day and night effort to establish communications with Israel. On the way he talked to me about his shop in Los Angeles, about his family and his nostalgia for the youthfulness and vigor of America in constrast to the senile decadence of Europe. But in spite of his scorn, he still found the French countryside delightful and burst into rapturous paeans as every fresh turn of the road revealed a vista more breathlessly enchanting than the previous one. When we arrived at the chateau, Joe surprised me still further by his completely un-American attitude towards it. He took an immense delight in pointing out to me the noble proportions of the rooms, the antique furniture and old paintings, and was not distracted by the obvious signs of decay and disrepair in the house itself and in the magnificent wilderness which still showed signs of having once been a stately garden. Joe positively enthused over the chateau in contrast to his contemptuous dismissal of Parisian architecture as resembling a Christmas cake with its iced scrolls and rosettes and filigree work, and his even more contemptuous dismissal of elegant Parisian apartments as resembling museums. I could not quite fathom the reason for his excepting the chateau from these criticisms, unless it was that the house had gripped him unawares, when his artificial defences were down, when his parochial pride did not force him to debase everything that was not American in order the more to acclaim what was.

I teased him about this and warned him that one day a non-American woman would capture his heart in the same way and despite his declared intention of marrying only a Californian girl. I even suggested finding him a beautiful girl in Israel who would keep him tied to the country and prevent him from leaving as soon as he felt his job was done. But Joe simply laughed good-humoredly at my good intentions.

I was not allowed to remain idle in Paris for any length of time. My first commission was to go to Basle to transfer some money to Israel. A good part of the IZL money was concentrated in Switzerland from where it was transferred, either to Paris or to Tel Aviv as the need arose.

I immediately took the night train to Basle and arrived there just as the banks were opening. In spite of the long and complicated instructions which Benyamin had given me, the operation was a very simple one and took only a few minutes. The final stage of the process, however, had to be done through Zurich. The manager of the bank suggested that if we were in a hurry it would speed matters up considerably were I to go to

Zurich myself with a letter from him and complete the transfer. I readily agreed and forthwith took a local train from Basle to Zurich. The train was local in more senses than one. It stopped every ten minutes—at every small village, at every large farm, at every cluster of houses, in fact at every excuse. At first I kept myself amused and interested by studying the Swiss country-folk and, of course, by drinking in the beauties of the scenery. I was suitably impressed by the mountains and the grandeur, but what struck me particularly was the exquisite tidiness of the countryside. Even the few factories that we passed were picturesquely built and surrounded by trees and gardens tended with loving care. I thought sadly of the countryside of my own Israel with its dumps of old tins, iron and refuse, and of the factories surrounded by barrels, boxes, discarded jerry-cans, old sacks—all deposited carelessly, with anything but loving care. I suppose that when we stop being a volatile, highly-strung, excitable people and become as settled, almost to the point of stodginess, as the Swiss, that our countryside too will become less hectic and slovenly; or, maybe, we need those years and years of peace and prosperity which the Swiss have enjoyed before we too can plant flowers and trees in front of our factories.

The slowness of the train began to send me into a fever of impatience lest the banks in Zurich should close before I could get there. This was a complete waste of energy, as we arrived with a good half-hour to spare and I was able to complete my business without any undue hurry, and return to Paris that same night.

Shmuel met me with bad news. He had just heard, through South Africa, that Matie Silber had been killed near Jerusalem, six weeks previously. It was typical of the times in Palestine that we should hear of Matie's death through South Africa and six weeks after it had happened. At the time we left Israel, Jerusalem was completely cut off from the rest of the country. The city received no provisions, no fresh supplies of water and no reinforcements. It was being continuously shelled by the surrounding Arab forces and the very slender means of communications were reserved exclusively for military purposes.

Matie was a young South African whom I had met for the first time on my visit there two years previously. He had lived in the coastal town of Port Elizabeth and was the only child of well-off parents, who doted on him and lived only for him. They sent him to the University and looked forward eagerly and proudly to the day when they would see him graduate as a full-fledged engineer. But Matie dreamed only of going to Palestine to join the IZL. To this end he learned flying and caused his mother end-less anxiety every time she knew he was in the air. To his parents' acute distress he wearied of his studies at the University. His one obsession occupied him completely to the exclusion of all other interests. He had to get to Palestine; One might have thought that a simple operation for a boy whose parents could afford to pay for his passage. But, firstly, Matie's parents were very reluctant to part with their only child, and, secondly, for a Jew to go to Palestine in those days needed the permission of the Mandatory Government in the form of an immigration certificate. These certificates were doled out very sparsely and the "safe" countries, such as America, the Dominions and the British Isles got only a handful each year. Their immigration needs were not pressing and each certificate they received meant one less for the tortured people of Europe, who had exchanged Hitler's concentration camps for British and American Displaced Persons' camps. His only hope lay in persuading his father to send him to Palestine on a business trip or as a student at the Hebrew University. Eventually he succeeded in doing the latter and turned up at our flat in Ramat Gan towards the end of 1947, just after the outbreak of the unofficial war with the Arabs.

I remember Matie's telling me with great glee how, while he was walking through a street in Tel Aviv, two bullets suddenly whizzed past his ear. He simply did not associate himself with death. He drove a motor-car with dangerous speed and carelessness and he flew a plane recklessly and daringly. His belief in his own immortality was both childish and child-like. Very few of us go through life continually expecting and fearing death; but always, at the back of our minds, is the thought that one day our turn must inevitably come. Not so Matie. He simply did not believe that it could happen to him and he must have died incredulously, thinking to the last that it was but a nightmare or else some horrible mistake on someone's part.

Soon after Matie arrived, he insisted on going to Jerusalem—at least to register at the University, if not to study. Shmuel and I tried to dissuade him. We knew that Jerusalem was due for a difficult time and the lonely parents were always at the back of our minds. I suggested that if he stayed in Tel Aviv he might get the chance of using his flying ability when the IZL eventually got planes. But he was not to be moved. Jerusalem was the place for him—and to Jerusalem he went.

We met him there on our last visit in March 1948. He was in uniform

139

and looking better and happier than he had ever been. So as not to be a financial burden on either his parents or the IZL, he had got himself a part-time job at Reuter's and was at the same time taking an intensive course in the IZL. At the completion of his course he went into full-time service with the IZL as a junior officer. He was killed a month later in the gallant IZL defence of Ramat Rachel.

Matie's mother carried her grief with pride and dignity. Her first reaction to the news of his death was to say quietly that if her son had to die in war, she was glad he had not given up his precious young life for others, but had died fighting for his own people. But she never recovered from the shock of her bereavement. A year later her broken heart gave up its struggle with sorrow and quietly ceased beating.

*   *   *   *   *

I was welcomed back in Paris by Eliezer with new instructions—to go post-haste to Brussels. Besides taking arms to Israel, the Altalena was to carry about 900 young men and women to swell the fighting forces. As in the case of the deadlier portion of the ship's cargo, the human cargo, too, had to be gathered in from all over Europe, had to be taken across borders and into France. This was a monumental undertaking successfully entrusted to the capable administration of Eliezer, who had the control of his European organization at his finger-tips. Timing was the essential factor in dealing with the human element. The people had to be gathered together in their country of origin, the necessary passports and transit visas had to be available, not too soon to make the latter invalid before the date of departure and not too late to upset the time-table. At the same time, once the travellers were concentrated in a transit camp, they became a financial burden on the IZL who had to feed and provide for them, so that the shorter the time they spent in the camps, the less would they strain the IZL resources. In some cases, as in Germany, where most of the people were in Displaced Persons' Camps in any case, or in Italy, where the IZL had been maintaining a training and transit camp for months, this latter consideration did not apply; but in places like Belgium and Holland, or North Africa and the South American States, it was essential that the concentration of people should take place at the latest possible date.

In Marseilles, too, where the final foregathering before embarkation would have to take place, there were also many complicated problems to be overcome. A camp had to be provided for 900 people, with sleeping accommodations, eating facilities, proper hygienic arrangements and medical care. Then again, care had to be exercised so that young men and women should not have to spend too much time in Marseilles. The objections to this were three-fold: Firstly, there was the same financial consideration. Secondly, a large gathering of foreign, young people for some length of time would naturally arouse a good deal of comment. While this could not be kept a secret from the local population or from the prying eyes of the British Intelligence, it was nevertheless not thought advisable to give the latter sufficient time in which to pass the information on to their Government and so cause the French Government considerable embarrassment. Thirdly, the strain of keeping nearly a thousand people who were tearing at the leash to get to Israel and have a go at the Arabs, confined to a camp for any undue length of time would have been an extremely unenviable one, and could only result in a flaunting of discipline with its inevitable aftermath of demoralization.

So Eliezer's task was gigantic and as it depended so much on the element of timing he had to be continuously despatching envoys to all corners of Europe to coordinate, to organize, to give last-minute instructions. For this purpose I was sent to Brussels.

I had to obtain a full list of the people intending to come on the Altalena, see that they had passports and arrange for them to get transit visas for France and exit visas from Belgium. Most of the young people were Belgian-born and not a few of them intended leaving without the knowledge of their parents, as they were convinced that the latter would not give their consent. I did not approve of this and tried to persuade them to talk to their parents and overcome their opposition. But they were adamant in their anxiety not to be prevented from going with the others. Strangely enough, those who were keenest to go and understandably most concerned lest they should be stopped, were the girls. Or perhaps this was not so strange for the girls lived more sheltered and secluded lives than the boys, and here they were being given a glorious opportunity to take part in an epic such as they had only read about or seen in the cinemas. And for once they were not "mere girls," but human beings who could contribute and suffer as much as the boys. I read this enthusiasm and this eagerness for a life of thrills and adventures in their beaming, excited faces and sparkling eyes, and I felt sad and depressed. How could I explain to them that Joe was right, that they would find no glamor in this adventure, but only heartache and hardship. How could I explain that there would be times when they would bitterly regret having run away from their

141

comfortable homes and the protection and solace of their parents. Such explanations would have sounded trite and flat in face of their youthful ardor and idealism. But, nevertheless, I felt I owed it to them, or to their parents, or to my own conscience to describe to them what war against the Arabs meant and also to warn them that a small ship on the high seas would be extremely vulnerable to attacks from the air and from enemy ships of war. I told them this, not so much to frighten them off as to prepare them, to provide them with some kind of shock-absorber against all eventualities. They absorbed all the details with rapt attention as children will listen to fairy stories of cruel witches and malevolent ogres, but they did not, and possibly could not, grasp the implication.

However, my job was not to scare the wits out of our future soldiers; it was to see that they arrived safely and on time in Marseilles. So, after I had done what I considered to be my duty in attempting to dissuade those who were running away from home from joining the rest, I set about the more concrete aspects of the undertaking. Firstly, however, I did put my foot down and insisted that no-one under eighteen should be allowed to go and that two girls in particular—one with tuberculosis and the other with heart-trouble—should on no account be taken. Yosef, the boy in charge of the group, agreed with me whole-heartedly and was greatly relieved at the chance of using my veto, which could be identified with Eliezer's, to reinforce his own arguments and so overcome all tears and pleading.

My concrete tasks proved somewhat complicated. Firstly, not all the boys and girls had passports and some could not hope to get them without their parents' consent. Secondly, the question of exit permits from Belgium was rather a ticklish one especially for those with Belgian passports, who were all of military age and so liable for temporary conscription into the Belgian army; and for those without any passports at all, whose departure from any country would in normal circumstances be regarded as impossible, it was doubly ticklish. This was obviously not an undertaking for amateurs to dabble in, so Yosef and I decided to call in the local expert on these matters. He was a certain Mr. Z., who had organized the traffic of "illegal" immigrants for the Haganah. Mr. Z. worked in an obscure little office in one of the suburbs of Brussels and it took Yosef a day or two to trace him through the tortuous channels of the Haganah underground. Having eventually located his lair, we had to call on him four or five times and leave cryptic, carefully veiled messages until we eventually ran him to earth.

He received us very kindly and undertook to help us. According to the plan which he outlined, he would arrange a collective French visa for the 35 or so boys and girls and would then take them clandestinely out of Belgium. They were to be dressed as hikers and to carry only rucksacks and food and water with them. After they had "jumped" the border, the party would take the train to Paris, where they would become our responsibility. We fixed on a date during the first week of June.

I left Yosef to work out all the details with Z. and returned to Paris to report to Eliezer. The Belgian party did not arrive upon the appointed day. I was beginning to worry badly about them when, 36 hours later, Eliezer walked into the office and asked in his matter-or-fact, nonchalant manner whether I would like to go with him to the hotel to see the Belgian boys and girls who had just arrived.

At the hotel all was chaos and confusion and spirits which, in Brussels, had reached the top of the barometer were now pushing a way out through the bottom. Ardor was practically dripping with dampness and enthusiasm had petered out completely. They had had their first taste of the "glamor and romance" of the underground and had found it bitter and rather frightening. The story I heard was somewhat garbled by the introduction of excited interjections, in even more excited French, into a narrative told in already imperfect Yiddish. I managed to pick out from the jumble of jargon and jabbor that they had had to wait around the border for nearly twelve hours until they saw a chance of crossing. Meanwhile they had eaten up all their food and drunk all their water and had not dared replenish their stocks. They grabbed at their first chance of jumping the border, jumped, and were caught on the other side by a French patrol. After hours of argument and discussion they eventually persuaded the French to let them go, as their French visas were in order. By this time they were dead tired, hungry, cold and still not recovered from their fright. When they arrived in Paris, a new catastrophe awaited them in the form of a posse of French police. In Brussels, the stricken parents of those who had run away had set up a hue and cry and called in the aid of the police, who had, in turn, passed on the appeal for assistance to the French Prefecure. Once more there was vehement argument, tears and protestations and, at last, emotionally and physically exhausted, and with most of their luggage mislaid in the general melee, they were allowed to go— except for two girls who were minors. The latter were taken into custody and eventually returned to their parents.

After two days in Paris the rest regained their youthful ardor and enthusiasm and, deliberately forgetting the dark depression and resolutely shutting out their brief glimpse into the realms of fear, set out for Marseilles in great spirits to add their mite to the history of their times.

*   *   *   *   *

While I was in Paris I acted as Eliezer's driver. I would have sworn, before I tried it, that driving in Paris was a physical impossibility for any comparatively sane and normal person. To the naked eye of the pedestrian in Paris, any driver of a moving vehicle appears either as some kind of miracle-working demi-god or as a sheer lunatic completely careless of his own life and utterly oblivious of the existence of his fellow-creatures. In point of fact, when one is actually sitting behind the wheel and driving, everything seems to fall into its natural place—pedestrians do appear to have minds and even occasionally to know them, rival motorists actually do not appear to regard it as their life's work to knock out as many vehicles as possible, and even the taxi-drivers appear to be almost human instead of the diabolical hell-cats one always pictures them to be. In short, except for one or two cunning devices designed to confuse and confute the unwary visitor, Paris is a much easier and pleasanter city to drive in than Tel Aviv.

I got some of my worst headaches from a habit the French have of hiding away their traffic-lights in some unobtrusive corner, or of suspending them somewhere in the stratosphere well out of the range of vision of anyone without a portable telescope or periscope. Fortunately, the French police are generally very polite and long-suffering, and even more so with foreigners who, besides not being able to talk a word of French, seem also to be generally half-witted and below par.

Eliezer had only one fault to find with my driving,—a fault of omission rather than of commission—my complete lack of a bump of locality. I must, in self-defence, deny that I am completely devoid of a sense of direction, but I have to confess that I could never remember where all Eliezer's offices were. For this I would have required not only a knowledge of topography and compass reading, in which I am considerably shaky, but also a neat pigeon-hole mind which I certainly do not possess at all.

When I was not driving Eliezer I helped Shoshanah, the widow of David Raziel. Bad luck had dogged Shoshanah since the ill-omened day in 1941 when David was killed in Iraq by a splinter from a bomb. In Paris her bad luck held good, though it no longer operated on the plane of tragedy, but merely set the stage for Opera Bouffe. She was put in charge of the cash—a duty she carried out with scrupulous conscientiousness—which did not serve to endear her to those who had to pass through her inquisitory researchers into the whys and wherefores before they got what they asked for, but did, undoubtedly, save the IZL many thousands of francs.

I helped Shoshanah mainly in counting money which very often ran into hundreds of thousands of francs, without meaning very much in purchase value. Fortunately for my sanity and the customary tranquility of my nerves, Eliezer did not let my driving licence and my British passport go to waste in the mechanical process of counting the roots of evil for any length of time. I drove and I travelled—twice more to Switzerland. On the second occasion I brought back with me $50,000 which I declared quite openly and honestly in Basle. I then spent a most uncomfortable night clutching it tightly to my bosom in case some predatory robber-of-women on the train had overheard my declaration and cast covetous eyes on what was a small fortune in Europe. My avid consumption of detective stories in which people are murdered for a good deal less reason than $50,000 did not exactly serve to quieten my fears. But James Hadley Chase notwithstanding, I reached Paris quite safely and with the money all there—to the last dollar.

Meantime the feverish efforts to prepare the Altalena went on apace. Shmuel was in a perpetual state of anxiety. At first he was all a-fever to get the ship off as soon as possible in order to get its precious cargo into the hands of those who were fighting tanks with sten-guns; and then another equally urgent reason for haste suddenly loomed up ominously. Rumor was rife that the United Nations were about to enforce a truce on the Jews and Arabs and that one of the terms of that truce would be an embargo against arms and immigrants of military age. Shmuel, Benyamin and their confederates spent hours discussing this problem and weighing the pros and cons of sailing or not sailing in those circumstances. There was always at the back of each one's mind that nagging worry about the safety of the precious human cargo on the ship—always open to attack on the high seas, and possibly in even greater danger during a truce. One did not need a great deal of imagination to envisage the horrible carnage which a few direct hits on a ship loaded with arms and ammunition could effect. There was also the danger of confiscation by the UN after the ship landed in Israel. But confidence in the ability of the ship's captain, a

145

veteran of the war in the Pacific, on the one hand; and the dire need of Israel for arms, on the other hand, proved decisive. It was not yet known in Paris what the attitude of the Israel Government would be, but it was agreed that the arms must be brought to the shores of Israel. If the Government then decided against landing them—the IZL would at least have done their duty.

Pressure came from another direction too. The French authorities were insisting on the immediate departure of the ship from French waters.

It was already the beginning of June and for the first time a sailing date was tentatively set—for approximately the tenth of the month. In Paris the fever was reaching its crisis. Benyamin was put in command of the men on the ship and left for Marseilles together with Joe, his faithful henchman. Monroe Fein, the young American captain of the Altalena, came up to Paris to make last-minute arrangements. With him came Avraham Stavsky, the beloved Abrasha — affectionately known as "Nebraska" by his English-speaking young friends—who spread an aura of cheerfulness, good-will and flashing wit in his generous and capacious orbit. He was the nominal owner of the ship, which had been bought and registered in his name on behalf of the Hebrew National Committee in America, and he was going to see the venture through to the very end— to the minute when arms and men were landed on the shores of Israel. And each day and every day the late-comers trickled in—small parties from England, from the United States, from Canada, from the Argentine. They were sent off to Marseilles to swell the growing ranks of fighters.

The original final date of arrival for volunteers, the 31st May, was extended by Benyamin to the 7th June, but this too did not suffice. On the 9th of June a small party of intrepid young men arrived from Cuba. Shmuel told them they were too late. Their disappointment was bitter as gall. They pleaded passionately for a chance to try and make it. Their eloquence and sincerity won the day and they wrung reluctant permission from Shmuel to go to Marseilles and try to persuade Benyamin to take them along. Though they arrived at Marseilles almost at the last moment, they succeeded with Benyamin too—and sailed on the Altalena to fulfill the unalterable dictates of Fate.

In Marseilles the embarkation camp was an ants' nest of activity and order. Each party, as it arrived from one of the four corners of the world, was housed, medically examined and given the necessary injections. Arms poured into Port de Bouc where the Altalena was anchored, and were loaded on to the ship. Suddenly, on the morning of the 10th June, there was consternation and alarm. The port workers, among whom were many Lascars and Moslems from North Africa, had gone on strike and refused to load arms intended for use against the Arabs in Palestine. The panic was short-lived. Willing hands and eager backs took over. Our boys tackled the unfamiliar job with the fury of galley-slaves under the whip, making up for lack of experience and skill with inspired zeal and energy. The work of loading went on under the blazing Mediterranean sun and the amateur dockers sang as they worked, in a tongue strange not only to the dockside loungers and the curious sightseeers, but even to many of those who sang. But the spirit of the song transcended the incomprehensibility of its words. It rang out into the hot summer air, speaking of a new freedom, of a new race, resurrected from the ignoble, maltreated skeleton of what had been a proud and dignified people, and of an old tongue re-born to unify the scattered shreds of a nation and turn Babel into Concord.

On the morning of 11th June, 1948, a truce came into force between Israel and the invading Arab States, and on that same evening the Altalena sailed for Israel and destruction.

The next morning Shmuel received a cable from Israel to hold up the ship! In great dismay he cabled back that it was too late and suggested that the ship be contacted from Israel as he had no means of communication with her. Shmuel spent another three anxious and unhappy days before the arrival from Israel of Arieh Ben Eliezer who brought the welcome news that, after a meeting between the IZL and representatives of the Israel Government, the latter had asked that the ship be brought with all speed and had promised to help with the unloading arrangements. Atlas did not lay aside the burden of the world on his shoulders with greater relief than we cast off the stones from our hearts. We were all jubilant. We were now able to set about our preparations for returning to Israel, which we hoped to reach in time to welcome the ship on its arrival there.

There was to be a virtual exodus from Paris. Except for a skeleton staff, headed by Arieh Ben Eliezer, who would liquidate all IZL activities in Europe and close down the ramification of offices and organizations, everyone was leaving for Israel, for home. A special plane was chartered to take the 30-odd passengers.

We remained in Paris another week tying up the loose ends and waiting for the planes from Canada to arrive. When Shmuel declared that we would wait no longer and set a final date for our departure, two planes

147

arrived with a dramatic last-minute flourish, on the eve of our impending flight. Their ultimate fate was affected by the disaster of the Altalena. Instead of being flown to Israel as soon after our departure as possible, they were kept in France and the crews, whom Yechiel had with painstaking perseverance kept off the tiles and on the straight and narrow, were sent home. Eventually, the planes were handed over to the representatives of the Israel Government in France.

*　　*　　*　　*　　*

As we boarded the bus which was taking us to the airport the next day we got news that the Altalena had arrived safely off the coast of Israel. The news was supplemented by a vague report of shooting at the ship. This puzzled and worried us considerably. We tried to analyse the situation without any of the facts at our disposal and came to the following conclusion: It could not have been the Arabs who fired at the ship as there was a truce on; it could not have been the Israel forces who fired on the ship as she was arriving with the full knowledge and consent of the Government; therefore it must have been a pre-arranged and pre-conceived blind on the part of the Government to give the UN observers the impression that Israel was sticking strictly to the spirit of the truce even though a handful of "wild cats" were breaking it in the letter. This wishful thinking satisfied most of us who had neither the imagination nor the politcal acumen to foresee the tragedy in all its horror; but I could see that Shmuel was worried and was not prepared to accept this facile conclusion with the glib ease with which the more light-hearted amongst us accepted it.

Amongst our thirty fellow-passengers were Eliezer, returning after years of self-imposed exile to see whether he could find a place once more in a country of which his memories were black and bitter; Major Weiser, who had courageously defended the exploits of the IZL in the very teeth of the enemy—on the public platform in Hyde Park; and Konrad Bercovici, the well-known American author whose imagination had been fired by the deeds of these modern heroes of a modern bible.

Eliezer and I joked and laughed together about our fear of flying and decided to sit next to each other and be frightened together. We joked outwardly but our fears were real enough deep inside us. Mine are more superficial and are based on a primitive dislike of being hurtled into space without any obvious means of self-protection against the elements and against gravity. I have never feared the sea, even when we crossed the ocean in the midst of a war, with enemy submarines as thick and slippery as sharks, for the very childish, but nevertheless comforting, reason that I can swim and so feel that I have some chance of survival in the event of catastrophe. So, until I can fly, I shall nurse a secret fear of going in a plane.

Eliezer's fears are much deeper and are backed by weightier reasons. He was once involved in a plane crash and had a miraculous escape from death. Just as he suppressed his general fear complex and lived dangerously in spite of it, so did he suppress his fear of flying and travelled by air where anyone else might, with justification, have pandered a little to an understandable phobia and travelled by ship.

The plane was enough to strike terror into the hearts of the most hardy and intrepid travellers. In appearance it looked less than an aeroplane than anything I have ever seen and more like a truncated elephant than a truncated elephant itself, with its big, swollen belly, and little, piggy propellor eyes. It had originally been intended as a cargo plane and had none of the refinements usually found in a passenger plane. Its sides and ceiling were completely bare and resounded tinnily to our timid tappings. This lack of insulation and padding deprived us of any protection against the noise and vibration of the engines, so that we were deafened and dizzied by the devilish clang, our feet danced frenziedly on the agitated floor and our hands beat a crazy tattoo on the sides every time we absent-mindedly clutched at them to steady our rolling bodies. But there were seats, and even padded ones, to console us for the bare rigors of the journey.

We spent the night at Ajaccio in Corsica where the news of our coming had mysteriously preceded us. At the hotel, two members of the Haganah's overseas division awaited us and asked that we should not make ourselves conspicuous in Ajaccio and so perhaps draw attention to the fact that a group of Jews, of whom the majority were obviously of military age, was proceeding to Israel. We agreed readily, although most of us were returning residents and so entitled to travel to Israel, while the remainder had absolutely legal visitors' visas in passports of un-impeachable authenticity.

* * * * *

The next day we touched down at Haifa airport. We were welcomed by screaming banner headlines in the first newspaper which fell into our eager hands: "ALTALENA STILL BURNING! AVRAHAM STAFSKY DEAD." The blow was stunning. We could not and did not believe that

149

the Altalena, our ship, was burning off the shores of Tel Aviv and that Abrasha, the embodiment of the zest and joy of life, our beloved Abrasha, was dead. Nor could we understand why or how. The paper could not answer our questions. It merely gave the bald facts. The Altalena was still burning after being shelled and set on fire by shore-batteries, and Avraham Stafsky had died in hospital of the wounds he received when the ship was fired on from the shore by Israel forces.

We dared not ask any questions nor show any undue interest or agitation; for, if the Altalena were burning, then our comrades may all have been arrested too and we were reluctant to share that fate before we had an opportunity of finding out what had happened.

So we all maintained a stony calm behind which we were sick with worry and anxiety about the fate of the others on the ship. We stayed in the airport for hours waiting numbly and wearily for the customs officials to sort themselves out of the mess. The State of Israel had been in existence for only a month and any disorder and disorganization in the customs arrangements was understandable. In any other circumstances we would have forgiven them this. But we were embittered against a Government which could have killed Abrasha and fired the Altalena, and the chaos at the airport set a final seal to our disillusionment.

I felt deeply sorry for the newcomers in our party. We old Palestinians had experienced the hate of our brothers before. Our shock lay not so much in the recognition that fraternal hate existed, as in the fact that it should manifest itself at such a time and in such a manner. But they had come to Israel full of hope and idealism. They had come to visit the new state which they had helped create and to pay their respects to its Government which was not one of their own choice but was nevertheless the Government of Israel, and therefore pervaded by an aura of sanctity. They came to respect and revere and stayed to shudder and despise.

But most of all, I was sorry for Eliezer. He had left Palestine after an epoch of fratricidal brutality in which he had been one of the main victims. He returned to Israel hoping he would forget the horrors of the past and pick up the threads of his old life—and he found himself caught once more in the web of hate. During his first few days in Israel he lived in terror of being recognized by some of his former tormentors and of falling once more into their clutches. His fear was unreasonable—no one would have hurt him; but it was none-the-less understandable and pitiable. The

150

scars which had gradually healed during his years in Europe were brutally scorched and re-opened by the burning Altalena.

Besides those killed and wounded, five so-called ring-leaders were arrested. They were Benyamin, Yaacov Meridor and Amitsur who had supervised the off-loading, and Hillel Kook and Moshe Hasson, who had merely come to welcome the ship and its passengers.

In Tel Aviv we learned that, besides Stavsky, another seventeen young men had been killed by the bullets of the Palmach, some of them in the sea as they tried to escape from the burning hulk. Amongst those killed were two of the boys from Cuba, the boys who had begged and pleaded to be given a last-minute chance to keep their appointment with death. We learned, too, that Avraham Stavsky had died—not from the wound in his leg or the subsequent loss of blood, but from a broken heart. That stout heart refused to go on beating in a world where brother murdered brother in cold blood, where wounded men were shot at in the water, not by a cruel, insensate enemy, but by their fellow-citizens.

It is futile now to go into all the arguments, the insinuations and the libels which have raged about the tragedy of the Altalena and will continue to do so for many years to come. But two facts stand out starkly and nakedly: even if the Israel Government were correct in their highly imaginative argument that the IZL had acted illegally or even that they were preparing a revolution, there was absolutely nothing to prevent them from helping to unload the Altalena, confiscating all the arms and, if necessary, arresting all the leaders of the IZL who were in any case known to them personally. Instead of doing this, they set brother to murder brother. And then, as a crowning infamy, they fired on a ship loaded with ammunition which, but for the presence of mind of the captain, could have exploded and blown up the whole Tel Aviv front, besides shattering to smithereens the men and women in the ship—and they fired on this ship as it flew the white flag of surrender and continued to fire at the small boats which carried the wounded away from the blazing powder magazine.

For both these acts of stupid brutality the members of the Provisional Government of the State of Israel will one day have to answer to their own consciences even if the people, whose memories are notoriously short-lived, should never call them to answer in more formal fashion.

CHAPTER XII

THE ARMY OF THE IZL

As soon as we had recovered somewhat from the shock of the Altalena, I went to look for Joe. He was staying at the Savoy Hotel on the Tel Aviv sea-front, together with the crew of the ship. With Benyamin interned in an Israeli prison, Joe felt lost and lonely. In addition, he was terribly bitter, with a bitterness that encompassed everybody—both Ben Gurion and Begin, both humanity in general and the Jews in particular. He hated the world with a mature, adult bitterness—not the kind that would dissipate itself under the soothing hands of time, but the searing kind which leaves everlasting scars, and in its heat anneals the character into a hard and vitreous substance. I could not find words of explanation or comfort for him, and eagerly grasped at the suggestion which he himself put forward—that he should go to Jerusalem and join the IZL forces there and, perhaps, get rid of some of the poison in his system through the sweat of mental and physical activity. This seemed a better idea than sitting in the Savoy Hotel under the shadow of the hulk of the Altalena, where he had time and opportunity to brood and envelope himself still further in his morass of gloom and depression.

Joe had two other courses open to him: he could return to Amerca, as did Monroe Fein and many others of the crew, or he could join the Israeli Army. He did not even consider the first as he felt, despite his bitterness, that he had come to do a job and he did not wish to leave before he had finished it. As for the second course—but here it is necessary to digress a little and explain how this came to be an alternative as opposed to joining the IZL in Jerusalem.

When the State of Israel was declared on the eve of May 15th, Jerusalem was not included in its boundaries. Under the Partition scheme, it was to be an international city. So cut-off and besieged Jerusalem, while it remained attached by sentimental and practical ties to the main body of the State, was nevertheless legally an autonomous city not bound by the laws of the new state nor subject to its Government. When Begin, therefore, declared the dissolution of the IZL in Israel and its absorption into the Israeli Army, the IZL in Jerusalem was perforce excluded and

152

continued to exist as an independent organization, operating in conjunction with the Haganah against the Arabs. Its ranks were considerably swelled by the cream of the ex-IZL forces in Israel whose gorge rose up at the thought of serving under Ben Gurion's administration after the Altalena incident. Many of them walked the fifty miles between Tel Aviv and Jerusalem over the bare crags of the Judean hills in order to continue the fight against the Arabs amongst friends and comrades.

Joe, for this reason and even more so because the thought of liberating Jerusalem had captured his imagination, chose to fight with the IZL in Jerusalem rather than join the Israel Forces in Tel Aviv. Perhaps he would have been wiser to choose the latter or return to Americta. Those who believe in the inexorable inevitability of Fate will say it would have made no difference to his ultimate destiny. We are, unfortunately, never given the chance of testing the fallibility or otherwise of these theories.

* * * * *

Menachem Begin was a completely broken man after the Altalena incident. He came to stay with us in Ramat Gan for a few days to re-cuperate in the quiet, unfevered atmosphere. In all the time I had known him in the days of the underground, I had seen him worried and dis-tracted, but never depressed and hopeless. During this crucial period in his life he touched the very depths of depression and only his natural resilience and buoyancy bore him back to the surface of the swirling, dark pool of horror and despair.

During this visit, Arthur Koestler came to see Begin. He obviously thought he was at the Begin home, not at ours, and I had some little difficulty in persuading him that I was not Ala Begin. I suspect that he went away with the definite impression that we were still suffering from a hang-over from the conspiracy days and had deliberately mixed ourselves up in order to confuse him.

That we really were suffering from a carry-over, rather than a hang-over, from the underground days was borne home rather forcibly to us by an incident during Koestler's visit. We were having tea out in the garden and he was holding forth rather loudly and aggressively on his theories about the Latinizing of the Hebrew script and the introduction of classics into the school curriculum. In order to emphasize a point he was making he banged on the table and said in loud emphatic tones: "I tell you, *Begin* . . ." A shocked silence fell over the assembled company and each one swivelled his eyes surreptitiously round to see if any of the

153

neighbors had heard the forbidden name. So strong were the taboos and restrictions of our conspiratorial days that even after the British had left the country we were still horrified at the broadcasting of the name and identity of their erst-while arch-enemy. A visible, communal sigh of relief quivered through all of us as we realized that our fears were completely anachronistic.

As Shmuel was away most of the day, I kept Begin company. We talked together a great deal but never about the tragedy which was foremost in our minds. I threw out a half-baked idea that he should go to Jerusalem where the IZL still existed and where the young men in charge were crying out for guidance and leadership in a task which was as much political as military and for which they did not feel qualified, particularly in view of the highly delicate and tense internal situation which had arisen out of the Altalena tragedy. I am sure that Begin had considered this possibility too but in the exigencies of the moment had shelved it. When I brought it up again, it began germinating and maturing in his brain and eventually emerged as a full-fledged plan. When he propounded it before his erstwhile colleagues in the IZL High Command, they opposed it vehemently on the ground that he was needed in Tel Aviv to straighten out the post-Altalena confusion and to lay the foundations for the formation of a political party from the ex-adherents of the IZL. Begin saw the justice of these arguments and proposed, instead, that Shmuel take over the leadership in Jerusalem and become the last of the Commanders of the IZL. This alternative was readily accepted as being suitable from all points of view, not the least of which was the fact that Shmuel was by heart and inclination a Jerusalemite and that he was still virtually a Jerusalem resident on temporary loan to Tel Aviv.

Shmuel eagerly agreed to the suggestion and I started packing again— for both of us. I had to overcome some initial resistance on his part to my accompanying him—resistance which was more formal than actual as there really was no doubt in either of our minds that I would go with him to Jerusalem—in spite of the shortages of food and water and in spite of the fact that the truce was due to end in a few days' time. We took it for granted that where he went, I went. Some of our friends thought it a bit scatterbrained of him to take me, but my mother, who arrived from Haifa just in time to greet us on our return from Paris and bid us farewell before our trip to Jerusalem, agreed that I must accompany Shmuel on what she considered another of our mad, death-seeking schemes. "If you must be crazy," she said, "then at least be crazy together." With that maternal blessing we completed our preparations.

* * * * *

Before describing our journey to Jerusalem it is necessary to depict, in brief, the background of the situation in the city before the truce. Abdullah's Arab Legion had occupied Latrun on the main highway, thus preventing any passage of traffic between the capital and the coast. At the same time, they cut off the city's water-supply by capturing the pumping station at Ras-el-Ein. On the south, the city was cut off by the armies of the Arab States—the Iraqis, the Egyptians and the Arab Legion.

Besieged Jerusalem tightened her belt. All the food-stores available in the city were collected and rationed out daily. The city's water wells were sealed to the public and tapped only by the local authorities, who distributed the water at the rate of a few cupsful per head per day.

The position of the city became desperate. The food stocks were petering out, the wells were drying up, and the population was subjected to day and night shelling from the heavy mortars of the surrounding Arab armies. The Old City fell, but the New City held on tenaciously. Then, just as the desperate population were reaching the end of their tether, manna fell from the heavens—food supplies and reinforcements reached the city from the coast. They had come over the mountains by way of a road built by the willing hands of thousands of soldiers and civilians—a new Burma Road, built by Jews in emulation of the inspiring example set by the Chinese.

The first convoy to break the siege was greeted by wild scenes of enthusiasm. Men and women wept with relief. Children shouted with joy when they saw real chocolates and knew they had no longer to exist on beans every day in every possible way.

But, even then, Jerusalem's troubles were by no means over. There was still no water, though new pipes parallel to the "Burma Road" were being feverishly laid. There was still no electricity and, worst of all, the Arabs still all but surrounded the city and hurled death into it every hour of the day and night. Then came the truce and this danger was temporarily removed.

With the truce, thousands of Jerusalem residents, who were not required for fighting or defence, packed their belongings, took their children and fled from this city of death to the coastal area—to Tel Aviv, to Haifa, to the settlements, to wherever they had friends and relatives, who could give them a roof, a bath and fatten up their children again. The "Burma Road" hummed with activity.

But these were the minority. The bulk of the civilian population remained in the city, among them those who had been born there, who had their roots there and were so physically and emotionally bound to the city that they could not dream of existence anywhere else. They did not blame those who left. The months of horror had impaired the physical health and nerves of many; the economy of the city was completely ruined, and there was very little from which to make a living. These two factors were sufficient to justify the exodus of those who did leave, but even they did not frighten the stalwarts of Old Jerusalem into seeking out the comforts of the "New Jerusalem" of Tel Aviv.

As the truce period drew to a close the stream of traffic on the Burma Road was reversed. Food supplies and reinforcements poured into the city from the coast together with returning residents who had rested for a while and were hurrying back to arrive in the city before all civilian transport was stopped.

* * * * *

Any non-resident of Jerusalem had to get a permit from the authorities to travel to the city. Soldiers travelled on army permits, civilians on permits from the Jewish Agency. Shmuel was very dubious about the possibility of my getting such a permit and warned me that he might have to leave me behind after all. But I was not easily put off by stories of permits. I went to the office of the Jewish Agency and asked for a permit as a returning resident, which was, after all, almost true: we had been living away from Jerusalem only some twenty months. The clerk informed me that I did not need a permit any longer—all I required was a voucher from the bus company to say that I had been granted a seat on a bus and I could then travel under the collective permit carried by the bus-driver. There were not many people going off to Jerusalem to be in the war, and I got my voucher easily. In fact, I got one for Shmuel too and had a little legitimate gloat over people who exaggerate the difficulties of a situation.

We arrived at the bus station looking like modern counterparts of the Lithuanian Jews who emigrated to South Africa in my parents' time. In deference to our age of progress we had, instead of the barrels of herrings, zip-bags full of tinned foods, and, instead of the feather mattresses, we had

156

rugs and cushions. Motye, the grocer, turned out all his precious food-stores so that we should not go hungry in Jerusalem. He refused to take payment, saying we could pay him when (I could almost hear him adding inwardly "and if") we returned.

My mother came to the bus-station to see us off. She ought to have been used to our continual comings and goings and to what she considered our crazy escapades. But she was not. Her heart still failed her every time she thought we were in danger and she looked very sad and forlorn as she waved us on our way, quite convinced that this time we had gone, finally, never to return.

The first part of the journey was on an old road through Rehoboth, one of the older Jewish villages. This road needed repairing badly, but in comparison with what was to come it was as smooth as a billiard table. Beyond Rehovoth, the road degenerated into a cart-track, and this still was not the famous Burma Road. At last we reached the latter. What had been originally a rough track dynamited and hewn out of the rocky hills had, with the passage of weeks and pressure of heavy traffic, become a veritable switch-back of holes, bumps and hillocks. To add to the dis-comfort of travelling, the dust rose in thick layers every time the wheels of the bus dislodged it from its resting place in the choked pores of the sun-baked earth. We travelled so slowly that we caused no disturbances of air by our velocity and so got no benefit from artificially created wind. After a particularly bad patch I looked at Shmuel who was the only passenger in the bus with an uncovered head. He had gone completely grey! It is true that the journey had been anything but comfortable and at times, when the descents had been particularly steep, had even been fraught with danger, but not to such an extent as to turn one's hair grey. It took me quite a few seconds to realise that it was dust and not pigmentation which had turned Shmuel from brown-haired youthfulness to grey-haired distinction.

But if our discomfort was acute it was as nothing compared with that of the toiling, sweating men who were laying the pipes which were to bring blessed water to parched Jerusalem. It was already July, when the heat of summer approaches its peak. There was not a breath of wind to fan the blazing atmosphere, and in all those miles and miles of blistering rock and hill there was not a tree to give some temporary shelter and shade to those who toiled beneath the broiling sun. These men, stripped to the waist, blackened and shrivelled by the rays of the sun, their only

157

protection the inadequate and varied head-coverings which they wore, are the real, unsung heroes of the liberation of Jerusalem.

It always irritates me considerably to hear some of my chauvinistic friends say that "only the Jews could have built the 'Burma Road' and laid the pipe-lines." The very nick-name which that road earned, and I say "earned" advisedly, belies the truth of this boastful statement. (It is perhaps a good deal nearer the truth to say that only the Chinese could have built the real Burma Road.) But whether others could have carried out the same back- and heart-breaking task or not, does not detract from the magnitude of that task nor from the courage, perseverance and endurance of those who fulfilled it.

Another group of people who deserve the unstinted praise of the people of Jerusalem are the bus and lorry drivers who, during the days of the siege, risked, and lost, their lives to break through to the city with supplies; and, during the days of the truce, strained every nerve and muscle in their bodies to control their leaping, bucking vehicles up steep and rocky inclines and down still steeper and slippery declines on the improvised mountain road to Jerusalem.

Just before the Burma Road joined the partly-asphalted strip connecting it to the old Jerusalem highway, there was a particularly treacherous decline. All the passengers alighted from the bus and walked the short distance, leaving the bus-driver to negotiate the slope and the sharp V-bend without being hampered by the additional responsibility of thirty human beings who would plunge with him to death over the edge of the precipice should he misjudge his distances by so much as a few inches. The bus groaned and shivered down the slope, in first gear, over the wire netting providently placed there to obviate any slithering, and reached the level part of the road successfully; but the effort proved too much for her already failing strength. With a good deal of coaxing and petting she crawled as far as the old Jerusalem highway at Bab-el-Wad and then gave up the ghost completely.

As on our previous journey to Jerusalem four months previously, we found ourselves stranded at Bab-el-Wad, but this time the circumstances were much more pleasant. Israel forces had cleared the area of Arabs, whose nearest elements were a couple of kilometres away. We could get out and stretch our legs without fear of the sniper's bullet. When the sun drove us back to the bus we could sit there with windows wide open to catch what little breeze there was.

158

A few hundred yards behind us was the barbed-wire entanglement marking the beginning of the part of the road controlled by the Arab Legion. Besides the barricade stood a UN sentry-box. It flew the blue insignia on the white background which symbolised universal peace and goodwill for all peoples on earth—a symbol whose sanctity was belied by the very barbed-wire barricade over which it floated.

As we waited to be rescued by some means or other, a bus coming from Jerusalem pulled up alongside us while its driver alighted to talk to ours. Inside the bus were the horrible remnants of what had been handsome, glowing young men and women. They were being taken to Tel Aviv for plastic operations which could not be performed in Jerusalem. Many of them had badly scorched faces, others had mutilating scars and staring empty eye-sockets. One in particular turned me sick and nauseous with horror. The lower part of his face, where once he had had a chin, was nothing but a pulpy mess.

This bus-load of human misery injected an icy deluge into the general buoyancy and gaiety which had prevailed amongst the passengers. Many began to fret and chafe at the delay and to urge the driver to "do something."

He, as he could not repair his bus without the necessary spare parts, had sunk into lethargic repose—and remained completely unperturbed. The hard core of grumblers grew more and more irritated and exasperated. We stood on the road for an hour before the first sign of traffic to Jerusalem appeared. It was an army jeep. Our driver bestirred himself sufficiently to give the driver of the jeep a note to the bus-garage asking them to send out another bus or a mechanic with the necessary spare parts, and fell once more into a coma, completely oblivious to the muttering and scowling of his restless sun-baked passengers. Another two hours passed before a bus arrived from Jerusalem to take the passengers and tow the patient. Shmuel and I rode in our old bus, both to keep the driver company and because we had formed quite a sentimental attachment to the stout-hearted broken-down old lady.

When we reached Abu Ghosh, an Arab village near Jerusalem which had remained friendly to the Jews throughout the war, I received a momentary shock at seeing Arabs standing openly on the road and selling their fruit and vegetables to passing Jews. I had become attuned over a period of months to thinking of Arabs as murderous and vicious purveyors of death and had to do some quick mental re-orientation to conceive of

159

them as peaceful vendors of the fruits of life. Our buses stopped and many of the passengers poured out to make last-minute purchases of fresh vegetables and fruits from the Arabs.

We arrived in Jerusalem as the sun was setting, eight hours after leaving Tel Aviv which is thirty miles away as the crow flies. The city looked dead and desolate but surprisingly undamaged, except for Ben Yehuda Street which had been practically destroyed by a load of explosives planted by the British, and for the various manifestations of the anti-British activities of the IZL which still gaped widely to the skies. The Arab shelling appeared to have caused very little external damage to the solidly-built stone buildings. This first, superficial impression was quickly dissipated when we arrived at the old IZL Headquarters (where we had drunk the toast to the newly-arrived Sten-guns four months previously) to meet Raanan. Here the gaping holes in the roof and the havoc in the courtyard gave the lie to the untouched and unruffled exterior of the building.

Shmuel immediately plunged into the maze of troubles and difficulties the IZL were experiencing in Jerusalem. So that I should not, meanwhile, have to sit on our suitcases in the street, we took a room at the Eden Hotel until such time as Shmuel could take off a few minutes from his more pressing worries to think about where we were going to live. The proprietor of the hotel welcomed us effusively. His welcome was probably all the more cordial for the fact that in his large and comfortable hostelry built to house nearly a hundred guests there were, besides us, exactly three others: Konrad Bercovici and Major Weiser who had arrived by jeep a few days before us, and Shoshana Raziel who had returned to her home in Jerusalem only to find it evacuated because of its uncomfortable proximity to the Arab front lines and her family scattered in the homes of relatives and friends. Even if we did not make much difference to the adverse balancing of his budget, we did at least serve to swell the crowd and provide more company for him, his wife, and the two solitary remaining waiters.

As night fell, there was not a soul in the dark streets. With just eighteen hours to go before the end of the truce, the population was bracing itself for the renewal of the war and for the horror of day-and-night shelling. In their candle-lit homes they sorted out their stocks of food in preparation for a self-imposed house-arrest as soon as death started raining down in the exposed streets.

160

The next morning, that was Friday the 9th of July, Shmuel went off early to hold councils of war with the IZL officers, while Shoshanah appointed herself temporary guide and mentor to Bercovici, Weiser and me, and took us on a tour of inspection of the city.

To say that the city exuded a somewhat unpleasant aroma would be a euphemism. Everywhere were heaps of refuse which had been overlooked in the general confusion and disintegration of public services. As soon as one entered a house, one was assailed by the smell of Lysol or Dettol which was still not quite powerful enough to camouflage or drown the insidious odor of latrines. That "chemicalised" smell of latrines epitomised for me the daily drudgery and discomfort of life in Jerusalem, and since then I have an illogical, instinctive abhorrence of the smell of all disinfectants.

The people were all nervous and on edge. The anticipation of the resumption of the war was a good deal worse than the actual fact. Rumors and contradictory stories were the order of the day. At first the Arabs had agreed to the extension of the truce, then they had not. Then UN had declared that they would enforce an extension, then they had not. Hopes soared aloft, then fell sickeningly. Ordinarily this swift transition from the high plateau of hope to the valley of despair produces demoralization. But here this was not so. Those civilians who had remained in Jerusalem had done so deliberately, with their eyes open. They had not been trapped there inadvertently and by the misfortunes of war, as in the first Battle of Jerusalem. They deliberately chose to share the fate of their city. But, nevertheless, no one could blame them if they hoped for a last-minute release, while at the same time preparing themselves for the worst with courage and steadfastness.

The four of us worked our way through the maze of barricades and barbed wire, circumvented road-blocks, making long diversions around military enclaves in the heart of the city, until we arrived at Katamon. Here the dreary piles of rubble, scattered liberally all over the place, were evidence of the ferocity of the fighting. But what most excited and impressed us was that here was the Empire of the IZL.

Here soldiers of the IZL lived, cared for by IZL medical personnel, disciplined by IZL officers and Military Police, respected by the whole community and cooperating, on an equal footing, with the Haganah. After the horrors of the Altalena, this was a blessed sight to our weary, embittered eyes. To us, mere spectators in the drama of history, this was a magnificent spectacle, but to Shmuel it meant the burden of a terrific responsibility. It meant many hundreds of people whose lives were in his hands: who had to be deployed in battle, who had to be armed, fed, clothed and housed. It meant a terrific financial strain on an organization which had not the monetary backing of World Jewry for twenty years, as the Haganah had had. The maintenance of this Army in Jerusalem eventually drained the reserves of the young Herut Party in Tel Aviv (the political party formed by members of the disbanded IZL) and prevented it from building itself up on the sound economic lines so essential for the success of any political party in Israel.

At twelve noon that day the truce ended and the first shells fell on the New City of Jerusalem. The streets were practically deserted except for soldiers and army vehicles, people scurrying hurriedly to finish their essential business and then to seek the safety of their stone-walled houses, and the four "tourists"—Bercovici, Weiser, Shoshanah and I, who continued our unofficial tour of inspection.

Undoubtedly, the fact that the civilian population stayed indoors as much as possible tended to keep casualties down to a minimum. There were comparatively few Jerusalem civilians killed during the eight days of the second round of the war, in spite of the frequent heavy bombardments and almost continuous sniping.

Those who have experienced both bombing from the air and shelling claim that the latter is a good deal more nerve-wracking by virtue of its unpredictability. I, too, have experienced both, but I confess I would be hard put to choose between death from a bomb or death by shelling. As for the comparative difference in the effect on one's nerves—that too is difficult for me to gauge. The air raids which I experienced were during the war in London when all the furies of Hell seemed to have broken loose. The bombs took the shape of screaming bombs, fire-bombs, blockbusters, flying-bombs and aerial rockets—in short, every diabolical form calculated to shatter the human-being psychologically, mentally and physically. The shelling of Jerusalem was on a comparatively small scale and the shells were rarely of a sufficient calibre to penetrate well-constructed buildings. On the occasions when I was out in the open during an air-raid in London, I did not like the experience at all, just as I did not like seeing a shell fall a few yards ahead of me in Jerusalem. But indoors, I took the air-raids in London with philosophical fatalism, as I did the shelling in Jerusalem. On the one and only occasion when I was

162

shot at by a sniper and felt the bullet whistle through my hair and strike a wall at my side with a sickening thud, I found it rather an unnerving experience, but I was assured by my veteran friends that one could get used even to that. Fortunately, I did not have to, Bercovici had a similar experience and I was grateful to learn that he too felt his stomach keel over and his knees sag weakly.

As for Shmuel, he always maintained so calm and dispassionate a front that it is difficult to know his reactions. He had two very narrow escapes. On one occasion he was in a car with Major Weiser when a shell fell directly behind them, killing a young man standing next to the car. Weiser, who was a seasoned campaigner, was considerably shaken, so I presume that Shmuel was not as unruffled inside as he appeared to be outside. On another occasion he was just stepping into his car outside the GHQ in Katamon when a shell fell on the pavement a few yards away from him.

The war-experienced Jerusalemites conceived of all manner of ingenious devices for confounding the snipers. I had the opportunity of seeing one of the most brilliant of these when we drove Shoshanah to her home to collect a few of her personal belongings. Her flat was in a district which faced the notorious Sheik Jarrakh suburb, from where the Arabs had ambushed the convoy to Mount Scopus. As pedestrians crossed the street, they afforded the snipers across the narrow valley a wonderful target. In order to obviate this, the dwellers in that neighborhood had hung up mammoth curtains made of sack-cloth across the exposed streets. This enabled them to run across in safety unless by some very unfortunate chance they were hit by a sniper trying out his luck in a blind, targetless shot.

After two days of "sight-seeing" and visiting all our old friends, I decided it was time I did some useful and constructive work. I could not seriously offer my services as a soldier, so, instead, I volunteered for work in the hospital.

The IZL women volunteers had rigged up a first-rate little hospital with about forty beds in a villa which had previously been occupied by General Barker, one of the best-hated GOC's of many who were sent out by the British to wipe out the "terrorists." This was a piquant piece of poetic justice which I was always at great pains to point out to visitors to the hospital.

In this hospital we received all our wounded who had been through

Hadassah or one of the other hospitals, been X-rayed, operated on when necessary and pronounced out of danger. In this way we made more beds available for urgent cases and helped, to some small extent, to narrow the dangerous gap between the hospital accommodation available and the thousands who needed it. It must be remembered that the large, modern Hadassah hospital on Mount Scopus had had to be evacuated and temporary make-shift premises had been hastily equipped in town. Even in normal circumstances this disorganization would have caused a shortage of beds. How much more, therefore, was this so when, in addition to ordinary cases of sickness, there were hundreds of wounded soldiers and civilians.

Soon after the recommencement of the war, Shmuel had visited the IZL wounded in the Hadassah Hospital and I had accompanied him. I had seen films of emergency war hospitals from the days of the Crimean War to modern times and had been warned by our friends of what to expect; yet, nevertheless, I was shocked and sickened when confronted by grim reality. As so often happens in moments of great stress it was something quite trivial which produced the greatest effect. I stood the sight of doctors and nurses stumbling over beds which filled the passageways in the wards, which filled the corridors and the verandas; I stood the sight of bloody, oozing bandages; I bore with difficulty the groans and cries from the chock-filled wards, but what eventually broke my nerve and sent me scurrying out for air was the shock of seeing men and women in the same ward. This departure from all accepted practice suddenly brought home to me the cruel and crucial difficulties under which the sick and wounded and their medical attendants existed.

My work in the IZL hospital was of a very elementary nature. My only qualifications were a First-Aid Certificate and a Home Nursing Certificate, both of which I had received in South Africa ten years previously, plus enthusiasm and willingness. I was allowed to draw only on the two latter qualifications. In the course of time I became an excellent meal-server, an even more excellent bed-maker and I could even remove a bed-pan without immediately wanting to vomit. I took temperatures with the skill of an expert and gave sleeping-pills as if I had been born to it. In fact, my patients always insisted that they found my pills more effective than those they received from the other nurses. This was probably due to the fact that they were nothing more than bread-pills, especially set aside for my administration by Yael, the head-nurse, to ensure that I did not, inadvertently, poison some of the patients. Such was my enthusiasm and willingness that Yael even let me help her with the dressings as soon as I got over feeling sick every time I saw an exposed wound. But when she tried to teach me to give injections my enthusiasm disappeared. The very sight of the quivering flesh waiting for the needle to be plunged in by the ruthless hand sent cold shivers down my spine. Nevertheless, under Yael's encouragement, and because I was still willing, I did try once to give an injection. My target was a particularly well-covered behind, which could not suffer any very great ill-effects even from my amateurish efforts. I tried once, and merely pricked my victim. Yael exhorted me to put some force into it, so I closed my eyes and plunged the needle in. To my horror, the patient let out a blood-curdling yell. This completely unnerved me and I fled from the room, leaving Yael to finish off the gruesome task of injecting the liquid from the syringe. In spite of the fact that she assured me I had done an excellent job and that that particular patient always yelled, I would never again touch an hypodermic syringe.

I always tried to be cheerful, patient and kind according to the tenets of the text-books, but I soon discovered why hospital nurses have the reputation of being hard-hearted, cruel monsters. This is sheer self-protection against the willfullness, irritating egotism, bad temper and, in fact, hard-heartedness and cruelty of their patients. Very sick people are no trouble at all. The constant attention which they need, but never demand, is given gladly and willingly, with unselfish devotion, by the nurses. But convalescent patients are the bane and detestation of every nurse's life, and our patients were mostly convalescent or near-convalescent. The number of times a day I ran up and down the stairs bringing glasses of water, administering phoney headache pills, washing fruit, tightening loose bandages and giving assurances that the doctor would most certainly come that day, were legion. By the end of the day my legs ached, my back ached and my spirits were dangerously near to breaking-point. I made a solemn vow there and then that if I should ever have the misfortune to be hospitalized, I would lie quietly reading a book, I would wait my turn to be fed and washed patiently and not clamor for preference and, above all, I would never criticize the nurses or accuse them of neglect.

* * * *

Two days after the recommencement of the war, Shmuel and I went to stay with Raanan, the Jerusalem Regional Commander of the IZL prior to Shmuel's arrival, and now, in effect, Chief of Staff. This was more convenient for Shmuel who spent a good deal of time at Raanan's flat in any case, and a good deal more in keeping with austerity conditions in Jerusalem in general and in the IZL in particular.

Shmuel was in the throes of solving the problem of the five British officials of the Jerusalem Electric Corporation who had been arrested by the IZL on suspicion of spying for the Arabs. Due to the inexperience of the intelligence officer, there was not sufficient evidence in the hands of the IZL to convict them in any court of law. The IZL Intelligence officers maintained, however, that the Haganah had enough additional evidence to convict the five in a fair trial. Shmuel studied all the evidence very carefully, including a confession of guilt from one of the five. He came to the conclusion that the IZL as such could not put the five on trial with the evidence in their possession.

Meanwhile the British government was demanding the release of the five men and Ben Gurion and his government went into their usual hysterical panic when confronted by an "international situation" and demanded, through the Military Governor of Jerusalem, Dr. Bernard Joseph, that the five be handed over to them. In their hysteria, they instructed Dr. Joseph to take the men by force, if necessary.

There were two courses open to Shmuel: to keep the five and try to collect additional evidence, or to hand them over to the Haganah. He inclined to the second course because, with the vision of the Altalena still vividly before him, he did not want to risk another blood-bath which would probably on this occasion have been reciprocal. But he hesitated about taking it because he did not trust the Haganah and feared they would not bring the five to trial. So he directed negotiations with Dr. Joseph until the latter declared publicly that if the five British were handed over to him he guaranteed they would be brought to trial and, presumably, that the Haganah would introduce the evidence in their possession to complete the link.

This public statement must have earned Dr. Joseph a literal drubbing-down and a figurative kick-in-the-pants from Ben Gurion who was, in consequence of it, landed with the responsibility of bringing the five to trial. This was a situation which appealed irresistibly to Shmuel's sense of the ridiculous. Certain now that, whatever happened, the five would be out of mischief, he ceremoniously handed them over to the Haganah who, in turn, took them to Tel Aviv and delivered them, in the form of a quintuple headache, to Mr. Ben Gurion.

Two of them were immediately released on the grounds of insufficient evidence. Three were brought to trial in a very amateurish fashion. Of these, two were acquitted and the third, Sylvester, was found guilty and sentenced to seven years imprisonment.

This sentence had its repercussions in Britain where a young man by the name of Monty Harris was on trial for being in possession of explosives, ostensibly for purposes connected with Israel. Soon after Sylvester was sentenced, Harris too was found guilty and given the inordinately heavy sentence of seven years. The similarity between the two sentences was, of course, strictly coincidental.

Sylvester's conviction was subsequently squashed by the Court of Appeal, who found insufficient evidence, and the last of the five British was released and returned to England, thus ending an episode which was typically Israeli in its bathos.

*   *   *   *

Joe came to visit us several times. He was not happy in Jerusalem either. His ignorance of Hebrew and of local conditions militated against his being given an administrative job, and yet his military qualifications entitled him to something more than a soldier in the line. I saw that he was unhappy at having to live once more in barracks and suggested to Shmuel, in my naive ignorance, that we invite him to come and stay with us. Shmuel pointed out patiently that he was the Commander of the IZL and Joe was a soldier; that he could not make any exceptions to the military regulations because Joe was a friend of ours, that there would be a lot of murmuring if Joe was taken out of the barracks and sent to live with the Commander. I saw the justice of his arguments and, in any case, I am sure that Joe himself would never have accepted any preferential treatment. At his own request, however, he was transferred to a mortar unit where his job was to be that of observer and liaison between the artillery and the infantry.

Except for the constant shelling and sniping from both sides, there was very little martial activity during the first three days of the final phase of fighting. Late at night we could hear the patrols going out, singing. From the songs we knew just exactly who they were—Haganah, IZL or the LHI. Each had their own distinctive tunes and regarded it as a point of honor not to sing those of the rival organisation.

167

This operetta, with loud accompaniment from the rival mortars, came to an end on the night of Tuesday, 13th July, when combined forces of the IZL and Haganah attacked and captured the Arab village of Malcha, about two miles to the southwest of Jerusalem. The IZL forces were led by Yishai, who had led the successful attack on Yehudieh. On Thursday, through some mistake on the part of the Haganah, the mortars supporting the IZL flank were withdrawn without the knowledge of the IZL Commander. The Arabs saw their opportunity, took it and launched a counter-attack which was beaten off after severe fighting and the loss of 22 IZL men killed and a number wounded. Amongst those killed were five boys who had come on the Altalena.

That day the Haganah Commander, after being pressed in vain by the IZL from the very first day of the war to launch a joint attack against the Old City, finally declared that they were ready to put into operation the plan of attack which had been drawn up jointly by them, the IZL Command and the Command of the LHI. The attack would be launched the next evening, the last before the second truce already ordered by the UN. It was already late in the day and many of their front-line soldiers were relieved at Macha only on the Friday afternoon, but the IZL Command worked like beavers to have everything in train by zero hour. They hoped that by means of a lightning attack at three points, the Old City could be occupied and held before the declaration of the truce.

The attack was due to start at 10 p.m. on Friday, the 16th July, seven and a half hours before the beginning of the new truce. The Arabs, either aware of what was afoot or determined to have a last fling, had started shelling the New City at dusk with a ferocity hitherto unparalleled. The Jewish mortars took up the challenge and all the furies of Hell were loosed. The din was terrific and even the solid Jerusalem buildings trembled and shook as the ground heaved with the impact of countless shells and the very air moaned and shuddered each time a cruel shaft pierced and parted it in screaming ecstasy.

The night was made all the more hideous by the terrible cries of one of our neighbors whose husband, missing after the attack on Malcha, had been found that afternoon in a gulley, killed by a shell.

Raanan's wife and I had the unenviable woman's task of merely sitting and waiting for news, which we got from Shmuel who was in constant contact by phone and messengers with the IZL staff. As zero-hour approached we heard a terrific explosion which we took to be the blowing

168

we very soon learned that this was the first of a long list of misfortunes up of the Old City gates as per plan and the initiation of the attack. But which foredoomed the success of the attack from the start. A shell had fallen on a LHI truck loaded with ammunition and had blown it sky-high, taking its toll of human lives too. Ten o'clock came and went, eleven o'clock came and went and the attack did not start. Shmuel grew more and more worried. Messengers came with news that the LHI still were not ready, that the Haganah were not ready. Meanwhile the precious hours slipped by and with their passing the chances of capturing the Old City before dawn grew more and more slender. At last, at three in the morning, both the Haganah and LHI informed the waiting IZL officers that they were ready to attack.

The plan called for the simultaneous blowing-up of three of the Old City's gates, one by each of the three attacking groups, and a three-pronged advance. The IZL blew up their gate without any difficulty and within a short time were fighting within the precincts of the Old City itself. But the Haganah and the LHI through some miscalculation of the amount of explosives necessary to do the job, failed to blow up their gates. The small IZL forces, which had already made a considerable bridgehead, were thus left without any protection on their flanks due to the miscarriage of the plan of the campaign. When, consequently, the truce came into force at 5:30 a.m. and the Haganah Command, which had the over-riding voice in all joint operations, gave them the order to retire, they had no alternative but to do so, and the Old City remained in the hands of Abdullah's Arab Legion.

All this I subsequently heard from Shmuel, as I went to bed shortly before three. Shmuel had the unpleasant task of breaking some other news to me: Joe had been killed! I behaved very badly when he told me of it as gently as he could. At first, I refused to believe that it could be true. How was it possible that a man who had survived the horrible war against the Japanese, could have been killed in what was a dolls' war in comparison When Shmuel dolefully insisted that it was not only possible, but that i had really happened, I turned upon him and berated him for having sen. Joe to his death. This was a cruel and unjust accusation made in the bitter-ness and despair of the moment. In spite of his deep hurt, Shmuel realised that I spoke in the wildness of sorrow and never felt any resentment that I, of all people, should so have added to his burden of grief and responsibility: He was not the first officer to be arraigned by the bereaved

169

friends and loved ones of those soldiers whom he had sent into battle; nor will he be the last, unless, by some miraculous mystical power, mankind should be persuaded that there are other ways of settling differences than by pulverizing one's opponents.

* * * * *

On Saturday, the 17th July, the official war came to an end in Jerusalem. People emerged from their homes into the bright sunshine, the laughter of the children rang out again in the streets, and through the whole city ran a tremor of relief.

But the pall of smoke and dust still hovered in the air—symbols of the destruction which had rained down in the night. And to the Jerusalem-smell of latrines and disinfectants was added another, sickly-sweet—the smell of death seeping out from the as-yet unburied bodies of the city's heroes and victims. The lack of water and the shortage of ice combined to bring home forcibly the horror and sordidity of man's continual strife against man. That smell of death pervaded the whole city. When it was not an actual sensory sensation, it remained with one as an olfactory memory, recurring at odd times and in peculiar places as if to insinuate the transitoriness and ephemerality of all things mortal and cast a shadow over the brief, forgetful moments of merriment and laughter.

On Sunday, I went to Joe's funeral. It was the first time I had ever been to a funeral. All our other bereavements had occurred in South Africa, while we were in England. Joe was buried, together with eleven other men of the IZL, among them one other from the Altalena who was killed by the same shell as claimed Joe's life. These two had no families in Jerusalem and only a few friends to see them off on the long road to eternity. But most of the others had been local boys and their mourners were many, amongst them Ashkenazi, Sephardi and Oriental Jews. The scenes at the Bikur Holim Hospital, where the plain deal coffins were piled up in the courtyard while their contents received the last tributes to the dead in the little adjoining synagogue, were ghastly. According to their customs and traditions, the Oriental Jews set up an endless heart-and-spirit-rending wail, while they tore their clothes and banged their heads with frightening effect against the walls of the synagogue. The immediate relatives of the dead men insisted that their coffins be opened and they fell upon their dear departed ones, kissing their hands and faces in a shrieking ecstasy of grief. To add to the horror of these macabre scenes,

170

the professional mourners who attend all oriental Jewish funerals, sat cross-legged on the ground, alternately beating the earth with their palms and flinging their arms wildly to the skies, all the time singing in high-pitched, quavering voices a blood-curdling funeral dirge. The noise of this un-fettered, primitive and elemental grief, combined with the sickly smell of death, became a nightmare. I found myself thinking about Joe and his love for the beautiful and the spacious, for cleanliness and modernity, or the lovely Californian shores—and I heard myself moaning aloud: "God, how he would have hated all this!'"

The funeral procession started off. The military trucks, on which lay the draped coffins attended by guards of honor, were preceded by slow-marching, tense-faced soldiers of the IZL. Behind the cortege walked the relatives and friends of the dead. All along the two-mile route, the citizens of Jerusalem lined the streets to pay their last respects to the faithful defenders of their city. A silly, sentimental refrain rang with maddening perisistency in my thoughts: "Joe, I promised to dance at your wedding, and instead I'm weeping at your funeral." This refrain accompanied me the whole length of that grievous journey in the blazing, phlegmatic sun. I felt it to be unworthy of the occasion, but it had occupied my brain, drained and exhausted as it was with emotion, as a disease will take possession of a weary, unresisting body.

At last we passed the outskirts of the town and reached the temporary war-time cemetery of Sheikh Bader. The communal grave. blasted out of the rocky wastes, gaped widely and hungrily. As the volley of the military escort echoed through the valley of death, the coffins were lowered one after the other, to rest in close proximity until such time as peace should return to the tortured city of Jerusalem and enable her to bury her dead in graves marked with the dignity of headstones in a setting in keeping with the tranquility and sanctity of death.

CHAPTER XIII

DISSOLUTION

THE battles were over, but Jerusalem's struggle with dirt and disease and with the daily hardships of life continued. We still had our water brought round in lorries and distributed at the rate of a pail a head for week-days and nothing on Saturdays. In order to convey what a pail of water represented, I must point out that in the heat of summer, in normal times, the average Jerusalem adult would drink—in the form of tea, coffee and cold squash—a half a pail of water a day. This severe scarcity produced a veritable water philosophy, with rival schools of thought, on the order of importance of various functions of life such as drinking, washing and cleaning. In our own household we followed a principle which was probably that of most practical housewives. First of all, I had the bolts in the drainpipes of the kitchen sink and the bathroom wash-basin removed and placed pails beneath the open pipes so that every drop of precious waste water should be collected, instead of being allowed to rush into oblivion through the absent-minded pulling out of a plug. The daily water ration was emptied into a small tank especially prepared for that purpose. From the tank it was drawn according to a strict routine. Clean water was used for cooking and for personal hygiene. Water in which vegetables had been boiled was re-used for washing dishes and then went into the waste water pail in the kitchen. Water in which we had washed ourselves was collected for the daily laundering of clothes, was used again for washing the floors and then went into the waste-water pails. This waste water was the housewife's most valuable asset, for it went finally into flushing the toilets. I hated those symbols of twentieth century civilization in Jerusalem—the modern conveniences. They were a devilish anachronism which contrived to inflict on the fastidious the most subtle of all tortures—the torture of the aesthetic sense.

Getting at the water was not so simple an operation either. Our bath-room, where the sacred tank was kept, was a clutter of ladles, saucepans and kettles—by means of which the water was transferred from the tank to wherever it was needed; while empty, unresponsive taps gleamed mockingly and tantalizingly in their useless glory. For Raanan's three-year-old daughter, these taps symbolised the magic of distant, half-forgotten Tel Aviv, which was known to her as "the place where the water comes out when you turn on the taps."

On the other hand, getting at the water was not nearly so much of an undertaking as getting the water. The distribution took place in the street and the problem of conveying the water from there to one's own home was the responsibility of each individual. While we stayed with Raanan this was not so serious a problem, as there was always a procession of young IZL men coming to see Raanan and Shmuel and Sarah, Raanan's wife, and I exploited them quite mercilessly. But we soon moved into our own flat, chosen because of its availability and not with an eye to the water problem. The building itself was set in a garden and was quite two hundred yards from the street. To cap this, we lived on the third floor and there was no lift. (Not that a lift would have made any difference, as there was no electricity). Shmuel was very busy and very rarely available to help me with the water; and the young men seldom arrived at the opportune moment. So I had to manage on my own. Two pails of water are very little in terms of water, but a great deal too much in terms of weight. At first, in a burst of youthful energy, I carried both pails at one time. After a great deal of gasping and spluttering I managed to get them to the foot of the stairs after having slopped away at least a third of their precious contents. Then I carried them one at a time up these three interminable flights, lurching drunkenly from side to side as the uneven weight unbalanced me.

But I soon worked out a much better technique. I made two trips instead of one, carrying a half-full pail in each hand at each trip. The distance from the street to the foot of the stairs I traversed in two hops. I would run—or rather my legs would make the motions of running, but due to the weight which bore me down, the effect was more that of a tripping scuffle—until my arms felt as though they were being pulled out of their sockets. Then I would rest for a few seconds, pick up the buckets again and repeat my curious scuffling-cum-tripping performance until I reached the foot of the stairs. Here I would rest again for a while, then grasp one bucket firmly in one hand and, using the other hand and the bannisters both as guiding and propelling forces, I would hurtle up the stairs, praying that no one would get in my way and so break the impetus. Having got the second half-bucket up in the same way, I would then repeat the whole wearisome process again until I had our two buckets of water safely deposited in the tank. How I would have managed if these had been more than the two of us in the family, and consequently more buckets to carry, I dread to think. As it was, it took me fully twenty minutes stretched out on the couch to recover my breath and the use of my arms after this daily performance.

The food position improved considerably with time. During the week of the war we lived on our supplies of tinned foods, supplementing these by very little else than bread and egg-plant. I collected recipes from all my acquaintances and served egg-plant practically every day as chopped liver, or chopped herring, or fried steak or fried fish or Vienna Schnitzel or in one of many other camouflaged forms. These ersatz dishes had one common characteristic—they all tasted like egg-plant. I have since added this deceptively versatile vegetable to the list of my taboos, together with Dettol and Lysol.

The lack of electricity easily earned second place in the list of discomforts. At first we had electricity twice a week. On those wonderful occasions we invited visitors and made extra-special tea—from water boiled in an electric kettle. It was quite customary to tell our friends to "come round on the night we have lights." Entertainment was coupled with the week's ironing—this precious opportunity could not be wasted. On the nights we did not have electricity we got used to sitting around the oil-lamp and even to reading in bed by candle-light. But we never got used to the gloomy, depressing atmosphere occasioned by the murky, shadow-casting lamps and candles. One has to be in the right mood and atmosphere to appreciate the romantic quality of soft candle-light; and no one with any soul or even with the most vivid of imaginations could possibly see "atmosphere" in cooking some soggy mess over an oil-stove in a murkily-lit Jerusalem kitchen or, still worse, in a Jerusalem bathroom with its conglomeration of Heath Robinson water contraptions, sufficiently obscured by the dim lights as to cause many a bruised ankle or shinbone to the unwary.

*　　*　　*　　*　　*

Although the battles were officially over, minor clashes continued to occur. We were constantly getting fresh casualties in our hospital, mainly from Mount Zion, a high point overlooking the Old City, the responsibility for guarding which was in the hands of the IZL. The changing of the guards took place at night so as not to expose them to the mercy of Arab snipers on the Old City walls. And yet there were incidents. On one night in particular we suffered heavy casualties in wounded when the Arabs tunnelled underneath a strong-point and then blew it up, burying its Jewish guards in stone and rubble. Some of the boys were interred for hours until their comrades could dig them out. There were no fatal casualties that night, but Yaacov Mizrachi, of whom more later, was permanently blinded, a second boy developed tetanus and hovered on the brink of death for days, and eight were so badly cut about and bruised that they spent weeks in the hospital before they were able to walk around in comfort.

The snipers, too, continued to take their toll of lives. Our flat, to which we moved a few weeks after the truce started, faced the Old City walls. Anyone who stood on our kitchen balcony for any length of time was either a hero or an idiot, depending on one's point of view. The number of bullet-marks on the ouside of the wall testified to that fact. As I have never pretended to be a hero, I used to crouch low and practically crawl whenever I wanted anything on the balcony, taking care not to expose even the minutest part of my anatomy above the low wall.

In between my chores, I continued working in the hospital. But with the advent of "peace," the girls in the First Aid units found the time heavy on their hands and many of them asked to be transferred to work in the hospital. This sudden abundance of helpers made me dispensable and I became, instead, a Welfare Officer. My duties consisted in visiting the wounded IZL boys in hospitals other than our own, bringing them chocolates, cigarettes and books, listening to their complaints and tending to their needs. As soon as they could be moved, I had to arrange for their transfer to our own hospital.

There were very seldom any complaints, and as for their needs—they always assured me that they, themselves, had none; but most of them worried about their families. I was continually asked to find out if parents were getting their allowances, or whether families who had had to evacuate their old homes had found new ones, as the boys realised that their parents or other relatives would not want to worry them with these things and so would not divulge the true state of affairs. And always they would ask how soon they could be transferred to our own hospital—not because they did not get good treatment or were unhappy where they were, but because they wished to be with friends, at "home."

In accordance with an unwritten, tacit law which we women had our-selves evolved, we made a point of looking our best whenever we came

175

into contact with outside authorities such as the Municipality, the welfare organisations, public medical authorities and the Haganah. This was a reaction to the real truth—that due to the chronic shortage of funds our forces looked rather a rag-tag and bobtail crew, in an amazing assortment of "uniforms," ranging from Cossack-booted partisan attire to Australian swash-buckling hats and bush-jackets. But we women were extremely jealous of the reputation of the IZL, so Noar, my visiting companion, and I always kept our uniforms as immaculate as possible in the circumstances, when we made our rounds of the hospitals. We were always received cordially and respectfully and our wounded were never in any way discriminated against, not even in the military hospital which was under the sole aegis of the Haganah.

I managed to wheedle permission from Shmuel to use his car for our hospital rounds and this enabled us to spend more time with the sick and wounded and less in tramping in the hot sun from one hospital to the next. And yet as much time as we spent with the boys and girls was never enough. They liked to see us in our trim uniforms and caps with the IZL badges prominently displayed. It made them feel less cut-off from their friends and still a part of the great, underground family, in spite of their temporary disablement. I am always happy to think that we did do something to lighten the long, painful days these boys and girls spent in the hospitals.

But we did not only give. We received too—spiritual gifts much more precious than the mere chocolates and cigarettes which we brought. There was Yaacov Mizrachi. He taught me how one can suffer pain and affliction with courage and forebearance. At eighteen he had lost one eye completely and thse doctors were fighting a losing battle to save the sight of the other. Yaacov underwent one operation after another, each one successively diminishing his and the doctors' hopes of restoring sight to his eye. And always it was he who was cheerful, he who talked animatedly and vividly when our spirits faltered, he who encouraged us when he sensed our dismay at the failure of another operation. I used to sit at his side, holding his hand to maintain contact with him, and tell him, in my faltering Hebrew, about what the Gedud (the Brigade) was doing and how his friends, who had been wounded with him at Mount Zion, were faring. Noar would read to him. Then he would speak of the "old days" and how different things would be in the future. Poor Yaacov, for him they certainly are different. But when last I saw him his spirit was as strong and

176

youthful as ever as he studied in the School for the Blind to become a useful citizen of the State for which he gave so much.

Then there was Yitschak, whose surname I have forgotten. He was sixteen years old altogther and was in hospital for the second time, this time with a shattered leg. He had been in the IZL since the age of fourteen and had not managed to finish his schooling. Now he was making up for lost time by reading voraciously and indiscriminately whatever he could lay his hands on. In addition, he had found that he had a remarkable aptitude for clay-modelling and was making rapid strides under the tuition of the hospital therapy instructor. Yitschak was simply simmering with enthusiasm at the wonderful new vista of learning and education which was opening before him. I always felt thoroughly ashamed at the thought of the careless matter-of-factness with which I and my South African friends had accepted our schooling and University educations. At sixteen we had sat at desks having education drummed into us, had gone home to waiting meals served by colored maids, then out again to play tennis and hockey, to swim or to ride. Or to our music lessons, our dancing lessons, our elocution lessons—most of which we detested thoroughly, but had to suffer in subservience to the ambitions of our dear Mammas. And here was Yitschak, twice wounded in battle at sixteen, serving in an underground organisation since the age of fourteen, and now lying and dreaming about the magical world which education could open to him. This contrast calls for more than a sigh and a pseudo-philosophical acceptance of the fact that there is no justice in the world. It calls for an understanding and appreciation of the fact that a very great proportion of the youth of Israel has suffered from Yitschak's disadvantages, has had no thorough educational grounding, has had no joyous, carefree play-time and is, consequently, separated by an immense gulf from the Jewish youth of the Diaspora—that is the youth of the Diaspora which did not receive its education and upbringing in Hitler's concentration camps. This abyss can engulf us if we more fortunate ones do not realise that it exists and try to bridge it with patience and tolerance on the one hand and help and encouragement on the other.

* * * * *

Soon after the truce came into effect, Menachem Begin came on a visit to Jerusalem. This was the first time he had made an official public appearance. Jerusalem has never given any man a welcome such as he received.

Wherever he went, to the hospitals to visit the wounded, to the religious Meah Shearim, to Mahne Yehuda of the Eastern communities, even to a Palmach training school, his car was surrounded by a cheering, yelling crowd who practically mobbed him in their enthusiasm. In the late afternoon he addressed a mass meeting in Zion Square, in the centre of the city. Tens of thousands of people came to listen to him, whether out of curiosity to see what he looked like, as his opponents maintained, or because they were interested to hear what he had to say, is not important. What is important is that this man, who symbolised the struggle against the British, had so fired the imagniation of the people of Jerusalem that they accorded him an ovation and a reception which had never till then been equalled and has not been equalled since.

After the meeting, Begin's escorts fought a way through the crowds to enable him to go to a near-by restaurant for dinner. The restaurant had to be protected by armed guards to prevent the enthusiastic mob from breaking in and surrounding him once more. In the street milled hundreds of people waiting for Begin to emerge so as to give him a final cheer. Sarah and I chose this strategic moment to try and join the party inside, according to arrangement. When we had successfully fought through the crowd to the restaurant door, we found our way barred by armed guards, who did not know us and showed no inclination to get to know us. In spite of our pleas and protestations they firmly, and none too gently, turned us away from the door. Just as we were both getting a little heated at the double indignity of being both unrecognized and dinnerless, Shmuel and Raanan came to our rescue, to the discomfiture of the guard whose wry apologies hardly made up for our ruffled tempers, disordered hair and clothes, and manifold bruises gathered from all the buffeting we had received. I decided then and there to eschew the life of fame and pursue the simple pleasures of a simple woman.

The next day Begin performed the ceremonial function of handing the IZL flag over to Raanan, as Chief of Staff of the Jerusalem IZL and thus of the IZL in toto. The duty of receiving the flag should nominally have been Shmuel's, as Commander, but he had no pretensions to being a military man and did not even have a uniform; so he gladly retired in favor of Raanan. This ceremony was one of the most touchingly impressive I have ever witnessed. On the large sports field in Katamon, which the IZL used as a parade-ground, row upon row of rifle-bearing men and women soldiers stood at attention. There were mortars and bren-guns, armored cars and jeeps, radio equipment and first-aid detachments. Everything gleamed in the sun, from the highly-polished boots to the freshly-laundered and almost uniform uniforms. To the casual observer this was no more than a very mediocre, small-scale military parade. But to those of us who knew how much blood and sweat and toil had gone into producing every rifle, every pair of boots, every uniform, every one of the brand-new berets with their different colored pom-poms—to us, this was a miracle. And as the flag of the IZL unfurled, revealing the gleaming golden emblem of the hand grasping the rifle against a background of white and blue silk, the miracle became an emotional cataclysm whose intensity was broken only by the sudden whirring of cameras as the newspaper photographers sprang back into life and resumed the feverish activity which they had suspended for a few minutes when even they had fallen under the spell of the solemnity of the moment.

For the foreign correspondents and photographers, Begin's visit to Jerusalem was a field-day. After days of uneventful post-war inertia, punctuated only by the clashes and snipings which had lost their news-value by their frequency, here was an event which hit front-page headlines. The newspaper men made the most of their opportunities; and the press- and movie-photographers were by no means outdone by them. Facts were sometimes sacrificed to sensation—as in the case of one movietone newsreel, which featured Begin's visit to Jerusalem and the ceremony of handing over the flag, and showed pictures of Begin and Shmuel, together with the commentary that Shmuel was Begin's double and went everywhere with him in order to foil assassination.

This resemblance between Begin and Shmuel created quite a sensation in Jerusalem. I myself see no resemblance whatsoever other than that they both have moustaches, not of the same length or shape, that they both wear glasses, not with similar frames, and that they both wear trousers. It was the trousers that must have clinched the argument for the news-photographers. By an unfortunate coincidence Begin and Shmuel were wearing identical suits brought for them from South Africa by my mother. This, coupled with the superficial facial resemblance, caused a good deal of confusion. Shmuel found himself cheered and congratulated and accosted unwarrantedly—a somewhat painful experience for one as modest and retiring as he is. Newspapermen asked him if he was Begin's younger brother and the photographers snapped him furiously, to his acute embarrassment. For weeks afterwards, small boys would stop and stare at him in the street

179

and then argue furiously about whether he was Begin or Artsi (Shmuel's pseudonym in Jerusalem).

Shmuel's reaction to the Begin's-double story was typical: he took it very calmly, remarking merely that they certainly must think him a damn fool if they thought he would serve as a bullet-proof vest for Begin.

* * * * *

Begin returned to Tel Aviv the day after the ceremonial parade. He was accompanied on part of his journey by an IZL guard of honor complete with white-helmeted motor-cyclists, and left the city in a triumphal procession, cheered on his way by the waving citizens.

Life returned to normal or to the equivalent of normal. For me it meant more work in the hospitals and the daily drudge of housekeeping. Not that this was dull and monotonous. On the contrary, every day brought something new and exciting. First we started getting ice—a great event in the heat of an Israeli summer; then we got more and more electricity until the nights of the candle were completely forgotten; and, finally, the shops filled up with all kinds of luxuries, such as tinned foods, fruit and vegetables and we even got rations of chicken to supplement our meat allocations. Only the water-pipes remained silent and obdurate and continued to remain so until a week after we left Jerusalem.

To brighten our lives still further, the cinemas re-opened, visitors started trickling in from the coast and even from overseas. Sometimes they stayed with us—and I forgave them wholeheartedly for the amount of our water-ration that they used as they cheerfully took over from me the burden of carrying it.

During this period I made my first trip back to Tel Aviv and Haifa. The Burma Road by this time was on its last legs and had practically returned to its primaeval state. But the jolts and bumps were fully compensated for by the half-hour I spent under a shower in Tel Aviv and the hour in a hot bath in Haifa.

For Shmuel, the return to normal meant the increasingly difficult struggle of maintaing the IZL camp in Jerusalem. Besides the immense difficulty of feeding and clothing hundreds of people, with very limited resources, there was the growing battle against demoralisation which afflicts every idle army. The men were bored and restless and exaggerated the usual soldiers' grumbles into minor tragedies. The hardships they had borne cheerfully in the days of fighting now became irksome and irritating. Those who had spent the last six years fighting—first against the British in the underground and then against the Arabs, chafed against this enforced idleness and strained to get back to civilian life and make up for the loss of precious time. Those who were newcomers to the IZL weighed up the comparative advantages in food and uniforms in the three military organisations—the IZL, the LHI and the Haganah. Not a few found the prospects in rival organisations more inviting and simply transferred themselves thither.

Discipline in the days of the underground had been self-imposed. The IZL was then a comparatively small organisation bound together by common ideals and a common purpose. This unity and harmony obviated the need of any imposed discipline. The soldiers of the line obeyed their officers because they recognised that through their plans and their leadership the common aim would the sooner be achieved. The junior officers obeyed their senior officers for the same reason. In everyone burned unquestioning devotion to the ideal and fear lest he should fall down in any task allotted him and so turn back the wheel of time by even one spoke. In such a company of men and women disciplinary measures were not only redundant, but ridiculous.

In the war against the Arabs, the common danger and the habit of self-discipline combined to make the task of controlling the IZL army a comparatively simple one for its officers. But by the end of the war this army was no longer a closely-knit body of friends and comrades, fired by a common ideal. It had become a large, unwieldy, heterogeneous body with the small hard core of underground fighters surrounded by the fleshy pulp of prodigals returned to the fold after many years of absence and of newcomers who joined the IZL instead of the Haganah for sentimental reasons, or for reasons known only to themselves. This mixed bag of idle men not only needed the ordinary elements of military discipline, but they needed the extraordinary rigor of a strong-fisted regime to keep them under control, just as any other conscripted civilian army required in time of peace. And the IZL officers had not the means of applying this much-needed discipline. They had no prisons, no fatigue duties, no punishments, in fact no army regulation sufficiently comprehensive to meet this situation.

To an objective observer the obvious solution to the immense two-fold problem of upkeep and discipline was the dissolution of the last rearguard of the IZL and its incorporation into the Army of Israel. But the objective observer does not always see the imponderables, one of which was the serious political purpose behind the maintenance of the IZL in Jerusalem.

This city, beloved of all the Jews of the world, which has inspired the magnificent vow: "If I forget thee, may my right hand forget its cunning," was still not incorporated into the State of Israel, was still mutilated by the amputation of its oldest limb from the body corporate. To many this justified the continued existence of the IZL in the hope that they would create a political situation which would convince the Israel Government of the desirability of incorporating Jerusalem in the State, or at least that they would serve as a symbol of resistance to internationalisation. Then there was, too, the powerful feeling of attachment which the old members still felt for the IZL and their great reluctance, none the less weighty for its sentimentality, to see it dissolve and carry away in its dissolution so large and real a part of their lives.

But these imponderables merely delayed the course of events—they did not change the inevitable decision which Shmuel and his colleagues had to make. The fact that the Israel Government, too, was demanding that the IZL arms should be handed over to the Israel Army and its soldiers incorporated therein, forced the issue.

The only remaining problem was that of getting the best possible terms for the soldiers. Negotiations were started on how the incorporation should take place. The negotiations were carried on between Mr. Gruenbaum, the Minister of Interior in the Provisional Government, and Raanan and Avinoam representing the IZL. Interminable discussions took place as to whether the IZL should go in as a battalion or whether the members should join as individuals; whether they would have their own officers or whether they would be officered by Army Command appointees.

The IZL planned to hold a monster military parade through the streets, bringing with them all their arms and armor which they would then hand over to the Haganah chiefs and so write a final glorious chapter to a glorious episode in Jewish history.

But fate willed otherwise. On the 17th September, while negotiations were still in progress, Count Bernadotte, the United Nations Mediator between Israel and the Arab States, was killed by unknown persons. That evening a group, claiming to be an off-shoot of the LHI, took upon itself the responsibility for the assassination. The Government was quick to grasp its chance of liquidating the dissidents once and for all. They rounded up and arrested all the members of the LHI, and to the IZL they gave a 24-hour ultimatum: "Hand over your arms, dissolve your organisation unconditionally, or else. . ." Undoubtedly the Government had good reason to demand the liquidation of the dissident groups in order to save face before world opinion which accused it of not being capable of preserving order amongst its own people. But the IZL had already made clear its readiness to dissolve of its own accord, and this peremptory, clumsy "we'll show you who's boss!" demand on the part of the Government put up their backs. Many of the more hot-blooded, jealous of the prestige of their beloved organisation, insisted that the Government's challenge be taken up. And without doubt the IZL's position in Jerusalem was sufficiently strong to have enabled them to cause havoc in the ranks of the Haganah. Without doubt, too, this would have precipitated a bloody civil war in the whole country. But these were in the minority, and Israel was saved from the horrors of internecine war by the level-headedness and cool judgment of the young IZL leaders in Jerusalem (a similar tragedy had been averted by the IZL leaders after the Altalena incident), rather than by the hysterical behavior of the members of her Government whose superiority in age and experience should have taught them better.

The ultimatum was accepted. And on Monday, the 20th September, 1948, the Irgun Zevai Leumi ceased to exist as an independent military organisation. The handing-over of the arms was carried out without incident in spite of the fact that the military authorities, with characteristic gaucherie and tactlessness, sent a unit of Palmach (who had carried out the brutal attack on the Altalena from the Tel Aviv shore) to receive the arms. Perhaps one day, when our Government reaches maturity, they will learn how to be gallant and gracious, and how to recognise and acknowledge worth even in their political opponents.

The Haganah in Jerusalem which, although Jerusalem had not been incorporated into the state, was a part of the Israel Army, carried out "Operation Liquidation" with amazing speed and efficiency. They dismantled the barracks in Katamon, they removed our wounded to their own hospitals, in one day, and then began swearing-in the individual members. This latter process took quite a considerable time, owing to the numbers involved.

The liquidation of our little hospital was a very sad event for the women volunteers, especially for Rachel and Nata who had built it up from an empty, neglected villa to a well-equipped, well-run modern establishment. They felt it should have been possible to keep it going for the Army, but by the very nature of the place this was impossible. The IZL was dead, and anything associated with it had to be destroyed, so that its name should not be perpetuated. This was good party politics on the part of the Government, even if it was not good ethics.

I had the dismal task of conducting the Haganah swearing-in officers round all the hospitals and explaining to our sick and wounded that they had to take the oath to the Israel Army and become part of it. (The Army had agreed to accept responsibility for all our wounded, including those who were permanently disabled.) I knew that the dissolution of the IZL was inevitable and that death had been quiet and painless, but, nevertheless, I had natural compunctions about assisting at the death-rites. Somebody had to do this, however, and who was more suitable than I who knew all the boys and had been accepted by them as a friend.

The task was not a simple one. Some of these boys had been in hospital for months and had lost touch with events. They could not understand why we had dissolved and, still less, why they should join the army. I explained as simply and clearly as I could and pointed out that, as the IZL was no longer in existence, there was no one to take care of them, to see they had the necessary medical attention, if they did not join the Army.

The Haganah officers behaved with exemplary patience and tact. They gave me all the time I needed to explain away all doubts and fears, adding their assurances that there would be no discrimination in care and attention against anyone. But what explanations or assurances could I find for 18-year-old Zion who cried and said that he had been in Betar and the Irgun half of his life, and what could he possibly do without an underground? This cry of Zion's struck fear in my heart. I confess that for one moment of blind panic I was afraid of what would happen to these young men, whose lives had been wrapped in an ostensibly illegal organisation, when they should have to revert to normal lives in normal circumstances. Would their revolt against the authority of tyranny become a revolt against authority in general, or would they revert back to peace-loving, order-abiding citizens of their new, young State. I could have spared myself such misgivings. These young men integrated themselves into their new society without any of the trials and difficulties which confronted others in every other revolutionary movement throughout the annals of history. They did not become breakers of law and defiers of authority as many of our opponents prophesied in their Jeremiads. This is one of the many phenomena in which the IZL abounded and which, in itself, deserves the learned attention of future historio-philosophers.

When we came to Yaacov Mizrachi, both the Haganah officers and I were deeply moved. I explained the situation gently to him. He accepted it philosophically, expressing amazement that the Army should want him: "I don't think I shall make much of a soldier again, but if you want me to swear, I'll swear." As the swearing-in officer guided the pen in Yaacov's hand to seal, with a sprawling, unnatural signature, his induction into the Army, the tears rolled unabashedly down my cheeks.

At the end of the day I walked home with the Haganah officers. One of them, a nice young man, seeing my dispiritedness, tried to console me: "Never mind," he said, meaning to be kind, "we might still need you people again if Jerusalem is internationalised." He was thoroughly snubbed for his pains. "Next time," I said tartly, *"you* and *your* friends can go underground. We shall not do Ben Gurion's dirty work for him again."

I met Shmuel at the Eden Hotel where he had been holding a Press Conference to explain the background to the liquidation of the IZL. We were both in cheerless moods and decided to dine at the hotel in an effort to restore our spirits. I was in uniform for the last time and the badge on my cap attracted the attention of a man sitting by himself at the next table to ours. He leaned over and asked me, in impeccable Southern English ,whether I would let him have my badge as a souvenir. I detached it and handed it to him, remarking dryly that I would not advise him to wear it publicly in England as that was the badge of the notorious Irgun Zevai Leumi. Instead of showing signs of agitation he perked up interestedly and introduced himself as a British Labor Member of Parliament on an unofficial tour of Israel. He told us that his sympathies had always been with the IZL and that he was going back to England to tell Attlee that he was making a great mistake about Israel.

Shmuel invited him to come and visit us and continue the conversation. He readily accepted the invitation, but two days later the porter at the hotel phoned Shmuel to say that the British Member of Parliament regretted he was unable to dine that day as he had been urgently recalled to England. We were sorry. There was so much more we would have liked him to tell Mr. Attlee.

* * * * *

The assassination of Count Bernadotte provided my mother with just about the only experience she had not yet had in Israel.

At the time of the murder, Nathan Friedman-Yellin, the leader of the LHI, was on his way to Haifa to take a plane to Europe. When the Government ordered all members of the LHI to be arrested he, naturally, headed the lists. In view of his claim that he knew nothing about the assassination, it might have been more politic for him to hand himself over to the authorities and dissociate himself from the crime. Instead, he chose to go into hiding—a rather impractical undertaking under a Jewish regime, where everybody knows everybody else's political affiliations, and where there is no longer any solidarity amongst the local inhabitants against the rule of a foreign oppressor.

As the members of the LHI were too well-known to the authorities in Haifa, Friedman-Yellin could not take refuge with any of them. He turned to my sister-in-law, Katie, with whom he had a slight acquaintance. My brother, Michael, and sister-in-law had been members of the IZL and were now members of the Herut Party. When he arrived at their flat and asked for refuge, Michael and Katie did what any other decent people would do in similar circumstances—they took him in. How anyone as large as Friedman-Yellin (he is about 6 ft. and must weigh close to 200 lbs.) could possibly have hoped to hide in a three-room flat in which there were, besides Michael and Katie, also three children and my mother, I cannot imagine. But he stayed there, undetected, for ten days, during which my mother had the time of her life. She was able to tell him just exactly what she thought of him and his organisation, she pumped him dry on his ideologies, past and future, and she bombarded him with questions about the Bernadotte murder. The poor man could not escape and probably cursed the day he had chosen to go into hiding instead of sitting in a quiet, peaceful prison.

Friedman-Yellin continued to keep in touch with those of his colleagues who were still at large and was thus, quite inevitably, traced to Michael's flat, where he was dramatically arrested in the early hours of the morning, on the eleventh day of his sojourn there. The Israeli police were polite but firm. They searched the flat thoroughly—but quietly, as my mother threatened them, in her curious Anglo-Yiddish, that they would have to pacify the baby if they woke her. They left the flat an hour later taking with them Friedman-Yellin, all the papers, letters and photographs they could find, and Michael. They would probably have taken Katie as well if it had not been for the three little children.

So now my mother's cup of experience was full—she had actually witnessed, with her own eyes, the arrest of a member of the family. She took a very poor view of this experience.

186

As communication with Jerusalem was still very irregular, we heard of Micheal's arrest only days afterwards. Arieh Ben Eliezer came up from Tel Aviv to address a public meeting and it was from him that we heard the whole story. I immediately set out for Haifa to see if there was anything I could do.

This time we travelled on the new "Malaya Road," an asphalt road built to take the place of the old "Burma Road" which had practically disintegrated. (By now it is remembered only as a legend). The new road was built by labor squads of volunteers and conscripts from Jerusalem. The wits used to report on the daily casualties amongst the workers caused by over-crowding on the road and on the inability of the bull-dozers to maneuvre because of the hundreds of manual workers who kept on getting in their way.

When I arrived in Haifa, my mother's first words of greeting fore-warned me of melodrama: "Oh, so you've come at last!" I hastened to explain that we had only just heard the news and that mollified her some-what. Perhaps I should have been more tactful and sympathetic. Instead of associating myself with my mother's attacks on the Government, I said that I felt they were perfectly entitled to arrest Michael for harboring a man known to be wanted by the police. Katie, who was suffering con-siderably because she felt the responsibility had been hers as it was she who had known Friedman-Yellin, agreed with me. My mother took a poor view of this too. She took Michael's arrest badly because, as she explained, it was so unnecessary and such a waste. She agreed with us that thousands of mothers in Palestine had been through the same ex-perience and even worse, but in their cases, she said sadly, it was for some ideal, it was for the sake of freedom, for the sake of a cause, not just for something silly like this. It got a sneaking impression that she had been quite disappointed at not having had someone of hers in Latrun or Eritrea and Kenya. After all, a son in Bet Sach, detained at the pleasure of the Israel Government, was not so glorious an achievement as a rebel against oppression detained at the pleasure of H.M. Government. It certainly was a point of view.

Michael was imprisoned for six weeks and then released on bail. His case was eventually dropped and he was never brought to trial. The only complaint he had against his jailors was that they kept him in solitary confinement and that they would persist in giving him soft boiled eggs for breakfast without a spoon with which to eat them. Eventually, after ran-

187

sacking the whole place, the guard found a table-spoon and he had to make do with this.

*   *   *   *   *

We stayed in Jerusalem for another month after the dissolution of the IZL while Shmuel supervised the inauguration of the new political party and straightened out some of the tangles caused by the abruptness of the dissolution.

Then he was asked to return to Tel Aviv where the young Herut Party was in the throes of preparing for the first general elections in the State of Israel. And so we left Jerusalem, sadly, because we both love the city deeply, and returned to Tel Aviv. Shmuel immediately plunged into the intricacies and heart-aches of politics while I returned to domesticity. My days of being a "lady-terrorist" were over. They are now only a memory—but a sweet memory, wherein bitterness has been neutralised by time, where the hardships are overshadowed by the glories of achievement and where the sorrows are compensated for by the joys of comradeship and spiritual solidarity.

EPILOGUE

JUST before leaving Jerusalem we dined with Carter Davidson, of the Associated Press, and his wife. During dinner the conversation turned on books which had been written about Palestine, by people who had visited there for about a month and then gone away experts. I remarked that as it seemed possible for any idiot to write a book on Palestine, I saw no reason why I should not do the same. Davidson asked me what I would like to write about and I jokingly replied: "The home-life of a terrorist." He took up the idea with enthusiasm.

As I wrote, I found I had very little to say about the home-life of a terrorist, mainly because if there was one thing which a terrorist could hardly be said to have, it was a home-life. But I found other things jostling for place in my thoughts and tumbling over themselves to get put down on paper. There were the simple people like Ruhama and Yàacov Mizrachi who gave up uncomplainingly what they could ill spare—the first her loved ones, the second his sight—for the sake of a cause. There was the courage and endurance of the "forgotten men" of the revolution—the wives who sat at home and waited for the dread knock at the door. There was the great privilege which came to me fortuitously and which comes to but few—the privilege of seeing history being made and of witnessing, with my very own eyes, the courage, the glory, the inspiration—and the sordiness, the nastiness, the greed—which go into its making.

And, above all, there was the miracle and power of an idea which brought Joe from the sunny shores of California and Matie from the comforts of South Africa to a communal grave in the rocks of Jerusalem.

As I look back, now, on my own membership in the IZL, I find an incongruity which needs explaining. How was it possible that I, who have always hated violence and bloodshed to the point of over-fastidiousness, could have thrown myself heart and soul into a group which, on the face of it, employed both? The explanation of this is two-fold: because I hate violence and bloodshed, I shuddered at the cruel barbarity which has been inflicted on my people throughout the last two centuries, culminating in the unprecedented horrors perpetrated by Hitler and his henchmen; and

189

I sought a means of halting this monstrous genocide. I found it in a Palestine to which the persecuted Jews could come freely. (My Zionism has never been based on nationalism or on political considerations—it is strictly humanitarian). But Palestine—the last refuge of the Jews—was barred to them by Britain for her own selfish considerations. This obstacle had to be removed—and the use of moral appeals to the conscience of the world has fallen into abeyance in this twentieth century of progress. The only argument which is appreciated is that of war. I regarded this waging of war against the British as by far the lesser of two evils. When confronted with the choice of two forms of violence—that of sitting as a spectator at the arena and watching dispassionately the mass slaughter of a defenceless people by the mad bulls of Europe, or that of slaying the guards at the gates of the arena and allowing the tortured human victims inside to escape—I chose the latter.

This is one part of the explanation. The other lies in the concept of the IZL. I had read the writings of its leaders and eventually had the privilege of knowing them personally. Men like Begin, Benjamin, Avraham and Shmuel did not worship violence as a philosophy. They abhorred it with all their souls. But they made war, nevertheless, not for the sake of violence, but in the same way as a surgeon, with ruthless kindness, cauterises a festering growth, or amputates a rotting limb in order to save a precious life. Their violence was that of the Maquis who fought the hated German oppressor; that of the French people who stormed the Bastille, the symbol of tyranny; that of Joan of Arc who, in the name of Christ, fought the invader; that of the Barons who wrested Magna Carta from John; that of Yael who impaled the enemy general, Sisera, with a tent-peg, that of David who slew the giant, Goliath, by artifice. Those are all examples of violence, but violence as a means, not as an end. While I do not believe that the end always justifies the means, there are times when the negation of this Machiavellian philosophy may be used merely to cloak lily-livered cowardice and the fear of drawing correct conclusions. The end of saving a people from complete destruction was sufficiently high-minded and glorious to justify the means acceptable in our days as applicable to much less worthy causes.

A second anomaly in my adherence to the IZL was my "Englishness" —based on cultural and geographic ties. I had been brought up in an English-speaking community and educated by English teachers in English style. But love of the truly great culture and literature of England does not preclude hatred of those of her sons who defile freedom and liberty and some of the finest traditions of their people. The IZL did not fight against British culture and tradition. It fought against the bonds of slavery with which individual British task-masters attempted to manacle the people of Palestine. My hatred of the British was that of the American colonists and of the Irish Republicans, whose natal and cultural ties to Britain did not prevent them from revolting against her oppression.

There were two kinds of people in the resistance movements: those who had experienced oppression in one form or another and hated it with the violence of fear and bitterness; and those who had been brought up to revere freedom of spirit and thought and to abhor any restriction of human liberty and dignity with a cold, intellectual hatred. By accident of birth-place, by education and by home influence, I belonged to this second category. In the ranks of the IZL I found congenial spirits—young Palestinians who had been reared in the tradition of independence and nurtured on the teachings of Jabotinsky, who preached that every man was a king; Americans, French, Greeks, who, though themselves untouched by persecution and tyranny, hated it none the less.

It was this love of freedom, coupled with fierce national pride, which held together a body of men and women whose diversity of background, origin, education and mental outlook has never been equalled—the Polish visionary and the American go-getter, the Anglicised South African and the oriental Yemenite, the Russian atheist and the side-curled religious fanatic from Jerusalem, the hot-tempered and naive North African and the cool, sophisticated Parisian, to mention just some of the types who served with courage, devotion and complete selflessness in the IZL.

This selflessness aroused both my intense admiration and my annoyance. I admired and revered the complete obliteration of personal consideration, the complete sinking of the individual in the cause; but I rebelled against the sacrifice of family ties, against the neglect, to the point of causing them much suffering, of wives and children; against the complete subordination of all personal relationships, of all human desires, to an ideal. I rebelled because, at times, the suffering which this spiritual fanaticism caused to their own dear ones seemed to me to negate the great aim of liberation and freedom. I felt that these young men and women kept their eyes glued on a distant, glorious horizon and strained to reach it; but as they struggled along, with the dazzling, distant light both drawing and blinding them, they stumbled against and trampled unseeingly on those who sat at their feet. These occasional flare-ups of revolt against idealism were short-lived. I recognized them as the subjective, self-pitying cry of women throughout the ages—a cry which is none the less heart-rending for its subjectivity; but which, fortunately for history, has so often fallen on ears deafened to all else but the greater, more urgent, appeal of humanity as a whole.